Lotus™1-2-3™
User's Handbook

Lotus™ 1-2-3™ User's Handbook

Weber Systems Inc. Staff

Ballantine Books ● New York

Lotus 1-2-3 is a registered trademark of Lotus Development Corp. PFS is a registered trademark
of Software Publishing Inc., Visicalc is a registered trademark of VisiCorp Inc., dBASE II is a registered
trademark of Ashton-Tate Inc., IBM and DOS are registered trademarks of International Business
Machines Inc., Epson MX and FX are registered trademarks of Epson America, Inc., Hercules
Graphics card is a registered trademark, HP 7470A is a registered trademark of Hewlett-Packard,
Inc., Anadex 9620A Silent Scribe is a registered trademark, NEC 8023 is a registered trademark of
NEC Home Electronic Corp., Okidata microline 92, 93, 82A, 83A, & 84 are registered trademarks
of Okidata Corp., Prism Printer 80 & 132 are registered trademarks of Integral Data Systems, Inc.,
COMPAQ PC is a registered trademark of Compaq Computer Corp., COMPASS is a registered
trademark of Grid Şystems Corp., Portable Professional is a registered trademark of Texas Instru-
ments Inc., Professional Computer is a registered trademark of Wang Laboratories, Inc., Hyperion
is a registered trademark of Bytec Management Corp., Rainbow 100 & 100+ are registered trademarks of Digital Equipment Corp., Z-100 is a registered trademark of Zenith Data Systems, Strobe
Model 100 & 200 are registered trademarks of Strobe, Inc., Sweet P is a registered trademark of
Enter Computer, Inc.

ISBN: 345-32939-2

Manufactured in the United States of America

First Ballantine Books Edition: July 1984

10 9 8 7 6 5

Contents

Introduction & Acknowledgements

Lotus™ 1-2-3™ User's Handbook is meant to serve as a tutorial as well as an on-going reference guide to the operation of Lotus 1-2-3. All of 1-2-3's many features are discussed including:

> Installation
> Worksheet commands
> Graphing
> Printing graphs
> Database features
> Macros
> Functions
> File Manager
> Disk Manager
> Translate

A number of examples are included with the text to illustrate the topics being discussed. Terms that may be unfamiliar to the reader will be presented in bold in the text. These terms will be defined in subsequent paragraphs.

Chapter 1 of this book is meant to serve as an introduction to 1-2-3. Topics covered include 1-2-3 installation, the 1-2-3 Access System, 1-2-3 start-up, File Manager, Disk Manager, 1-2-3 keyboard usage, the spreadsheet, 1-2-3 monitor and printer output, 1-2-3 disk storage, and the 1-2-3 Help facility.

Chapter 2 is designed to provide the beginning 1-2-3 user with an overview of 1-2-3's worksheet. Worksheet movement, cell entry, command usage, cell ranges, and operators are all discussed in detail.

Chapter 3 describes 1-2-3's main command menu and its **W**orksheet commands. Chapter 4 describes 1-2-3's **R**ange, **M**ove, and **C**opy commands. Chapter 5 describes 1-2-3's **F**ile commands, and chapter 6 describes the **P**rint commands. The **G**raph commands and outputting graphs on the monitor are discussed in chapter 7. Sending graphs to the printer with the PrintGraph program is discussed in chapter 8. 1-2-3's Database commands and functions are discussed in chapter 9. The various functions available in 1-2-3 are described in chapter 10. Macro commands are discussed in chapter 11.

Chapter 12 contains several 1-2-3 models that can be entered by the user. Although these models can be used to solve everyday applications, their main purpose is to provide the reader with a practical example of 1-2-3 model design and entry.

We gratefully acknowledge Steven Miller of Lotus Development Corp. for his invaluable assistance in this project.

1

Introduction to 1-2-3

Introduction

Lotus 1-2-3, a product of Lotus Development Corporation, is one of the most significant developments in spreadsheet software. 1-2-3 combines electronic spreadsheet, database, and graphics capabilities into an integrated, sophisticated applications package.

An electronic spreadsheet is an electronic grid of columns and rows — very much like an accountant's columnar pad. However, the 1-2-3 spreadsheet with 2048 rows and 254 columns is much larger than any columnar pad. Any calculations that can be made using a columnar pad, pencil, and calculator can be made using an electronic spreadsheet — only faster and easier.

Hardware

1-2-3 can be run on an IBM PC or a number of PC compatible computers. As of this date, Lotus has announced that it will support the following computers:

IBM PC™	TI PROFESSIONAL™
IBM PC XT™	WANG PROFESSIONAL™
IBM 3270™	BYTEC HYPERION™
COMPAQ PC™	DEC RAINBOW 100 & 100+™
GRID COMPASS™	ZENITH Z-100™

Lotus recommends a minimum of two double-sided floppy diskette drives or one double-sided floppy diskette drive and one hard disk drive for use with 1-2-3. A monitor is also a necessity for 1-2-3 operation. A color monitor will be required to take advantage of 1-2-3's color graphics capabilities.

A printer and/or plotter will be necessary should the user wish to output hard copy from 1-2-3. Lotus includes drivers for a number of different printers with 1-2-3's PrintGraph disk. The following printers are currently supported:

- Epson MX 80™ and MX 100™ with GrafTrax Plus (single, double, triple density)
- Epson FX 80™ (single, double, triple, quad density)
- IBM Graphics Printer™ (single, double, triple, quad density)
- Okidata Microline 93™, and 84™ Printers with ROM step 2
- Okidata Microline 92™ Printer
- Okidata Microline 82A™ Printer
- Okidata Microline 83A™ Printer
- Anadex 9620A™ Silent Scribe
- NEC 8023™ Printer
- IDS Prism 80™ Color Printer (single or double density mode)
- IDS Prism 132™ Color Printer (single or double density mode)
- Strobe Model 100™ and Model 200™ Computer Graphics Plotters

- HP7470A™ Plotter
- Sweet P™ Plotter

Drivers for additional printers will most likely be developed by Lotus. Consult your 1-2-3 dealer for details on which printers are supported under 1-2-3. Details on configuring 1-2-3 for a particular printer are included in chapter 3.

1-2-3 Installation

The Lotus 1-2-3 package contains five diskettes — a System disk containing the basic 1-2-3 programs, a backup copy of the System disk, a Tutorial disk, a Utility disk and the PrintGraph disk.

The first step in installing 1-2-3 is to copy DOS to each 1-2-3 diskette. The procedure for copying DOS will be detailed in subsequent sections.

Once DOS has been copied, the proper **drivers** must be installed. Drivers are programs that send data to peripherals such as printers and video displays. Lotus 1-2-3 driver programs are stored in separate files on the Utility disk. Each driver's filename ends in DRV.

Since the procedures differ, separate instructions will be given in the following sections for copying DOS and installing drivers for systems with two diskette drives and for systems with one diskette drive and one hard disk.

COPYING DOS — TWO DISKETTE SYSTEM

In this section, we will describe the steps necessary for copying DOS onto 1-2-3 diskettes using a computer with two floppy diskette drives.

Step 1. Place the DOS master system diskette in Drive A. Power on the computer. The DOS prompt (A>) should appear after the date and time have been entered.

Step 2. NOTE: Perform this step only if DOS Revision 1.1 is being used and if the system contains 320K or more of main memory. The DOS system master should not be used since this step will cause two files to be changed on the DOS diskette. This step will correct errors in the programs named DISKCOPY.COM and DISKCOMP.COM.

Place the DOS diskette (or copy) in drive A with the write protect tab removed. Place the 1-2-3 Utility disk in drive B and type the following command:

B:FIXDOS ↵

Step 3. Make sure that the write-protect tab has been removed from the 1-2-3 System disk, and then place this diskette in drive B. After the A> prompt appears, type the following command:

B:INSTALL

A message will appear on the screen, asking if the disks are loaded properly. Check the disks and if correctly loaded, press any key to continue. After this procedure has been completed, a message will appear on the screen when the copying process has been completed. After the disk drive lights have gone off, remove the 1-2-3 System disk from drive B and place it aside in its protective jacket.

Step 4. Repeat Step 3 for each of the remaining 1-2-3 diskettes:

System disk (backup copy)
PrintGraph disk
Utility disk
Tutorial disk

Step 5. Remove the DOS disk from Drive A and return it to its protective jacket.

INSTALLING DRIVERS — TWO DISKETTE SYSTEM

In this section, we will describe the steps necessary for installing the drivers using a computer with two floppy diskette drives.

Step 1. Make sure that the A> prompt is active.

Step 2. Place the Utility disk in the source drive. For these instructions, we will assume drive A to be the source drive and drive B to be the target drive. To make sure that the source drive or drive A is the default drive, enter the following:

A: ↵

Step 3. Next, issue a driver installation command. This command consists of two words separated by a space. The second word must consist of a letter designating the target drive followed by a colon. The first word will determine the set of drivers that will be copied to the other Lotus 1-2-3 disks from the Utility disk. These include:

- MONO   Use this command if the system includes a monochrome display with an adapter card (no graphics capabilities). Example: MONO B:

- HERCULES   Use this command if the system includes a monochrome display with a Hercules graphics card. Example: HERCULES B:

- COLOR   Use this command if the system includes a color monitor with a color/graphics adapter card. Example: COLOR B:

- B&W   Use this command if the system includes a black & white monitor with a color/graphics adapter card. Example: B&W B:

- BOTH   Use this command if the system includes both a monochrome and a graphics display. BOTH allows two monitors to be connected to an IBM PC. When using BOTH, switches 5 and 6 must be positioned to off on dip switch 1. The color (external) monitor should be connected via the Color Graphics card. The monochrome monitor should be connected via the Monochrome Display/Printer Card.
   The color monitor will only display graphics. When graphics are not being output, it will be blank. The monochrome monitor will display the worksheet. Example: BOTH B:

- COMPAQ   Use this command if the computer is a COMPAQ portable. To connect an external Monitor with the COMPAQ, the COMPAQ driver should be used.
   In some cases where an external monitor is connected to the COMPAQ, the 80 x 25 display will not appear. By pressing the Ctrl-Alt-< keys simultaneously, the 80 x 25 character display will appear on the external monitor. Example: COMPAQ B:

Step 4. After the command has been entered, 1-2-3 will request placement of the remaining 1-2-3 disks into the target drive, one by one. Follow 1-2-3's instructions for each disk. After each disk has been processed, return it to its protective envelope.

COPYING DOS — FIXED DISK SYSTEM

In this section, we will outline the steps for copying DOS to Lotus diskettes using a computer system with one floppy diskette and one fixed disk.

Step 1. Place the DOS diskette provided with the system in drive A. Turn the power on. The prompt A> should appear. Enter the date and time.

Step 2. Change the default drive to the hard disk. If the hard disk is drive C, this can be accomplished with the following entry:

C: ⏎

Your prompt will now be C> rather than A>.

Step 3. Remove the DOS disk from drive A and replace it with the 1-2-3 System disk.

Step 4. If the DOS files had previously been transferred to the System disk, the following commands must be issued.

ERASE x:COMMAND.COM
ERASE x:FORMAT.COM
ERASE x:CHKDSK.COM
ERASE x:DISKCOPY.COM
ERASE x:DISKCOMP.COM

where x = the diskette drive (A,B,C,etc.).

Step 5. Issue the following DOS command:

COPY x:*.*.

where x = the diskette drive (A,B,C etc.)

Step 6. Repeat Steps 3 through 5 with the PrintGraph, Utility, and Tutorial diskettes.

---

*With a fixed disk system, DOS 2.0 should be used. If DOS 1.1 is used, errors in DISKCOPY.COM and DISKCOMP.COM must be corrected. This can be accomplished by placing the Utility diskette in drive A and executing the following:

d:FIXDOS ⏎

d represents the diskette drive identifier.

The files listed below should also be resident on the fixed disk:

FORMAT.COM   DISKCOPY.COM
CHKDSK.COM   DISKCOMP.COM

These files should have been transferred to the fixed disk when DOS was copied to it. If not, place a DOS system diskette in drive A, and use DOS's COPY command to transfer these. For example, the following command could be used to copy CHKDSK.COM:

COPY A:CHKDSK.COM ⏎

INSTALLING LOTUS ON A FIXED DISK

1. Turn on the computer. If DOS has not been installed on the fixed disk, do so. Refer to the DOS manual for installation instructions.

2. Enter the time and date as usual. The default drive should be that of the fixed disk. If not enter the following command:

    x:⏎   (x = fixed disk letter)

3. Set the default directory where Lotus is to be placed. This would be accomplished with the following entry:

    CHDIR directory/name ⏎

4. Place the 1-2-3 System disk in the diskette drive and close the drive door.

5. If DOS files were previously placed on the disk, issue the following commands:

    (x = diskette drive)
    ERASE x:COMMAND.COM⏎
    ERASE x:FORMAT.COM⏎
    ERASE x:CHKDSK.COM⏎
    ERASE x:DISKCOPY.COM⏎
    ERASE x:DISKCOMP.COM⏎

6. This step transfers the Lotus files onto the fixed disk. To transfer the files, issue the following command:

    COPY x:*.* ⏎

    where x = the diskette drive.

7. Steps 5 and 6 should be repeated for the other Lotus

disks. These are:

1-2-3 Print Graph disk
1-2-3 Utility disk
1-2-3 Tutorial disk

8. Remove the disk currently in the diskette drive and place a DOS master disk in the diskette drive.

9. Issue the following commands to transfer files used by the Disk Manager to the fixed disk:

COPY x:FORMAT.COM
COPY x:CHKDSK.COM
COPY x:DISKCOPY.COM
COPY x:DISKCOMP.COM

10. Install the drivers as described previously.

INSTALLING DRIVERS — FIXED DISK SYSTEM

The instructions for installing drivers on a two diskette system should be followed — except that the hard disk should be specified as the target drive. Since the files need only be copied from the utility disk to the hard disk once, during step 3, a prompt will be displayed requesting that the procedure be interrupted when appropriate.

INSTALLING DRIVERS — ONE FINAL NOTE

According to Lotus's documentation, any system hardware changes can be adjusted for by merely installing the proper new drivers. In the majority of such cases, this writer found it necessary to repeat the entire installation procedure, as when only the new drivers were installed, problems were encountered.

Lotus 1-2-3 Access System

ENTERING THE ACCESS SYSTEM MENU — FLOPPY DISK SYSTEM

Once 1-2-3 has been properly installed, the 1-2-3 Access System can be entered. To gain entry, first power on the computer with the 1-2-3 System disk in drive A. A prompt will appear calling for the date and time. Once these entries have been made, the Lotus Access System will automatically begin executing, and the screen will resemble that shown in figure 1-1.

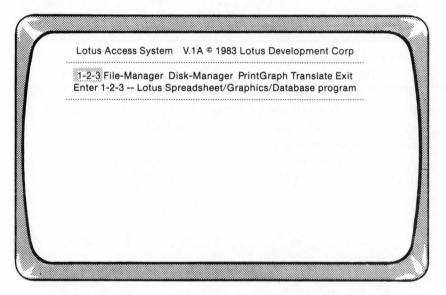

Lotus Access System   V.1A © 1983 Lotus Development Corp

1-2-3 File-Manager Disk-Manager PrintGraph Translate Exit
Enter 1-2-3 -- Lotus Spreadsheet/Graphics/Database program

FIGURE 1-1.   Access System Menu

If the computer system has already been powered on, the procedure for running the Lotus Access System is somewhat different. Place the 1-2-3 System disk in drive A and enter the following after the A> prompt:

LOTUS ↵

Again, the screen will resemble that depicted in figure 1-1. Figure 1-1 depicts the Lotus Access System Menu. A description of the menu selection currently highlighted by the cell pointer will be displayed beneath the menu choices. A description of the Access System menu selection process can be obtained by pressing the F1 function key. Once this key has been pressed, the menu choices can be displayed once again by pressing the ESC key.

ENTERING THE ACCESS SYSTEM MENU — FIXED DISK SYSTEM

To enter the 1-2-3 Access System menu on a fixed disk system, first load DOS from either a DOS diskette or fixed disk. Set the disk and directory default to where Lotus was transferred to. (The default drive and directory were set during installation.) Insert the 1-2-3 System disk in drive A. Type LOTUS ↵ to activate the 1-2-3 Access System menu.

Lotus is now ready for use. If 1-2-3 is selected on the Lotus Access System menu, the 1-2-3 System disk must be in the diskette drive. If not, the Access System menu will reappear. To continue, press any key. Lotus will then prompt for a disk to be inserted in drive B. Remove the System disk, and place a data disk in the diskette drive. Press the Enter key, and the worksheet will appear. If data is to be stored on the fixed disk instead of a floppy disk, press the following keys when the worksheet is present:

/FD

Lotus will display the current storage place. To change the storage place, enter the new drive and directory where the data is to be placed.

ENTERING 1-2-3

To enter 1-2-3, move the pointer to the first menu selection (1-2-3), and press the Enter key. 1-2-3's copyright information will be displayed followed by a screen similar to that shown in figure 1-2. This screen display is known as the **spreadsheet.**

The 1-2-3 program is contained in the file named "123.EXE". The various 1-2-3 help screens are stored in "123.HLP." Be careful not to alter or erase these files. The 1-2-3 System disk can be removed from drive A once the access menu appears on the screen. Never remove a disk while the red indicator light on the disk drive is glowing. If the System disk is removed, it must be replaced prior to exiting the access system.

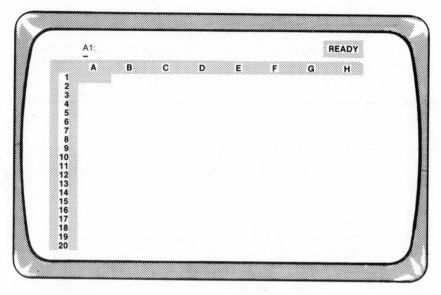

FIGURE 1-2. 1-2-3 Initial Screen

File Manager & Disk Manager

The two Access Menu selections, File Manager and Disk Manager, allow for various file and disk management functions. File Manager is stored on the Utility disk as FILEMGR.COM. When File Manager is selected from the Access System menu, 1-2-3 will request that the Utility disk be installed. Once this disk has been installed, the following prompt will be displayed:

Select source disk

A   B   C*

---

* Fixed disk.

At this point, a decision must be made as to which disk drive is to contain the source diskette. The source diskette contains the files to be processed by File Manager. Use the arrow keys to designate the desired source drive, A or B.

Once the source drive has been chosen, insert the source diskette in that drive and press the Enter key. A display similar to figure 1-3 will appear.

```
                                                                      ⑤
Lotus File Management System V.1A (c)1983 Lotus Development Corp   MENU

    ① Copy      Erase    Rename    Archive    Disk-Drive    Sort    Quit
    ② Copy    Selected   files   from   the   current   disk   to   another


     FILENAME    EXT      DATE       TIME     SIZE
     DONE        .WKS    01-Jan-84   1:10 am  43904
     IMPORT      .PRN    11-Jan-84   2:56 pm     61
     INVENTOR    .WKS    01-Jan-84   1:09 am  43904    ③  Current Drive:  B
   ④ LOOP1       .WKS    10-Jan-84   0:15 am   1664       Number of Files:  9
     MACRO       .WKS    09-Jan-84   2:06 am   2176       Total Bytes Used:   175104
     MACRO2      .WKS    09-Jan-84   1:05 am   2560       Total Bytes Free:   147456
     MACRO3      .WKS    01-Jan-84   0:13 am   2432
     OKAY        .WKS    01-Jan-80   0:57 am  49792
     SAMPLE      .WKS    09-Jan-83   0:13 am   1920
```

1. Menu Selections   2. Description of Current Menu Selection
3. Source Diskette Information   4. Source Diskette File Directory   5. File Indicator

FIGURE 1-3. File Manager Initial Display

Notice that the File Manager menu selections are displayed below the copyright line. These are described in table 1-1. The left-arrow and right-arrow keys can be used to move the menu pointer. A description of the current selection will be displayed directly below the menu selections. A directory of the various files residing on the source diskette occupies most of the screen. Notice that the current file is highlighted with the file pointer. The file pointer can be moved using the up-arrow and down-arrow keys.

File Manager's Copy, Rename, and Erase functions each require that one or more files on the source disk be selected for processing. The first step in file selection is to move the menu pointer to the desired menu choice and press Enter. Notice that the Function Indicator in the upper right-hand corner of the screen will change to reflect this entry.

The files to be processed must be selected by positioning the cell pointer to the desired filename, and marking it with # by pressing the space bar key. By pressing this key a second time, the # mark will be removed. The ESC key can be used to remove all # marks and return to the menu. When all desired files have been selected, press the Enter key to end the selection process. If copy was chosen, a screen similar to that depicted in figure 1-4 will be displayed.

If the file selection display is accurate, press Enter to verify the destination drive. File Manager will proceed to the file selection step where a final prompt will appear asking the user to verify that the function should in fact be performed (see figure 1-5). Three choices will be available.

No   ⟶ Return to file selection display.

Yes ⟶ Perform the function.

Quit ⟶ Return to File's Manager menu.

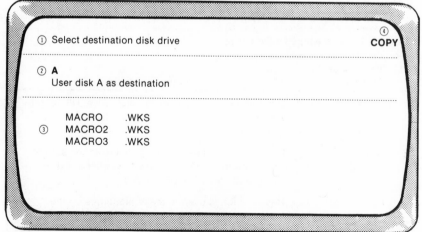

1. Prompt 2. Destination drive 3. Files previously selected 4. Function Indicator

FIGURE 1-4. File Manager Display — after File Selection

If "Yes" is selected, each filename will be highlighted as the function is performed. When the function has been completed, the File Manager menu will be displayed.

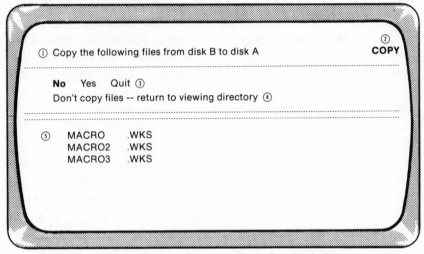

1. Prompt describing function to be undertaken   2. Function Indicator
3. Final verification choices   4. Consequence of each choice   5. Selected Files

FIGURE 1-5. File Manager Display — Final Verification

Table 1-1. File Manager Functions

File Manager Function	Function Description
Disk-Drive	This function specifies which disk drive will contain the source disk for the other File Manager functions.
Copy	This function is used to copy files from the source disk to another disk. The new files will have the same filename as the source file.
Erase	This function is used to erase filenames on the source disk.
Rename	This function is used to designate new filenames on the current disk.

TABLE 1-1 (cont). File Manager Functions

File Manager Function	Function Description
Archive	This function is used to create a second copy of the files on the current disk with new filenames.
Sort	This function is used to reorder the list of filenames. The files themselves are not affected. Sorting can be undertaken either in ascending or descending order based on the data contained in one or two designated columns. A submenu allows the user to indicate the columns to be used for the ordering process. P indicates the primary sort key. S indicates a secondary sort key.

When Disk Manager is selected from the Access System menu, a display similar to that depicted in figure 1-6 will appear. Disk Manager performs a number of disk operations. These are described in table 1-2.

Table 1-2. Disk Manager Functions

Disk Manager Function	Function Description
Prepare	Used to format a blank diskette so that it can be used as a data diskette. Formatting is a process in which the diskette is prepared so that data can be written to it.
Disk-Copy	Used to copy the contents of the diskette in drive A to the diskette in drive B.
Compare	Used after a Disk-Copy operation to corroborate that the duplicated diskettes are exact copies.
Status	Returns characteristics of a diskette (sectors free, sectors in use, etc.). Also, used to be certain that two distinct files do not use the same data sectors.

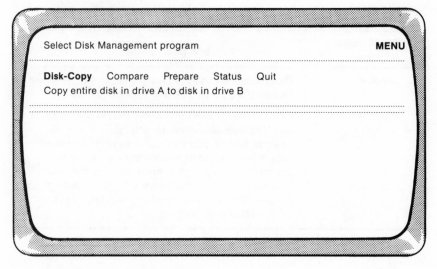

FIGURE 1-6. Disk Manager Menu

PrintGraph

The PrintGraph program is stored under the filename GRAPH.-
EXE on the PrintGraph program diskette. When PrintGraph is chosen
from the Access System, 1-2-3 will prompt the user to replace the 1-2-3
diskette in drive A with the PrintGraph diskette. When the PrintGraph
program has been ended, a second prompt will request that the 1-2-3
diskette be inserted in place of the PrintGraph diskette. The PrintGraph
program will be discussed in more detail in chapter 8.

Translate

The Translate program is stored on the PrintGraph program diskette. Translate enables the usage of 1-2-3 files with other applications
programs such as Visicalc and dBASE-II. Specific details on Translate
are given in appendix B.

Exit

The final choice in the Access System menu, Exit, allows the user to
exit the Access System and return to DOS.

The Keyboard

Before we begin a detailed discussion of the spreadsheet, we will discuss keyboard usage within the worksheet. In order to simplify our discussion, we will divide the keyboard into the following classifications:

Typewriter Keys
Cell Pointer Keys
Function Keys
Special Keys

The typewriter keys function in a manner almost identical to that of their counterparts on a typewriter keyboard. The Shift key is used to produce uppercase characters. Lowercase characters will be output when the keyboard is in unshift. The Caps Lock key causes all alphabetic characters to be output in uppercase. This key does not affect non-alpha characters.

The cell pointer movement keys, as depicted in figure 1-7, cause the movement of the cell pointer within the worksheet. Notice that these keys generally have a number as well as an arrow or group of characters on each key top. These keys have two characters because each key serves a dual function. The characters and arrows represent the cell movement function. The numbers represent the usage of these keys to produce numbers. Numbers will be output by these keys when the Num Lock key is depressed.

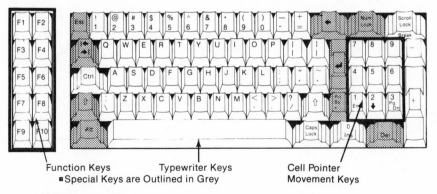

Function Keys   Typewriter Keys   Cell Pointer
■Special Keys are Outlined in Grey   Movement Keys

FIGURE 1-7. Keyboard

The arrow keys (← ↑ → ↓) move the cell pointer to the left, up, to the right, and down within the worksheet. Pg Up (Page Up) causes the previous page* within the worksheet to be displayed. Pg Dn (Page Down) causes the next page within the worksheet to be displayed. Home causes the cell pointer to move to the upper left-hand corner on the worksheet.

The function keys (F1-F10) are used to execute specialized 1-2-3 operations. These are listed in table 1-3. A template is provided with 1-2-3 which can be placed over these keys to serve as a reminder of their usage.

The special keys as depicted in figure 1-7 are described individually in table 1-4.

Table 1-3. F1-F10 Operations

Function Key	Name	Operation
F1	Help	Displays the Help screen
F2	Edit	Switches into or out of the Edit Mode
F3	Name	In the Point Mode, displays menu of range names
F4	Abs	In the Point Mode, designates cell addresses as absolute
F5	GoTo	Used to move the cell pointer to a designated cell
F6	Window	Used to move the cell pointer to the other side of the split screen
F7	Query	Repeats the Data Query operation last used
F8	Table	Repeats the Data Table operation last used
F9	Calc	Recalculates the worksheet
F10	Graph	Recreates the last graph drawn

---

* Explained on page 37.

Table 1-4. Special Keys

Special Keys	Description
Esc	Causes 1-2-3 to back-up one step
⊢ ⊣	Causes a leftward or rightward movement by the cell-pointer
⇧	Causes keyboard to assume the shift mode
Alt	Used in conjuction with alpha keys to invoke keyboard macros
Num Lock	Causes cell pointer keys to output numbers
←	In data entry, causes the last character entered to be erased. In pointing situations, sends cell pointer to the previous location
Del	Erases the character at the current pointer location
PrtSc	When pressed with the shift key, causes the data on the screen to be sent to the printer
↵ (Enter key)	This key is used to tell 1-2-3 that an entry or operation has been completed, and that the program should proceed accordingly

1-2-3 Display Screen

The 1-2-3 display screen, as depicted in figure 1-8, consists of three principal areas. The control panel is located at the top of the display. The border, located between the control panel and the worksheet, consists of the worksheet column and row numbers. The worksheet itself lies inside the border area.

Certain portions of the 1-2-3 worksheet are highlighted. These include the border area, cell pointer, mode, and key indicators. If an IBM Color monitor is used as 1-2-3's display device, different colors will be used to display different portions of the worksheet.

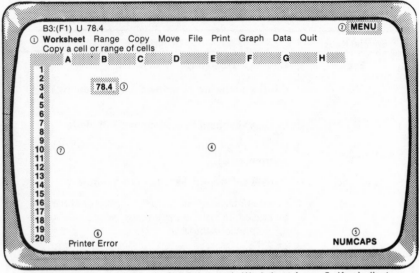

1. Control Panel 2. Mode 3. Cell Pointer 4. Worksheet Area 5. Key Indicators
6. Error Message 7. Border

FIGURE 1-8. Display Screen*

Spreadsheet & Border Area

The spreadsheet consists of a group of cells which are organized into a grid. Although this grid in fact consists of 2048 rows with 256 columns in each row, only a portion of the grid can be displayed on the screen at any one time.

Each cell in the grid is assigned an address consisting of its column location followed by its row location. Column addresses range from A to IV. Row addresses range from 1 to 2048. The current row and column addresses are displayed in the border area.

We already briefly mentioned the **cell pointer**, a highlighted cell which can be moved about the screen using the arrow keys. The cell address where the cell pointer is located is indicated at the top of the control panel (see figure 1-8).

---

*This display is meant only for illustrative purposes. Such a display would probably not be encountered in actual usage.

As we mentioned earlier, the entire spreadsheet cannot be viewed on the screen at one time. For viewing purposes, the spreadsheet is divided into **windows**. The column width (explained later) determines the size of the window. For example, when the column width has been set at 9, the window will consist of an area with a width of 9 columns and a depth of 20 rows.

CONTROL PANEL

The control panel contains three separate lines. The top line contains information pertaining to the current cell — the cell indicated by the cell pointer. The initial entry on this line gives the current cell's address. This line's second entry denotes that cell's display format.* The third entry indicates the current cell's protection status.** The final entry gives the current cell's actual contents.

The control panel's second line will display one of the following three items:

- Data as it is entered or edited
- Menu items
- Prompts

The third line on the control panel is used to display a short summarization of a command during the command entry process. Note that the contents of line three will change to reflect the current command choice as the menu pointer is moved about the menu.

Monitor Output with 1-2-3

Many 1-2-3 users choose to install two monitors with their system. When two monitors are installed, worksheet data will be displayed on the non-graphics (monochrome) display, and 1-2-3 graphs will be displayed on the graphics monitor.*** Such a system allows the display of 1-2-3 graphics and worksheet data simultaneously.

---

* Explained on page 41.
** Explained on page 111.
*** The graphics monitor is connected to the color graphics board. The monitor itself can be B&W, color, or RGB.

If only a graphics monitor is installed, it will be used to display both 1-2-3 worksheet data and graphs. If only a non-graphics monitor is in use, it cannot be used to display graphs. However, printed copies of graphs can be output with the PrintGraph program.

Printer Output with 1-2-3

A number of different text and graphics printers can be used with 1-2-3 to output data. When a text printer is installed, the following can be output by 1-2-3:

- Any portion or all of the worksheet
- A listing of cell entries in any portion of the worksheet

Data can either be output to the printer during the 1-2-3 session or that data can be saved in a Print file for output later under DOS's Ctrl-PrtSc feature.

When a graphics printer is installed and the PrintGraph program is active, a printout of any graph created under 1-2-3 can be obtained. If the system does not include a graphics monitor, a graph can still be output to the printer by defining that graph under 1-2-3, storing that definition in a file, and then invoking the PrintGraph program to produce output.

Disk Storage with 1-2-3

1-2-3's current worksheet* is stored in the computer's RAM memory. RAM serves only as a temporary storage area. If the computer is powered off or if the 1-2-3 program is exited, the current worksheet will be erased from RAM.

The current worksheet can be saved as a disk file for future use. It is a good practice to save your current worksheet as a disk file one or more times during its creation. This will prevent an accidental loss of the worksheet's contents in case of a power failure of some other hardware or

---

*The current worksheet can be defined as that visible on the monitor.

software problem. It is also a good practice to use Disk Manager or File Manager to make duplicate copies of your data diskettes. These should be stored in a secure area for use in case the orginals are misplaced or damaged.

A blank diskette must be formatted before it can be used to save a worksheet. This can be accomplished by selecting the Disk Manager program from 1-2-3's Access System. Select "Prepare" from the Disk Manager menu, and then press "Y".

This procedure causes DOS's FORMAT.COM program to format the blank diskette in drive B. Once the "Format Complete" message appears, Disk Manager can be exited to the Access System by pressing "N". Additional diskettes can be formatted by pressing "Y".

USING 1-2-3's HELP FACILITY

1-2-3 includes a Help feature which allows its users to reference a Help screen during program usage by pressing the F1 function key. The Help screen can be exited by pressing the Esc key. 1-2-3 will then continue at the exact point where the Help feature was invoked.

The individual Help screens include a number of additional related Help topics. These are interspersed throughout the Help screen's text. The Help topics are displayed with brighter characters so as to enable the user to identify them. The pointer movement keys can be used to position the cell pointer over the various Help topics. A menu of additional Help topics is also displayed at the bottom of the Help screen. Any Help topic can be chosen by moving the cell pointer to the desired topic and pressing the Enter key.

If a new Help topic is selected, the preceding topic can be displayed by pressing the Backspace key. Up to 15 screens can be reviewed in this manner. Each Help screen also includes a "Help index" choice which allows the user to reference any of 1-2-3's more than 200 Help screens.

2

Worksheet Basics

Introduction

This chapter is intended to provide the beginner with an overview of 1-2-3's worksheet. The following topics will be introduced:

- Worksheet Movement
- Cell Entry
- Command Usage
- Formula Entry
- Macros
- Ranges

The discussions presented in this chapter will be expanded upon in later chapters.

Worksheet Movement

In the following sections, we will discuss the various means of moving around the 1-2-3 worksheet. The topics discussed will include:

- Arrow Keys
- F5 (Goto) Key

- Home Key
- Page Keys
- Scroll-Lock Key
- End Key
- Active Area
- Titles and Split Screen

Some of the examples in this section will require that data be entered into a cell. To do so, move the cell pointer to the desired location, enter the desired data using the keyboard, and press Enter. Cell entry will be discussed in more detail later in this chapter.

ARROW KEYS

The arrow keys ($\leftarrow \uparrow \rightarrow \downarrow$) move the cell pointer by one position in the direction indicated on their key tops. Notice that any attempt to move past the worksheet's boundary will result in a beeper being sounded. Also, when the cell pointer is positioned at the right or lower edge of the worksheet window, the window will scroll when the $\rightarrow$ arrow or $\downarrow$ arrow keys are pressed. In other words, if the cell pointer was positioned at location H20 and the $\downarrow$ arrow key was pressed, the cell pointer would subsequently be located at H21. If the $\rightarrow$ arrow key was then pressed, the cell pointer would be located at I21.

F5 KEY

The cell pointer can also be moved to a specific location by pressing the F5 (Goto) key followed by the desired worksheet address. Notice that when F5 is pressed, the mode indicator will change from READY to POINT, and the following prompt will appear in the control panel's second line:

Enter address to goto: *xx*

xx indicates the current cell pointer location. When the desired address has been entered, the mode will change from POINT to EDIT. When Enter is pressed, the cell pointer will be positioned to the designated location, and the mode will change back to READY.

Position the cell pointer to A1, and then move to Y6 using the Goto key. Notice that the window adjusted so that Y6 constituted its upper left-hand location. Whenever the address indicated by the Goto key is outside of the current window, that address will be used as the new window's upper left-hand location.

HOME KEY

Pressing the home key causes the cell pointer to return to the upper left-hand location (generally A1).

PgUp, PgDn AND TABS ($\leftrightarrows$)

As we mentioned in chapter 1, the spreadsheet is divided into a series of windows or pages for viewing purposes. This concept is illustrated in figure 2-1. PgUp, PgDn, Tab and BackTab allow the cell pointer to be moved by one page at a time as opposed to one cell at a time. Notice that the cell pointer's relative position within the worksheet remains constant when the page keys are pressed.

When the → and ← arrow keys are used in conjunction with the Control key, they will have the same effect as Tab and BackTab respectively.

SCROLL LOCK

Earlier, we discussed the usage of the arrow keys to move the cell pointer within the worksheet. In certain instances, it may be necessary to move the window without moving the cell pointer. This can be accomplished by using the Scoll Lock key. Figure 2-2 demonstrates the effect of pressing the ↓ key when Scroll Lock has been pressed.

Notice that when Scroll Lock is pressed, "Scroll" is displayed in the screen's lower right-hand corner. When Scroll Lock is pressed again, the message will disappear.

Notice in figure 2-2 that when the ↓ key causes the cell pointer to reach the window's top edge, the cell pointer's location changes. The effect at the window edge with Scroll Lock on is the exact inverse as when Scroll Lock is off.

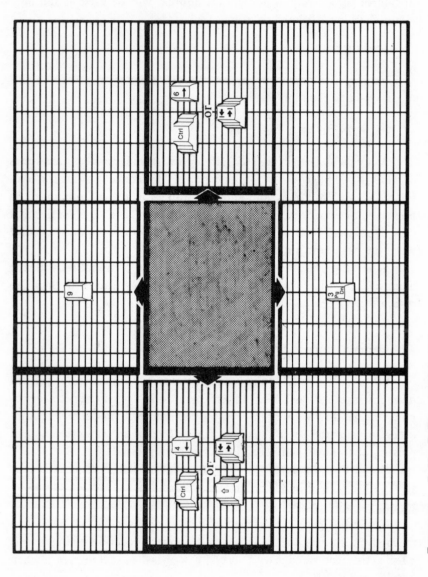

FIGURE 2-1. PgUp, PgDn, and Tabs ($\leftrightarrows$)

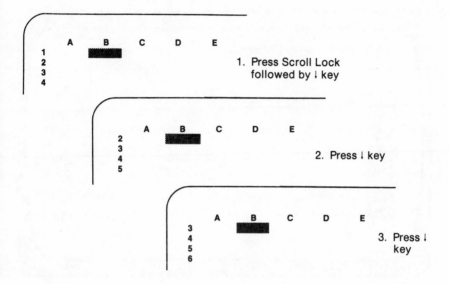

FIGURE 2-2. Scroll Lock

END KEY

The End key moves the cell pointer based on the worksheet's contents. End is generally used in conjunction with the arrow keys. When End is pressed the Ready or Point modes, the message "END" will be displayed in the screen's bottom right-hand corner. If an arrow key is pressed following End, one of the following events will occur:

- If the cell pointer is positioned on a blank cell, it will move in the direction indicated by the arrow key to the worksheet's next non-blank cell, or to the edge of the worksheet (see figure 2-3).
- If the cell pointer is positioned on a non-blank cell, it will move in the direction indicated by the arrow to the next* non-blank cell (see figure 2-3) or to the end of the worksheet.

---

* According to the Lotus 1-2-3 manual, this procedure will move the cell pointer to "The last non-blank cell before a blank cell". Our tests found this statement inaccurate using 1-2-3 revision 1A.

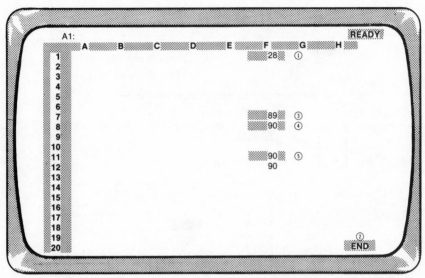

1. Initial cell pointer position 2. Press End key 3. Cell pointer position after pressing ↓ 4. & 5. Cell pointer after pressing End and ↓ keys

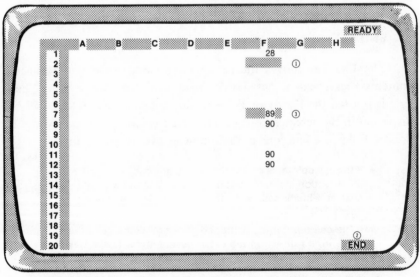

1. Initial cell pointer position 2. Press End key 3. Cell pointer position after pressing ↓ key

FIGURE 2-3. Cell Pointer Movement Using End Key with ↓ Key

ACTIVE AREA

Generally, only the upper left portion of the 1-2-3 worksheet is actually used. The portion of the worksheet where data has been entered is known as the **active** area. The active area can be defined by a rectangle with its upper left corner at cell address A1 and its lower left-hand corner at the cell address corresponding to the column farthest from the right and the lowest row where data was entered.

You will most likely encounter a number of circumstances where the cell pointer must be moved to the end or lower right corner of the active area. In the Ready or Point modes, this can be accomplished by pressing the End key followed by the Home key.

TITLES & CURSOR MOVEMENT

The Titles command allows the border area to be expanded so that it encompasses a portion of the worksheet. Titles will be explained in chapter 3. When 1-2-3 is in the Ready mode, the arrow keys cannot be used to move into the border set up by the Titles command. However, in the Point mode, the arrow keys can be used to enter the border area.

SPLIT SCREEN & CURSOR MOVEMENT

1-2-3's **Windows** command allows the worksheet to be split into separate working areas or windows. Within each window, the arrow keys and End key function as usual. However, to move from one window to another, the F6 (Window) key must be pressed.

Cell Entry

Now that we have learned how to move the cell pointer around the worksheet, our next step will be to learn the various methods of entering data into a particular cell. There are three primary means of doing so:

- Keyboard entry
- /Copy or /Move data from another cell
- Read data from a disk file

Each of these methods will be discussed later in this chapter. First, however, we will discuss the different types of data that can be entered into a cell.

ENTRY CLASSIFICATION

Cell entries can be classified as follows:

- Numbers
- Formulas
- Labels

ENTERING NUMBERS & FORMULAS

If the first character of an entry is one of the following:

$$0\ 1\ 2\ 3\ 4\ 5\ 6\ 7\ 8\ 9\ +\ -\ .\ (\ @\ \#\ \$$$

1-2-3 will consider it to be a number or a formula*. 1-2-3 indicates that a number or formula is being entered by displaying VALUE in the screen's upper left-hand corner.

The following rules should be observed when a number is entered into a cell:

- The number should begin with either a digit, plus sign (+), minus sign (-), period (.), or dollar sign ($).
- The percent sign (%) can be used to indicate a percentage value.
- Only one decimal point can be included in a number.
- Numbers cannot be entered with commas. These can later be inserted for display purposes using a Worksheet command (discussed later).
- Numbers can be entered in scientific notation using the following format:

---

* @ and # are used to create sophisticated formulas. $ is used to create an absolute cell address. These topics are discussed on pages 64 and 62, respectively.

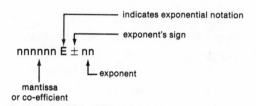

The coefficient can be entered as any positive or negative number. The exponent must be entered as a positive or negative whole number.

@NA & @ERR

NA and ERR are special variations of formula entries. NA is an abbreviation for Not Available. NA generally is entered when the user is not sure what value is to be assigned to a cell. When 1-2-3 makes calculations, any cell whose value is dependent upon another cell with an NA value will also be assigned that value.

ERR is generally used to represent an entry that is outside of an allowed range. As with NA, any cell with an ERR value will be assigned that value. 1-2-3 will assign ERR to a cell when it contains a formula that cannot be calculated (i.e. division by zero).

ENTERING LABELS

Whenever a cell entry is made whose first character does not distinguish it as a number or formula (see page 59), 1-2-3 will assume that entry to be a label.* When a label is being entered, the mode indicator will change from READY to LABEL.

Several characters can be inserted at the beginning of a label entry which will cause that label to be positioned in a specified manner within the cell. These are known as prefix characters and include the following:

'(single quote)	Left aligned with cell border
"(double quote)	Right aligned with cell border
^(caret)	Centered within cell
\ (backslash)	Repeated within cell

---

* The exception to this rule is 1-2-3 characters preceded with the slash character (/).

A value that otherwise would be interpreted as a number or a formula can be entered as a label by beginning that entry with a label-prefix character.

At this point, you may well be wondering why 1-2-3 requires a distinction between a numeric or formula value and a label value. One reason is that a numeric or formula can be used in a calculation while a label is merely a set of characters which are to be displayed. If you are familiar with the BASIC programming language, you know this also to be the case in that language, where data is catagorized as numeric or string (characters). A second reason for this distinction is that 1-2-3 allows the user to indicate cells to be used in a formula with the cell pointer rather than requiring that their addresses be entered via the keyboard. This process will be described on page 52.

CELL ENTRY EDITING

1-2-3 allows the user a number of means by which to edit data entered incorrectly. When 1-2-3 is in either the Value or Label Modes, the current entry can be cancelled by pressing the Esc key. This will only work if the entry had not been completed. If a formula is being entered in the Point mode, it might be necessary to press Esc two or more times in order to cancel the entry. As an alternative, a Control-Break* can be issued.

If a cell entry has already been completed, the easiest means of correcting it is to move the cell pointer to the desired position and replace the erroneous data with a new entry. The **Range Erase** command can also be used to simultaneously erase the contents of a group of cells. This command will be discussed on page 103.

---

* A Control-Break is issued by holding down the Control key while simultaneously pressing the Scroll Lock/Break key.

1-2-3's Edit mode allows its users a more efficient means of correcting invalid cell data other than re-entering the entire cell. The Edit mode can be activated by pressing F2 (Edit key). The mode indicator will then change to EDIT. The Edit mode can be used either during the entry process or it can be employed to correct an existing cell entry. Move the cell pointer to the cell to be edited before pressing F2.

When F2 is pressed, a copy of the cell's existing data will be displayed on line 2 of the control panel. The cursor will be positioned at the end of that data. The following keys can be used to correct the cell's contents:

←	Moves cursor one position to the left
→	Moves cursor one position to the right
⊢	Moves cursor five positions to the left
⊣	Moves cursor five positions to the right
Home	Moves cursor to initial character
End	Moves cursor to final character
Backspace	Deletes the character preceding the cursor
Delete	Deletes the character beneath the cursor

In the Edit mode, new characters can be entered at the cursor position by merely pressing the desired key. Pressing the Ins key is not necessary.

Once editing has been completed, the corrected data can be placed in the cell by pressing the Enter key. If the Edit mode was entered from the Value or Label modes (while an entry was in progress), the entry process can be resumed by pressing F2 a second time.

F9 (Calc) IN THE EDIT MODE

The F9 key functions differently in the Edit mode then it does in the Ready mode. In the Ready mode, F9 causes a recalculation pass* to be performed. In the Edit mode, when a formula is being edited, F9 will convert that formula to its equivalent numeric value without a general recalculation occurring.

---

* Explained on page 49.

/COPY & /MOVE

The second method of entering data into cells, transferring data from another cell, can be accomplished using the *Copy (or/ C) and Move (or / M) commands. The first character of each of these commands (/) causes the main command menu to be displayed (see figure 2-4). The second character selects the corresponding menu item.

The prompt sequence for / C and / M are virtually identical. / C's sequence will be outlined below:

Enter range to copy FROM:A14..A14 ↵

The cell pointer movement keys can be used to extend the range.   Press Enter.

Enter range to copy TO:A14 ↵

Indicates the initial cell to be copied to. Use the cell pointer movement keys to change this location.   Press Enter.

Once these entries have been made, the operation will be performed, and the indicated values will be placed in the proper cell addresses.

READING CELL DATA FROM A FILE

As mentioned earlier, 1-2-3 allows worksheet data to be stored as a disk file. Data from a disk file also can be loaded into the 1-2-3 worksheet. This is generally accomplished with the File Save and File Retrieve commands which are used to save and reload worksheet data respectively. More complex data reading operations can be accomplished using the following commands:

/File Combine   Combine worksheet or load part of a worksheet
/File Import   Loads data generated by a program other than 1-2-3

---

* Generally, a 1-2-3 command's first character need only be entered to perform that operation. The characters to be entered via the keyboard to activate a command will be displayed in bold type in this book.

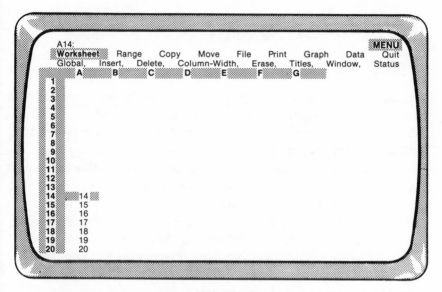

FIGURE 2-4. 1-2-3's Main Command Menu

1-2-3 Command Usage

We touched on 1-2-3 commands during our explanation of /**M**ove and /**C**opy earlier in this chapter. A 1-2-3 **command** can be defined as a specific instruction which when entered will be executed by 1-2-3. 1-2-3 commands consist of the slash character (/) followed by a **command keyword** describing that command. Examples are given below:

> /**M**ove
> /**Q**uit
> /**E**rase
> /**W**orksheet **W**indow

1-2-3 commands are arranged in a series of menus. The initial Main Command Menu (see figure 2-4) can be selected by pressing the slash key. This menu displays a set of submenus (i.e. **W**orksheet, **R**ange, **P**rint, **G**raph, etc.) which can be selected* by moving the menu pointer to the

---

* A command can also be selected by keyboard entry. For example, /**WS** would result in the execution of the **W**orksheet **S**tatus command.

desired option and pressing Enter. A menu item can also be selected by entering the first letter of the desired selection via the keyboard.

PROMPTS

Submenus can result in the display of either additional submenus or of **prompts**. A **prompt** can be defined as a message displayed during a 1-2-3 operation which requires a user response. See page 54 for an example of a typical prompt.

Prompts can take a number of different forms in 1-2-3. One common occurrence is a prompt for a filename. In this instance, 1-2-3 will assist the user by displaying a list of appropriate filenames retrieved from the current disk. A filename can be selected either by moving the menu pointer to the desired choice or by entering the desired filename.

1-2-3 may prompt for a range* name. Pressing the F3 key will result in a menu of the current range names being displayed. The range can be entered by any one of the following means:

- Moving the menu pointer to the range name and pressing Enter
- Entering the range name
- Entering the cell addresses of two of the range's diagonally opposite corners

Certain 1-2-3 prompts require that new data be entered. In these instances, 1-2-3 will enter the Edit mode in order to allow the user to correct the response as he or she enters it.

Sometimes, a 1-2-3 prompt will automatically display part or all of a possible response. This default response can be accepted by pressing Enter. In the Edit mode, the default response can be changed using the various editing keys. The default response can be erased by pressing the Esc key, thereby allowing the user to enter a new response.

In certain instances, a default response will be displayed which cannot be edited. The user can either accept the default value by pressing the Enter key, or he or she can replace that value by entering new data, Esc is not required to erase existing data.

---

* A range is a group of cells. This concept is discussed in greater detail on page 50.

COMMAND EXECUTION

Once the required prompt responses have been entered, 1-2-3 will execute the command. After the command has been executed, a **formula recalculation pass** may be undertaken. During a recalculation pass, every formula in the worksheet affected by a command will be recalculated. The worksheet calculation mode must be Automatic for a formula recalculation pass to be undertaken. 1-2-3's Worksheet Global Recalculation command allows the user to alter the recalculation procedure as follows:

Automatic	A recalculation pass occurs whenever a cell value is changed
Manual	A recalculation occurs only when the F9 (Calc) key is pressed
Natural	Recalculation order will be natural (see page 82)
Columnwise	Recalculation begins with column A, and proceeds down that column. Once column A has been recalculated, 1-2-3 will continue recalculating columns B, C, D, etc.
Rowwise	Recalculation begins with row 1, proceeds to row 2, row 3, etc.
Iteration	This setting denotes the number of times 1-2-3 will process the entire set of formulas when a recalculation is undertaken.

Once command execution has been completed, 1-2-3 will return to the Ready mode where a new command can be entered or a cell entry made.

REVERSING COMMANDS

As long as a 1-2-3 command has not actually been executed, the procedure for escaping from it is relatively simple. One means of doing so is pressing the Esc key. Each time Esc is pressed, 1-2-3 will back up one step. A second method for reversing a 1-2-3 command is to issue a Control-Break. This can be accomplished by holding down the Control key while simultaneously pressing the Scroll Lock/Break key. A Control-Break returns 1-2-3 to the Ready mode.

STICKY MENUS

In certain instances, after a command has been executed, 1-2-3 will display a menu of related commands rather than return to the Ready mode. These are known as **sticky menus.** 1-2-3 displays a sticky menu when it believes that the command just executed will necessitate further command entries.

Each of the various sticky menus includes **Q**uit as one of their choices. This allows the user to exit to the Ready mode. A sticky menu can also be exited by pressing Esc or issuing a Control-Break.

Cell Ranges

Situations often arise in 1-2-3 where a particular group of 1-2-3 cells is used as a group. A group of cells arranged in a rectangular block is known as a **range.** Examples of ranges are given in figure 2-5. You may already noticed in your experiences with 1-2-3 commands that they often specify that a range be entered. Ranges can be indicated in three different ways in 1-2-3.

- Entering cell addresses
- Expanding the cell pointer to highlight the range
- Indicating a range menu

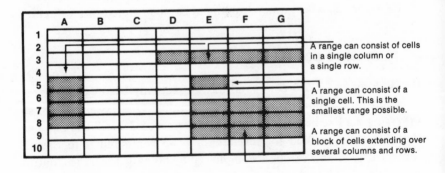

FIGURE 2-5. Cell Range

SPECIFYING A RANGE OR ENTERING A CELL ADDRESS

A range can be specified by typing the cell addresses of two diagonally opposite corners of the range separated by one* or more periods. For example, the range in the lower right-hand corner of figure 2-5 could be indicated with "E7..G9".

Earlier we noted that ranges are often prompted for by 1-2-3 commands. Ranges also can be used with formulas (discussed on page 64). When specified in the context of a formula, a range can be denoted in **relative, absolute,** or **mixed** terms. These formats are also available when individual cells are entered into formulas (see pages 61-63). Generally, 1-2-3 deals with ranges in absolute terms. For example, with the formula in cell A15, the following ranges:

A7..A11

would be interpreted as "those cells beginning in the cell 8 rows above the current cell and ending in the cell 4 rows above the current cell".

The $ can be used in 1-2-3 to specify all or part of a range in absolute terms. For example, the following:

A7..A11

would indicate the range from A7 to A11. Again, with the formula in cell A15, the following:

$A7..A$11

could be interpreted as "the range extending from the cell 8 rows above the current cell in column A to the cell in row 11 of the current column". Although 1-2-3 only differentiates between absolute and relative range specifications during formula entry, specifying an absolute range in response to a command prompt will not cause any problems.

---

* Regardless of the number of periods entered, 1-2-3 will display the addresses separated by two periods.

SPECIFYING A RANGE — EXPANDING THE CELL POINTER

When a range entry is called for during a 1-2-3 command or when a formula is being entered, the cell pointer can be expanded using the arrow keys to define a range. When the cell pointer is used to indicate a range, at least one corner of the range must be **anchored**. The procedure for anchoring one corner of the range is different for indicating a range in a command as opposed to entering a range in a formula. Procedures for both are outlined below:

- Example of command range entry using the cell pointer

  1. Move the cell pointer to E10.
  2. Enter /C.
  3. Notice the prompt, "Enter range to copy FROM: E10..E10". E10, the cell pointer's location when the command was invoked, will be the cell range's anchor.
  4. Using the arrow keys, move the cell pointer to location H20. Notice that the highlighted area and range indicator on line 2 of the control panel change as the cell pointer is moved. These represent the current range boundaries. Also, notice that the flashing underline is always positioned in the cell address diagonally opposite from the anchored corner. This position is known as the **free corner.**

- Example of formula range entry using the cell pointer

  1. Using the arrow keys, enter the following values:
     1,2,3,4
     into cells C5, C6, C7, and C8 respectively.
  2. Move the cell pointer to C10, and enter the following:
     @sum(
  3. Use the ↑ key to move the cell pointer to C8. Notice that C9 and C8 are indicated in the formula as ↑ is pressed, and that C8's value is displayed in line 1 of the control panel.
  4. Enter "." via the keyboard. This anchors C8 as one corner of the range. Notice that the formula is displayed as:
     @sum(C8..C8
     in line 2 of the control panel.
  5. Use the ↑ key to expand the range to C5. Notice that lines 1 and 2 in the control panel change as ↑ is pressed.

6. Enter ")" via the keyboard. This ends the formula entry process. The cell pointer returns to its original address, C10.

7. Finally, press the Enter key. Notice that the formula is calculated and its result displayed in C10. If we were to change the values stored at any of the cell addresses from C5 through C8 inclusive, the value displayed at C10 would vary accordingly.

A range can be specified in absolute terms while defining it by moving the cell pointer. This can be accomplished by pressing the F4 (Abs) key during definition.

MOVING THE ANCHOR WITH THE "." KEY

In the last section, we described how to anchor one corner of the cell range by pressing the "." key. Once the cell has been anchored, pressing "." once again will cause the anchor to move* to the next corner in the cell range. One visible effect of pressing "." is that the blinking cursor will move to the next corner. Since the free corner (with the blinking cursor) is always opposite the anchor corner, we know the anchor corner moves accordingly. Another visible effect of pressing "." is that the anchor and free cell indicators on line 2 of the control panel will change to reflect this movement. Figure 2-6 illustrates how to move the anchor cell by pressing the "." key.

REMOVING THE ANCHOR WITH THE ESC & BACKSPACE KEYS

As we mentioned earlier, pressing the Esc key causes 1-2-3 to return to the previous step. When a range is being prompted for, pressing Esc causes the expanded pointer to be reduced to the current cell and the anchor to be removed. This is illustrated in figure 2-7.

The Backspace key also can be used to reduce the expanded cell pointer to the current cell and to remove the anchor. This is illustrated in figure 2-7.

---

* The movement may either be clockwise or counterclockwise.

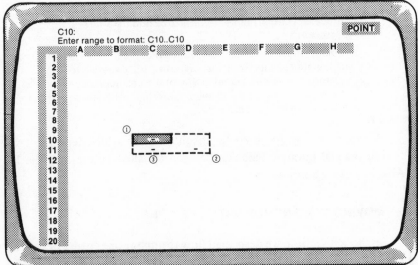

1. The command sequence to reach this point is /RFF ⏎.   2. Press ↓ followed by →.
3. Press ".". The control panel will change as follows:

         C11
         Enter range to format:D10..C11

FIGURE 2-6. Moving the Anchor with the "." Key

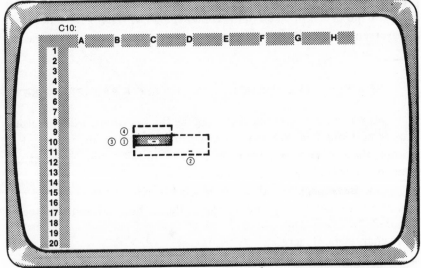

1. The command sequence to reach this point is /RFF⏎.   3. Press Esc or Backspace.
2. Press ↓ followed by →.   4. Press ↑.

FIGURE 2-7. Removing the Anchor with the Esc Key

Notice that pressing the Backspace key will return the cell pointer to the current cell — the position in which it was located before the command or formula was begun. In this respect, pressing Backspace differs from pressing Esc. Try running through the sequence outlined in figure 2-8. This example should illustrate the difference between Backspace and Esc.

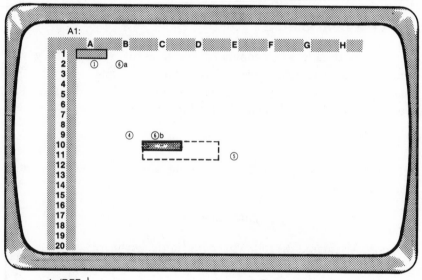

1. /RFF↵
2. Press the Esc key.
3. Use Arrow keys to move to C10.
4. Press "." to anchor cell.

5. Press ↓ then →.
6a. Press Backspace.
6b. Press Escape.

FIGURE 2-8. Removing the Anchor with the Backspace Key

RANGE NAMES

1-2-3 allows a range to be defined with a name consisting of as many as 15 characters. Generally, 1-2-3 users find a range name (i.e. SALES83) a more effective reference to a range than a pair of cell addresses (A5..A11).

1-2-3's **Range Name** commands are used to designate, alter, or delete range names. A menu of the current range names can be displayed by pressing the F3 key (Name). A range can be defined as being absolute during the naming process by preceding the name with $. If a range name is altered, all 1-2-3 formulas and commands referencing that name will be adjusted accordingly. For example, if SALES83 was altered so as to refer to (A5..A13) rather than A5..A11, any formula incorporating SALES83 (i.e. @sum (SALES83)), would be calculated using the revised range.

COMMAND RANGE

When certain 1-2-3 commands prompt for a range, they will remember the specified range and automatically display it if the command is subsequently re-entered. For example, suppose the **Data Fill** command had been specified with the following entry:

/DF

The following prompt would appear in the screen with the cell pointer stationed at A1:

Enter Fill Range:A1

Suppose we entered the following data via the keyboard:

A15..A20

The following prompts would appear. Press Enter in response to each.

*Start:0   Step:1   Step:2047

---

* This command is discussed on page 192.

The values 0-5 would then be displayed at A15-A20 respectively. If /**DF** were entered once again, the command range (A15..A20) would be displayed next to the prompt and would be highlighted with the expanded cell pointer. At this point, the command range could be left unchanged by pressing Enter, or it could be modified by altering the highlighted area as desired and then pressing Enter. If major command range alterations are required, the Esc key can be used to reduce the command range to the anchor cell, or the Backspace key could be used to return the cell pointer to the current cell.

A range other than the command range can also be specified by entering a new range name or by pressing F3 to define the range name menu and then selecting the desired name using the menu pointer.

CHANGING RANGE NAMES — /RANGE NAME CREATE

Once a range name has been assigned to a cell pointer using the **R**ange **N**ame **C**reate command, that name can subsequently be assigned a new cell range.

When a range name is changed, any other references to the initial cell range will be changed to the new range. These changes will be made regardless of whether the range was referenced by name or address name. These changes will include the following:

1. Other range names defined with the original cell range
2. Use of the original cell range in formulas
3. Command ranges using the initial cell range

This can be illustrated with the following example:

1. Enter 1000, 1100, 1200, 1300, 1400, and 1500 in A15 through A20. Enter 2000, 2200, 2400, 2600, 2800, and 3000 in B15 through B20.
2. Use /**R**ange **N**ame **C**reate to assign SALES83 to A15 through A20.
3. Assign the name REVENUE83 to these same cells.
4. Enter the formula @sum(SALES83) in A1.
5. Use /**R**ange **N**ame **C**reate to assign SALES83 to B15 through B20.

The following changes will be evident:

1. The formula calculation will change to reflect the new range name definition.
2. REVENUE83 will also be defined as B15 through B20. This can be verified by entering /**RNC** and indicating REVENUE with the menu pointer.
3. Subsequent execution of /Range Name Create will cause the expanded cell pointer to encompass B15 through B20.

When the name of a range consisting of just a single cell is redefined, any formula containing the original cell name will not be altered. This can be illustrated with the following example:

1. Enter 1000 in A15 and 2000 in B15.
2. Use /**R**ange **N**ame **C**reate to name cell A15 as SALES83.
3. Home the cell pointer and enter the following formula:

@sum(SALES83)

4. Use /**R**ange **N**ame **C**reate to redefine SALES83 as the range containing A15..B15. Notice that the formula will be displayed in line 1 of the control panel as:

A1:@sum(A15)

Also, the formula calculation in A1 remains constant at 1000.

EFFECT OF /MOVE, /WORKSHEET INSERT, & /WORKSHEET DELETE ON RANGE NAMES

When the upper left or lower right corner cell of a range is moved or deleted, the corresponding range name will be altered or erased respectively. This change will also affect any other range names defining that same range, any formulas incorporating the range name, and any command ranges.

The following example will illustrate the effect of the **M**ove command on range names and formulas:

1. Enter 1,2,3 in B5 through B7 and 4,5,6 in C5 through C7.
2. Define the aforementioned range as COUNT.
3. Enter @sum(COUNT) in A1.
4. Issue a **Move** command to move the value at C7 (the lower right-hand corner) to D9.
5. This will cause COUNT to be redefined as the cell range extending from B5..D9.

To illustrate the effect of / **W**orksheet **D**elete, erase the worksheet and repeat steps 1 through 3. Issue a **W**orksheet **D**elete command in step 4 again specifying C7. Notice that COUNT will no longer be defined as the range name for B5..C7. ERR will be displayed in A1 as well as in line 1 in the control panel when its contents are displayed.

Entering Formulas

Formula entry has already been introduced in this chapter. We will expand on that discussion over the next few pages. A **formula** can be defined in the context of 1-2-3 as an instruction which when executed will calculate a number. A formula can be entered in any 1-2-3 cell.

One method of entering a formula is to enter the actual values to be calculated. For example, the following formula could be entered in A10 to calculate the contents of A1 through A3 (see figure 2-9).

$$2000 + 4000 + 6000 \,\,\lrcorner$$

When Enter is pressed, the answer will be calculated and displayed in A10.

An easier means of undertaking this formula entry could be accomplished by indicating the cell address rather than the actual values. The following formula:

$$+ A1 + A2 + A3 \,\,\lrcorner$$

would yield identical results. Notice that we prefixed the formula with the + sign. If we had not done so, 1-2-3 would have interpreted A1 as a label.

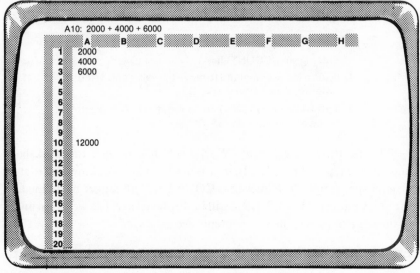

FIGURE 2-9. Formula Entry

Pointing is often an even more convenient means of entering a formula. For example, the following steps would result in the formula for adding A1 through A3 being placed in A10:

1. Position the cell pointer to A10.
2. Press +.
3. Move the cell pointer to A1.
4. Press +.
5. Move the cell pointer to A2.
6. Press +.
7. Move the cell pointer to A3.
8. Press Enter.
9. The cell pointer will automatically move to A10 and display the results of the calculation.

For certain formulas, a combination of pointing and typing is the easiest means of formula entry. For example, cells close to the cell pointer could be entered by pointing and those distant could be entered by typing. However, by using the TAB, PgUp, PgDn, and END keys, it may be just as convenient to use pointing exclusively. 1-2-3 allows the user to switch from pointing to typing as desired.

RELATIVE CELL ADDRESSING IN FORMULA ENTRY

Formulas are entered using relative cell addressing. In other words, if the following formula was entered into A5,

+ A1 + A2 + A3 ⏎

1-2-3 would interpret the entry as follows:

"The value in the cell four cells above the formula cell plus the value in the cell three cells above the formula cell plus the value in the cell two cells above the formula cell."

Notice that each cell in the formula is referenced relative to its position in relation to the formula cell. This is true regardless of whether the formula is entered by typing or by pointing.

Relative cell addressing is a big plus in formula entry as it allows the same formula to be moved from one area of the worksheet to another. This principle is illustrated in figure 2-10.

ABSOLUTE CELL ADDRESSING IN FORMULA ENTRY

In certain instances, it will be necessary for a formula to refer to a cell in absolute terms. A cell can be designated as absolute by prefixing both its column and row locations with the $ character. For example, if A10 was specified in a formula, it would reference cell A10 regardless of where that formula was subsequently copied. Figure 2-11 illustrates utilization of absolute cell addressing in formula entry.

If a formula is being entered by typing, a dollar sign can be incorporated with the formula by pressing that key. However, if a formula is being entered by pointing, the F4 (Abs) key must be used to insert the dollar sign character. Do not attempt to use the $ key.

MIXED CELL ADDRESSING IN FORMULA ENTRY

Mixed cell addresses are specified partly in absolute terms and partly in relative terms. When used with the Copy command, these can make formula entry much more efficient.

Figure 2-11 illustrates mixed cell addressing in formula entry. In

```
D3: + A3 * B3
         A         B         C         D         E         F         G         H
 1   Invoice   Commis.              Net
 2   Amount    %                    Commis.
 3    131.76    0.1                 13.176       ①
 4   2817.92    0.05                140.896   ⌉
 5    379.42    0.1                 37.942    │
 6   2112.17    0.05                105.6085  │
 7     47.17    0.1                 4.717     │   ④
 8    201.12    0.1                 20.112    │
 9    579.81    0.1                 57.981    │
10   5874.21    0.05                293.7105  ⌋
11
12
13
14
15
16
17
18
19
20
```

1. Enter +A3*B3.   2. /C↵   3. Specify D4..D10 as the range to copy to.   4. D4 through D10 will be calculated.

FIGURE 2-10. Relative Cell Addressing — Formula Entry

```
E3: + $A2 * D3
         A         B         C         D         E         F         G         H
 1   Commis.   Schedule             Invoice   Net
 2    0.05     Wholesale            Amount    Commis.
 3    0.1      Retail                131.76   6.588        ①
 4                                  2817.92
 5                                   379.42   18.97115     ③
 6                                  2112.17
 7                                    47.17
 8                                   201.12
 9                                   579.81
10                                  5874.21
11
12
13
14
15
16
17
18
19
20
```

1. Specify +A2*D3↵ in cell E3 either by typing or by using the cell pointer.   2. Execute the /C command.   3. Copy the formula from E3 to E5. The result will be calculated.

FIGURE 2-11. Formula Entry Using Absolute Cell Addressing

figure 2-11, we are solving for the present value of a future stream of income. For example, suppose that we had just bought a lottery ticket where the following four prizes were being offered:

- $1,000 per year for the next 25 years
- $2,000 per year for the next 25 years
- $4,000 per year for the next 25 years
- $25,000 per year for the next 25 years

E2: @PV($B2,E$1,25)

	A	B	C	D	E	F
1			0.08	0.10	0.12	
2		1000.00	10674.78	9077.04	7843.14	
3		2000.00	21349.55	18154.08	15686.28	
4		4000.00	42699.10	36308.16	31372.56	
5		40000.00	426991.05	363081.60	313725.56	
6						
7						
8						
9						
10						
11						
12						
13						
14						
15						
16						
17						
18						
19						
20						

FIGURE 2-12. Mixed Cell Address Entry

Although the total gross award for each prize could be easily calculated (i.e. $1,000 per year x 25 years = $25,000 prize), figuring the value of the stream of future payments discounted for different interest rates would be more difficult. 1-2-3's present value (@PV) function (see page 253) makes this calculation relatively simple. Suppose we wished to calculate the present value of each prize assuming interest rates of 8%, 10%, and 12%. One way of doing so would be to enter 12 separate formulas utilizing absolute addressing:

@PV(B2,C1,25)
@PV(B3,C1,25)
⋮

By using mixed cell addressing with the Copy command, this task could be accomplished by entering just one formula and then copying it to the other 19 cells.

For each formula, the annuity can be defined as "the value in Column B in the same row as the formula". If we were entering a formula into C2, the relative entry B2 would initially work for the annuity value. B2 can essentially be interpreted as "use the cell to the immediate left". Obviously, once the formula was moved to D2 and E2, the results would be erroneous. What is required is an entry that in effect states, "the cell in Column B in the current row". Such a statement could be accomplished with the following mixed address:

$$\$B2$$

Likewise, the interest portion of the formula would also require a mixed address. We need an entry that specifies, "the cell in the current column in row 1". Our formula entry for C2 would require the following mixed address:

$$C\$1$$

Try entering the following formula:

$$@PV(\$B2,C\$1,25)$$

in C2. Then, execute / Copy to copy this formula to the remaining cells in the table. The screen should resemble that depicted in figure 2-12.

USING CELL RANGES IN FORMULAS

Formulas can process cell ranges as well as individual cell addresses. Ranges, however, cannot be processed with the standard arithmetic operators (+ - / *).

@ FUNCTIONS

Functions can be defined as formulas which have been built into 1-2-3 and are predefined to perform a standard calculation. Functions can be used within a formula. Each function begins with the @ character.

1-2-3 functions are defined with function names. The function argument follows the function name. The argument contains one or more values which are called by the function in order to perform the calculation. Certain functions allow cell ranges to be specified as arguments. The function arguments are set off from the function name by parentheses. The various 1-2-3 functions will be discussed in detail in chapter 10.

CHANGING FORMULAS

Once a formula has been entered, it can later be revised. A formula can also be edited during the cell entry process. 1-2-3 will most likely be in the Value mode during the cell entry process. The following keys can be used to edit a formula entry in the Value mode:

- Backspace   Erases the character preceding the cursor
- Esc   Cancels the entry and returns 1-2-3 to the Ready mode

If values are being entered into the formula by pointing, these keys should not be used when the cell pointer-movement keys are active. 1-2-3 will be in the Point mode when these keys are active.

In the Point mode, pressing Esc causes the cell address to be deleted from the formula. The cell pointer will return to the formula cell, and 1-2-3 will return to the Value mode. Backspace also returns the cell pointer to the formula cell. However, the indicated cell's address will not be deleted. Also, 1-2-3 will remain in the Point mode. If the cell pointer is being expanded to indicate a cell range, pressing Esc will cause the free cell's address to be deleted from the formula. The expanded cell pointer will be shrunk to the anchor cell, and the anchor will be removed from that cell.

Pressing Backspace will cancel the entire cell range and will return the cell pointer to the formula cell. 1-2-3 will remain in the Point mode.

The Edit mode can be accessed during formula entry by pressing the Edit key. The editing function is described on page 44.

F9 — CALC KEY

The Calc key, F9, can be used during formula entry or editing as desired to convert the formula to its current value. No other recalculations will occur.

Calc can also be useful in other ways during formula entry. For example, Calc can be used as follows to display an entry outside of the worksheet viewing area:

- Enter +AI99. ◄── desired cell address
- Press F9.
- The value will be indicated.
- Press Esc to erase the display.

1-2-3 OPERATORS

As our examples have already evidenced, 1-2-3 allows the basic arithmetic operators to be used in formulas. A list of these in their order of precedence is provided in table 2-1. Precedence is the order in which 1-2-3 performs mathematical operations. When all operators have the same precedence, the operations will be performed from left to right.

The order of precedence can be changed by using parentheses. Operations within parentheses will always be performed first followed by operations outside of parentheses. When parentheses are nested, the innermost operations will be performed first. The effect of parentheses in formula evaluation can be observed by entering the following into 1-2-3's worksheet. Notice how the use of parentheses affects the formula's values.

```
+G5 +200*G4
+(G5 + 200)*G4
+G3 + G1 ^ 2
+(G3 + G1) ^ 2
+G3*G1/2
+G3*(G1/2)
```

*Relational operators are generally used to compare values. The following relational operators are available in 1-2-3:

    =   equal
    <   less than
    <= less than or equal
    >   greater than
    >= greater than or equal
    <> not equal

Table 2-1.   1-2-3 Operators in Order of Precedence

Operator	Description
^	Exponentiation
+	Positive
-	Negative
*	Multiplication
/	Division
+	Addition
-	Subtraction
=	Equal
<	Less than
<=	Less than or equal
>	Greater than
>=	Greater than or equal
<>	Not equal
#NOT#	Logical not
#AND#	Logical and
#OR#	Logical or

A relational operation evaluates to either true or false. For example, if the constant 1.0 was compared to the constant 2.0 to see whether they were equal, the expression would evaluate to false. The only values returned by a comparison in 1-2-3 are +1 (true) or 0 (false). These values can be used as any other integer would be used. The relational expressions listed below generate the following results:

---

* 1-2-3 terms these operators as logical operators. In most programming languages, this term is reserved for the various Boolean operators (AND, NOT OR, etc.).

```
5 > 7        0 (false)
5 > 2        +1 (true)
7 = 7        +1 (true)
```

Relational operations are evaluated after the addition and subtraction arithmetic operations. The order of evaluation of the relational operators is given in table 2-2.

1-2-3 also allows the use of the following logical or Boolean operations:

```
*#NOT#       logical not
 #AND#       logical and
 #OR#        logical or
```

NOT (logical complement), AND (conjunction), and OR (disjunction) return results as depicted in figure 2-13.

A logical operator evaluates an input of one or more operands with true or false values. The logical operator evaluates these true or false values and returns a value of true or false itself. An operand of a logical operator is evaluated as true if it has a non-zero value. (Remember, relational operators return a value of +1 for a true value.) An operand of a logical operator is evaluated as false if it is equal to zero. The result of a logical operation is also a number which, if non-zero, is considered true, and false if it is true.

---

* In 1-2-3, Boolean operators begin and end with the # sign. This is not the case in the BASIC programming language.

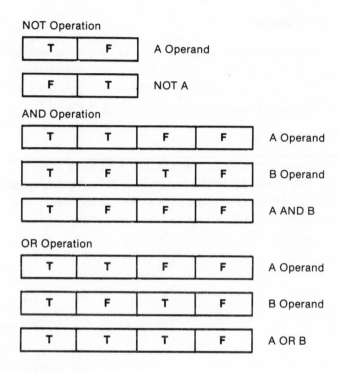

FIGURE 2-13. NOT, AND, OR

Logical operators are generally used in 1-2-3 to compare the outcomes of two relational operations. Examples of possible uses of logical operators in 1-2-3 are given below:

+flag1=1#OR#flag2=1	A value of +1 will be returned if the contents of either of the one-cell ranges named flag1 or flag2 contain a value of 1.
+A10>1000#AND#A11>200	A value of +1 will be returned only if the values stored at A10>1000 and A11>200.
#NOT#(E15)	If E15 contains a zero value, +1 will be returned. Otherwise, zero will be returned.

Keyboard Macros

1-2-3 allows its user to define a series of keystrokes as a **keyboard macro**. Keyboard macros can be used for entering commands, entering data, creating graphs, etc. As keyboard macros are a somewhat advanced topic, we will defer our discussion of them until chapter 11.

Conclusion

At this point, you should be familiar with basic 1-2-3 worksheet operation. The remainder of this book will be dedicated to expanding on these basic operations, discussing advanced 1-2-3 features and providing practical examples of 1-2-3 usage to solve specific applications.

3

Main Command Menu and
Worksheet Commands

Main Command Menu

In the context of 1-2-3, a command can be defined as an instruction, which when executed, will cause a specific operation to be undertaken. 1-2-3 commands are selected from the main command menu. This menu can be displayed on the 2nd line of the control panel when 1-2-3 is in the Ready mode by entering the slash character (/). The control panel's third line will contain a short explanation of the menu pointer. The main command menu display is depicted in figure 1-1 on page 19.

The various 1-2-3 commands are arranged in a tree-like structure. The main command menu selections correspond to the trunks of each tree. The various commands available in the submenus correspond to branches. Separate chapters in this book will be dedicated to the various main menu selections. These include:

Worksheet	Data
Range	Graph
File	Print
Copy	Quit
Move	

An illustration depicting the tree structure of each main menu command will be included at the beginning of each chapter. In this chapter, we will discuss the Worksheet commands.

Once the main command menu has been accessed, subsequent command selections can be made in either of two ways — by indicating the desired item with the menu pointer or by entering one or more letters correpsonding to the first name(s) of the command.

A command can be exited by pressing the Esc key. This will return 1-2-3 to the step previously executed. By pressing Esc repeatedly, eventually 1-2-3 will return to the Ready mode. The Ready mode can also be entered by pressing the Control-Break key sequence.

Worksheet Commands

The Worksheet commands are as follows:

Global	Erase
Insert	Titles
Delete	Window
Column-Width	Status

The tree structure of the Worksheet commands is depicted in figure 3-1.

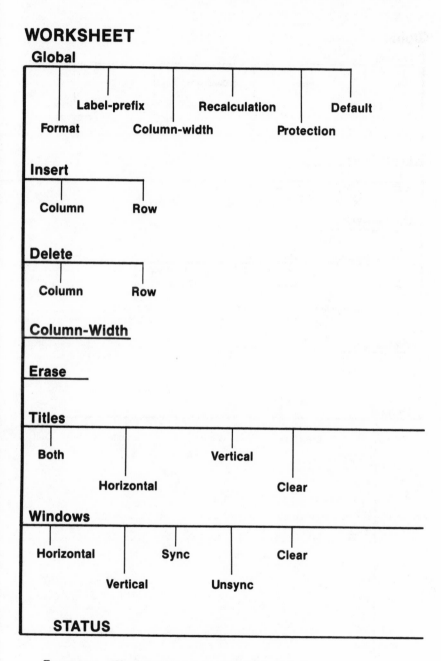

WORKSHEET

Global

Format · Label-prefix · Column-width · Recalculation · Protection · Default

Insert

Column · Row

Delete

Column · Row

Column-Width

Erase

Titles

Both · Horizontal · Vertical · Clear

Windows

Horizontal · Vertical · Sync · Unsync · Clear

STATUS

FIGURE 3-1. Worksheet Command Tree Structure

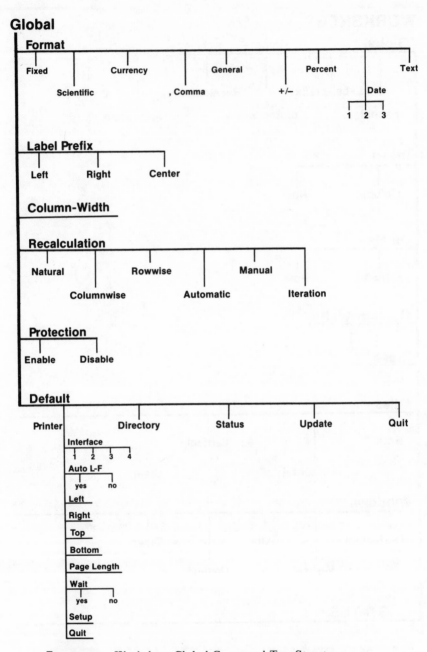

FIGURE 3-2. Worksheet Global Command Tree Structure

The Worksheet commands can be categorized as follows:

- **System Information Commands**
  These commands return information pertaining to the system hardware.
- **Determine Worksheet Settings**
  These commands determine the overall appearance of the worksheet.
- **Changing Worksheet Contents**
  These commands allow the user to alter the worksheet contents during a 1-2-3 session. Columns and/or rows can be inserted or deleted. Also, the entire worksheet can be erased.

/Worksheet Global Commands

The Worksheet Global commands allow the user to control the worksheet as follows:

- Format* in which numeric entries are to be displayed
- Alignment of labels within cells
- Column width settings

Whenever 1-2-3 begins executing, the global setting will automatically be initialized as shown in table 3-1. If these default settings are subsequently changed, they can be re-established by executing the Worksheet Erase command or by re-entering the necessary command sequences to reset those settings which had been altered. Of course, / Worksheet Erase causes the entire worksheet to be erased.

When global settings are changed, those changes will be stored along with the cell entries in any worksheet files created with / File Save.

---

*Worksheet commands only affect the way in which numbers are displayed on the screen. They do not affect the way in which 1-2-3 stores these values internally.

Table 3-1. Default Global Command Settings

Global Setting	Default Value	Other Values
Format	General	Fixed, scientific, currency, +/-, percent, date text
Label Alignment	Left	Right, Center
Column-Width	9 characters	1-72 characters

The Global commands control the five worksheet features detailed in table 3-1. Each of these will be discussed individually.

WORKSHEET GLOBAL FORMAT

The Worksheet Global Format (/ WGF) command controls the format of numbers and formulas entered into the worksheet. The various format options are detailed in table 3-2.

No matter which format option is selected and regardless of how it appears on the display, 1-2-3 will store the entire value (up to 15 decimal places) in memory. It is also possible to select two different Global Formats while using the Worksheet Windows command. This allows values to be viewed under different options at the same time.

For example, the results of formulas could be viewed in one window using the General Format Option while the formulas themselves could be viewed under the text option in the other window. Also, the serial numbers of dates using General Format could be viewed in one window, while the more common dates were displayed in the other window using the Date Format Option.

Table 3-2. Worksheet Global Format Command Options

/WGF OPTION	Description
Fixed	This option sets the number of decimal places to be included in number and formula displays. The user will be prompted to enter the number of decimal places desired. A default of 2 will be displayed. For example, if the /**WGFF** response was 5, a subsequent cell entry of 9 would be displayed as 9.00000.
Scientific	This option displays numbers and formulas in exponential scientific notation. The number of decimal places will be prompted for. A response of 2 (the default) will cause our previous entry to be displayed as 9.00E+00.
Currency	This option causes numbers and formula entries to be preceded by a $. Negative values will be displayed in parentheses, and commas will be inserted between thousands. The number of decimal places will be prompted for. If the default (2) was chosen, our previous entry would have been displayed as $9.00.
,Comma	With the , (comma) Option, values are displayed with commas inserted between thousands. Negative values will be enclosed in parentheses. The user will be prompted to specify the number of decimal places (0-15) to be displayed. If -9000 was entered and the default number of decimal places (2) was chosen, the number would be displayed as: (-9,000.00)* ——————————— *Assuming column-width of at least 10.
General	This is the initial global format. With this option, trailing zeros to the right of the decimal point are not displayed. Very large and very small numbers are displayed in scientific notation. The following are examples of numeric values entered using a column-width of 9:

/WGF Option	Description
	Value Entered **Display** 9.00 9 1200900000 1.2E+09 .00000000012 1.2E-10 .000000012 0.000000 9999999.9 9999999. 1/3 0.333333 -1234.567 -1234.56 The column width setting will determine the allowable number of digits in a numeric entry before it will be displayed in scientific notation.
+/–	This option can also be referred to as the horizontal bar graph option. If a numeric value is entered when this command is in effect, the cell will be filled with +, -, or. characters depending upon the value. If the value is a positive integer, the cell will be filled with that number of + characters. For example, an entry of 9 would result in the following display: +++++++++ If the entry is negative, the cell will be filled with that number of - characters. For example, an entry of -2 would result in the following display: -- Any entry in the range $-1 < 0 < +1$ will cause a period (.) to be displayed. For example, an entry of 0.9 would cause a single period to be displayed in that cell. If the absolute value of the cell entry exceeds the column width, the cell will be filled with the * character. An entry of 10 with a column width setting of 9 would result in the following display: *********
Percent	This option displays the value entered multiplied times 100. The number of decimal places to be displayed must be specified by the user. Examples of entries using the default decimal display of 2 follow:

/WGF Option	Description
	Value Entered **Display** 2 200.00% .5 50.00% .01 1.00% .006 0.60%
Date	The Date Format Option allows a **date serial number** entered into a cell to be displayed in one of the following formats: **Format** **Display** 1 Day-Month-Year 2 Day-Month 3 Month-Year To use the Date Format Options, the date must be entered as a **date serial number**. A date serial number is a number between 1 (Jan. 1, 1900) and 73049 (Dec. 31, 2099). These serial numbers represent dates to 1-2-3 and allow 1-2-3 to perform calculations using dates. For proper display of Date Format 1, the column-width must be set to at least 10. For Date Format 2 and 3, the column-width must be set to at least 7. Date Format example entries are provided below: **Format** **Serial Date Entry** **Cell Display** Date 1 30682 01-Jan-84 Date 2 2000 22-Jun-05 Date 3 40022 29-Jul-2009 To generate the serial number for a particular date, the @DATE (configuration: @DATE (*year, month, day*)) function must be used. For example, to generate the serial number for January 15, 1955, the following would be entered: @DATE(55,1,15) If @DATE (55,1,15) was executed with the general format command in effect, that function would return a serial number (20104) rather than a date. With Date Format Option 1 in effect, @DATE (55,1,15) would return the following: 15-Jan-55

/WGF Option	Description
	The @TODAY function can also be used to generate a date serial number. The @TODAY function returns the serial number of the date entered when the computer was started for the current session. If the date was 1-1-84, then when the @TODAY function was entered under Date Format Option 1, the following would be displayed:
	01-Jan-84
Text	The Text Option displays numbers in general format and formulas exactly as they were entered. Formula display is limited by the column-width setting. The following are examples of entries made with the Text Option active with a column-width setting of 15:

Entry	Display
2.00	2
2*A4/(3.5*B4)	2*A4/(3.5*B4)
@SUM(A1..A15)	@SUM(A1..A15)
+A1+A2+B1+B2+C1+C2	+A1+A2+B1+B2+C

WORKSHEET GLOBAL LABEL-PREFIX

The label-prefix indicates whether a label will be right-justified, centered or left-justified within a cell. The initial global label prefix is ', which indicates left-justification. With the Worksheet Global Label-Prefix command (/WGL), the global label-prefix can be changed to ∧ (centered), " (right justified) or back to the initial setting.

To override / Worksheet Global Label-Prefix, use / Range Label-Prefix or edit the cell entry by deleting the global label-prefix character and replacing it with another. Also, a new entry with a prefix character will override Worksheet Global Label-Prefix.

Once a label has been entered, it cannot be changed by altering the global label prefix setting. Changing the global prefix setting only affects labels entered after that change.

Table 3-3. Label-Prefix Characters

Label-Prefix Characters	Description
'	Denotes left-justification in the cell.
"	Denotes right-justification in the cell.
∧	Labels will be centered in the cell.
\	Label will be repeated across the width of the cell. For example, if BOB was entered in A1 and A1 had a width of 9 characters, the following would be displayed in A1: BOBBOBBOB The \ (backslash) label prefix must be entered initially with the label or by editing. It cannot be specified as a global label prefix or range label-prefix setting.

WORKSHEET GLOBAL COLUMN-WIDTH

The initial global column-width setting is 9 spaces. With / Worksheet Global Column-Width (/ WGC), the global column-width can be set to any width from 1 to 72 spaces. / WGC does not affect any columns that have been changed using the **Worksheet Column-Width** command. However, it does affect columns that have been changed but subsequently Reset to the global column-width. To change the global column width to 15, follow these steps:

User Step 1:	Select **/WGC**
1-2-3 Response:	Enter global column width (1..72):9*
User Step 2:	Enter column-width desired either by pressing 1, 5 or by pressing the → key until the desired width appears. To decrease the width, press the ← key.
User Step 3:	Press ↵

WORKSHEET GLOBAL RECALCULATION

The **Worksheet Global Recalculation** command controls the global recalculation setting. The **Global Recalculation** setting controls how the formulas in the worksheet will be recalculated, **Natural, Rowwise, Columnwise.** This command also determines whether the worksheet will automatically be recalculated or whether the user will have to press F9 to recalculate. The number of iterations 1-2-3 performs during each calculation is also controlled by this setting.

To change the **Worksheet Global Recalculation** setting, press **/WGR**. The following choices will be displayed:

Natural Columnwise Rowwise	Automatic Manual	Iteration
order of recalculation	initiation of recalculation	no. of recalculations

As indicated above, three types of choices can be made concerning recalculation methods under this command.

The initial setting is **Natural/Automatic/Iteration-1.** A discussion of the other options is provided in table 3-4.

---

* The number displayed is the current global column-width setting.

Table 3-4. Worksheet Global Recalculation Command Options

/WGR Option	Description
Natural	This is the initial global recalculation setting. In this setting, 1-2-3 considers all interdependent relationships between cells (example: formulas which reference that cell address). When /**WGR** has been set to natural, 1-2-3 will calculate all other cells that are referenced by a formula before calculating that formula. For example, if the following formula was stored in A5, $\qquad$ +A6*(D5/D6) 1-2-3 would recalculate cells A6, D5 and D6 before recalculating A5, as the formula in A5 is dependent on the values in A6, D5 and D6. This method of recalculation can lead to what is known as a **circular reference**. A circular reference occurs when two cells are dependent on one another either directly or indirectly. An example of a **direct dependency** follows: $\qquad$ **location** $\qquad\qquad$ **entry** $\qquad\quad$ A2 $\qquad\qquad\qquad$ +A4 $\qquad\quad$ A4 $\qquad\qquad\qquad$ +A3(A2*2) If these entries were made, the indicator, CIRC, would appear in the lower right portion of the screen. This would indicate a circular reference on the worksheet. To facilitate finding the formula(s) involved in the circular reference, it may be helpful to use the text format for display or to printout all the cell entries using the cell formulas option. An example of indirect dependency follows: $\qquad$ **location** $\qquad\qquad$ **entry** $\qquad\quad$ A2 $\qquad\qquad\qquad$ +A4+1 $\qquad\quad$ A3 $\qquad\qquad\qquad$ +A2+1 $\qquad\quad$ A4 $\qquad\qquad\qquad$ +A3*(B1/2) $\qquad\quad$ B1 $\qquad\qquad\qquad$ 4 A4 is indirectly dependent on A2 through the reference to A3, while A2 is directly dependent on A4. Enter the above entries in the worksheet and press F9 (Recalculation Key). Notice that each time F9 is pressed, the values in A2, A3, and A4 increase. Unless this type of interdependent relationship is necessary, circular references should be corrected.

Table 3-4.   (cont.) Worksheet Global Recalculation Command Options

/WGR Option	Description
Columnwise	This option can be used when control over the recalculation order is needed by the user. With columnwise recalculation, 1-2-3 will recalculate each cell in column order beginning with A1, followed by A2, A3, etc. ...A2048. Columns B, C, D, etc. will then be recalculated. If circular references are present, they will not be indicated by 1-2-3. The columnwise option assumes that any circular references were planned.
Rowwise	With this option in force, recalculation will be undertaken by rows. For example, A1 will be calculated first, followed by B1, C1, etc. through IV1. A2, B2, C2 etc. will then be recalculated. Circular references will not be indicated.
Automatic	This is a default option (in conjunction with Natural and Iteration of 1). With the Automatic recalculation option in effect, the entire worksheet will be recalculated each time a cell entry is made or changed. It is also recalculated each time the F9 Key is pressed.
Manual	Under this option, the user must press the F9 key to recalculate the worksheet. The CALC indicator will appear in the lower right area of the screen if any cell entries have been made or changed since the last recalculation of the worksheet. This option can save time when the worksheet is large and a great number of entries must be made. The user will not have to wait for 1-2-3 to recalculate each time an entry is made. Manual can be used when a worksheet includes intentional circular references, and it is necessary to recalculate only a specified number of times.
Iteration	This option controls the number of calculation cycles 1-2-3 will perform during each recalculation. The initial setting is 1, but when prompted, the user can enter any number between 1 and 50.

WORKSHEET GLOBAL PROTECTION

With the Worksheet Global Protection command (/WGP), a worksheet can be "protected" against unwanted changes. Global Protection can either be **disabled** (the initial setting) or **enabled**. If Global Protection is enabled, a cell entry cannot be made unless the Range Unprotect command has first been used to disable that cell protection.

If the user attempts to enter information into a protected cell, 1-2-3 will beep and enter the Error mode. The error message "Protected cell" will appear in the lower left corner of the screen. The same error will occur if the user attempts to execute /Worksheet Delete, /Worksheet Insert, /Range Erase, /Copy, /Move, /Data Fill, or /Range Justify. However, execution of /Worksheet Erase, even while protection is enabled, will result in erasure of the entire worksheet.

WORKSHEET GLOBAL DEFAULT

This command allows the user to choose the type of printer interface as well as the page format to be used by the printer. /WGD also allows the user to specify the disk drive to be used for saving and retrieving files.

Whenever 1-2-3 is started, the program reads a configuration file entitled "1-2-3.CNF" from the 1-2-3 System disk. This file contains a number of **default configurations**. These include details on the hardware being used, the printer output format, and the disk drive being used for data storage. The default configurations are listed in table 3-5. /Worksheet Global Default allows the 1-2-3 user to change the default configuration values.

Five options are displayed by /WGD. These are:

- **Printer**   Allows the printer default configurations to be set
- **Directory**   Displays the current directory and allows a new directory specification
- **Status**   Displays current default configurations
- **Update**   Stores configuration settings on 123.CNF
- **Quit**   Exits to worksheet

Table 3-5. 1-2-3.CNF Default Configurations

Default Item	Default Setting	Description
Printer		
Interface	Parallel	A parallel printer interface card is installed
Auto Line-Feed	No	The printer does not output a line feed after encountering the carriage return character.
Left Margin	4	The left margin is set to 4 characters.
Right Margin	76	The right margin is set to 76 characters.
Top Margin	2	The top margin is set to 2 lines.
Bottom Margin	2	The bottom margin is set to 2 lines.
Page length	66	The page length is set to 66 lines.
Pause at end of page	No	No pause will occur when the end of the page is reached.
Setup String	None	The printer does not require a special setup string.
Directory	B:	Worksheet files will be stored on the data disk in drive B.

Although most of the default configuration settings are self-explanatory, two of them, interface and setup string, warrant an extended discussion. To install a printer with a computer, an interface card and cable are generally required. These are generally designed as either serial or parallel devices. 1-2-3's default configuration must be set according to the type of interface being used. The default configuration options are as follows:

1 Parallel   Parallel interface used with IBM Monchrome Display/Printer Adapter card.

2 Serial   Serial interface used with IBM Asynchronous Communications card.

3 Second Parallel   Optional second parallel interface.

4 Second Serial   Optional second serial interface.

With most printers, a series of special characters can be sent allowing that device to produce specialized output (ex. expanded characters, compressed characters, color printing, etc.). Each printer recognizes a different set of special characters, or **control codes.**

In 1-2-3, these control code characters must be specified either as ASCII characters, or as the ASCII code for that character preceded by a backslash (required for ASCII codes 0-32). The ASCII codes are listed in appendix A.

The following setup string:

$$\backslash 027; \backslash 075$$

would represent the control string, ESC $\wedge$ 0. On a Epson MX printer, this string specifies condensed output.

WORKSHEET INSERT

The **Worksheet Insert** command (**/WI**) enables insertion of one or more columns or rows. The user, upon being prompted, must specify whether columns or rows are to be inserted. Then, he or she must specify the range into which the blank columns or rows are to be inserted. If columns are being inserted, any entries located within the specified range will shift to the right of that range.

The following example should clarify / **Worksheet Insert.** Suppose the worksheet appeared as follows:

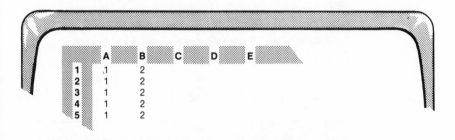

and the following steps were performed:

User Step 1:	Select **/WI**
1-2-3 Response:	Column Row
User Step 2:	Select **C**

1-2-3 Response: Enter column insert range: A1..A1
User Step 3:   Press ↵

The worksheet will then appear as follows:

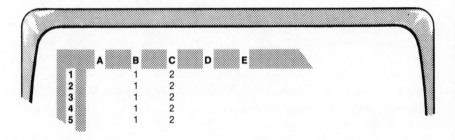

Notice that even though the range specified was A1..A1, an entire column of blank cells was inserted as though the range specified was A1..A2048. The **W**orksheet **I**nsert command inserts only entire rows and columns of blank cells.

When rows are inserted, any entries located within the specified range will shift down.

Using the figure pictured above as the starting point, perform the following:

User Step 1:   Select **/WI**
1-2-3 Response: Column Row
User Step 2:   Select **R**
1-2-3 Response: Enter row insert range: A1..A1
User Step 3:   Press ↵

The worksheet will now appear as follows:

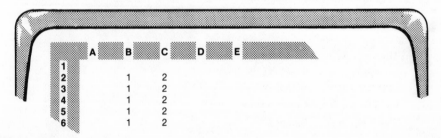

When the cell entries were shifted during this command, the values in the cells were not affected and any formulas referencing cell addresses were automatically changed to reflect the move.

WORKSHEET DELETE

The Worksheet Delete command (/WD) removes entire rows and columns. Since cell entries are deleted during execution of this command, it is recommended that the worksheet be saved on diskette using the File Save command to prevent accidental loss of a vital part of the worksheet. When columns are deleted using this command, all information located in cells within the specified columns is deleted, and the remaining worksheet shifts left to occupy the deleted area.

For example, if the current worksheet appeared as follows:

	A	B	C	D	E
1	1	2	3	4	
2	1	2	3	4	
3	1	2	3	4	
4	1	2	3	4	
5	1	2	3	4	

and the following entries were made,

User Step 1:	Select **/WD**
1-2-3 Response:	Column Rows
User Step 2:	Select **C**
1-2-3 Response:	Enter range of columns to delete:A1..A1
User Step 3:	Press Esc →.→⌐ or; type B1..C1⌐

the worksheet would appear as follows:

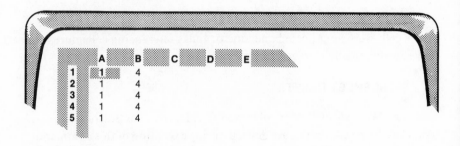

When rows are deleted, the entire worksheet will shift upward to occupy the deleted rows. The following example will illustrate the process of deleting rows. If the worksheet appeared as follows,

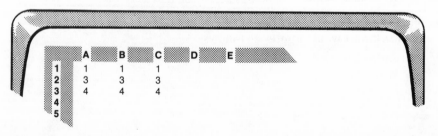

and the following entries were made,

User Step 1:	Select /**WD**
1-2-3 Response:	Column Row
User Step 2:	Select **R**
1-2-3 Response:	Enter range of rows to be deleted A1..A1
User Step 3:	ESC ↓. ↵

the worksheet would then appear as follows:

When cell entries were shifted during the execution of **Worksheet Delete**, the values remained the same and references to cells were automatically adjusted to reflect the change. If a cell that was deleted was referenced in a formula, the cell address was replaced by ERR.

WORKSHEET COLUMN-WIDTH

/ **Worksheet Column-Width** enables the user to change the width of any column in the worksheet or reset the column-width to the global column-width. Before selecting / **WC**, place the pointer on the column to be changed. When / **WC** is selected, the following will appear:

Set   Reset

Selecting **R**eset will return the width of the current column to the global column-width. If **S**et is selected, the following message will be displayed:

Enter column width (1..72):9

The last number denotes the current column-width. The desired column-width can be specified either by typing the number of spaces from 1 to 72 and pressing ↵ to execute the command or by using the left and right arrow keys. The left arrow key will decrease the column-width of the worksheet as the number decreases, and the right arrow key will increase the width of the column and the number. This enables the user to view the worksheet with different column-widths before actually executing the command. To execute the command, press Enter.

WORKSHEET ERASE

Worksheet Erase (/ **WE**) erases the entire current worksheet. All information contained in the worksheet will be lost. Saving the worksheet first on diskette with / **File Sa**ve will preserve the current worksheet for future sessions.

When / **WE** is selected, 1-2-3 will respond with the following menu:

No   Yes

If No is selected, the current worksheet will remain unchanged and 1-2-3 will return to the Ready mode.

Selecting Yes will cause the current worksheet to be erased from the screen. The screen will display a blank worksheet and all global settings will be returned to their initial settings.

WORKSHEET TITLES

The **W**orksheet **T**itles command (/ **WT**) will keep selected rows along the top of the screen and / or columns along the left edge stationary. The 'titles' created allow movement around the worksheet while row and / or column headings retain their visibility.

When / **WT** is selected, the following menu will appear:

Both Horizontal Vertical Clear

The details of the menu options and the effects of each on the worksheet are detailed in table 3-6.

Table 3-6. Worksheet Titles Command Options

/WT Option	Description
Both	This option sets both vertical and horizontal titles. All rows above the position of the cell pointer when /**WTB** was executed, and all columns to the left of the cell pointer will become "titles". Title columns can be scrolled up and down. Each title column heading remains with its respective row as it is scrolled up or down. Title columns can not move from left to right. Title rows can move from left to right, but will not move down or up.
Horizontal	The Horizontal option defines all rows above the cell pointer as title rows when /**WTH** is executed. Horizontal title row headings will scroll left and right with their respective columns.
Vertical	When the Vertical option is selected, all columns to the left of the cell pointer at the time /**WTV** is executed will become title columns. Vertical title columns will scroll up and down in harmony with the other columns, but will not move right and left.
Clear	This option clears the worksheet of any title settings and returns normal movement to the screen.

Pointer movement to the titles area is restricted. If the user tries to point to a cell in the titles area, 1-2-3 will beep and will not allow the cell pointer to move into that area. The F5 (GOTO) Key can be used to move the pointer into the title area while in the Ready mode. While in the Point mode (for example, while specifying a range while using / Copy), the user will be able to move into the titles area by using the arrow keys. When the pointer is moved into the titles area, either with GOTO or by pointing, two copies of the titles row and/or column will be displayed. When this occurs in the point mode, the second title row or column will disappear, once the user returns to the Ready mode.

The following example illustrates usage of / **Worksheet Titles Both**. Suppose the initial worksheet appeared as follows:

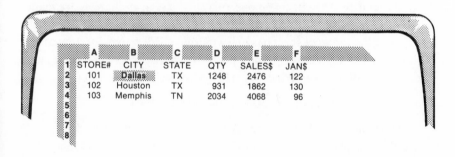

If the cell pointer was on B2 when / **WTB** was executed, the first row would become a title row. If the screen was scrolled up one row, it would appear as follows:

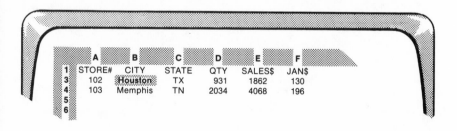

If the screen was scrolled to the left, it would appear as follows:

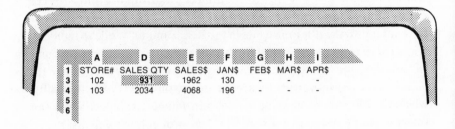

WORKSHEET WINDOWS

This command allows distant areas of the worksheet to be viewed simultaneously. The effects on one area can be seen as changes are made to another area.

Initially, the worksheet has one window. To view two different areas or two windows, place the pointer position where the screen is to be split and select / Worksheet Windows. The following menu will appear:

Horizontal Vertical Sync Unsync Clear

Horizontal and Vertical specify how the worksheet will be divided. If the pointer is placed on A50 and Horizontal is selected, the display will appear as follows:

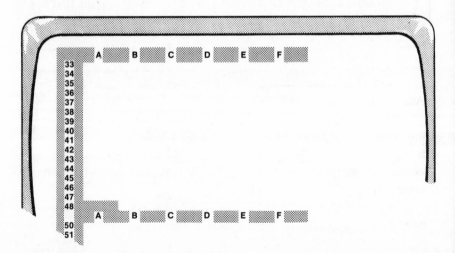

The two windows appear together. Each window has its own column and row headings. To move the cell pointer back and forth between the two windows, use the Window [F6] Key. Initially, both windows will have the same column widths and formats. These settings for global as well as individual columns can be changed on either window independent of the other.

To split the screen vertically, place the cell pointer at the position where the screen is to be split. In this example, the screen will appear as follows, after the user presses /**WWV**:

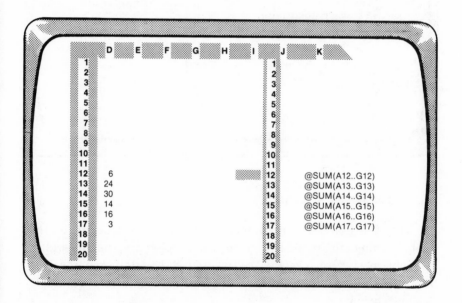

Again, to move the pointer between the windows, use the F6 key.

Sync and Unsync allow the user to select either synchronized scrolling for the two windows or unsychronized scrolling. Initially, the setting is synchronized. When the user scrolls horizontally split windows, the same columns appear on both screens. On vertically split windows, the same rows appear in each window.

When Unsync or unsynchonized scrolling is selected, the two windows scroll independent of each other.

The following figure depicts how / **WWV** would appear if scrolling was unsynchronized, and the right window was scrolled up.

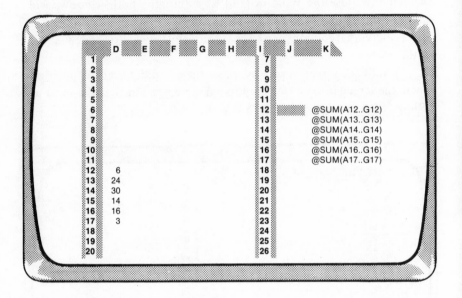

WORKSHEET STATUS

The Worksheet Status command provides a status report on the global settings for recalculation, format, label-prefix, column-width, available memory (in bytes) and cell protection. This status report will be located in the control panel above the actual worksheet area. An example is shown below:

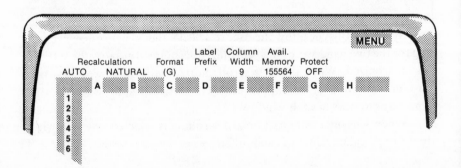

The example shows the initial settings for 1-2-3, except for Available Memory which will vary from system to system. Table 3-7 lists the possibilities for each area.

Table 3-7. / Worksheet Status Settings

Status Indicator	Options	Meaning
Recalculation	Auto Natural Auto Column Auto Row Manual Natural Manual Column Manual Row	
Format (where n = no. of decimal places)	(G) (Fn) (Sn) (Cn) (,n) (+) (Pn) (D1) (D2) (D3) (T)	General Fixed Scientific Currency , comma +/- Percent Date1 (Month-Day-Year) Date2 (Day-Month) Date3 (Month-Year) Text
Label-Prefix	' " ∧	Left Justification Right Justification Centered
Column-width	1-72	No. of spaces in each cell
Avail Memory	0 and up	Bytes available
Protect	ON OFF	Cell protection is on Cell protection is off

4

Range, Move, and Copy Commands

Introduction

The **Range, Copy** and **Move** commands allow the user to set up the worksheet exactly as he or she desires. With the various **Range** commands, the user can assign formats and label prefixes to ranges* that are different from the global settings, cells can be erased, cell protection can be removed and then turned back on, movement of the pointer can be restricted and blocks of cells can be assigned a name.

/ **Copy** enables the user to save keystrokes by copying entries from one part of the worksheet to another. With / **Move**, ranges of cell can be moved from one place to another, thereby allowing rearrangement of the worksheet. The **Range** commands will be discussed first. Figure 4-1 illustrates the **Range** command tree structure.

---

* A range can consist of a single cell.

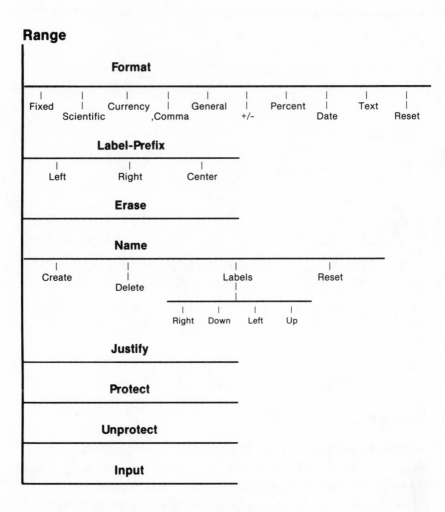

FIGURE 4-1. Range Command Tree Structure

/RANGE FORMAT

/ **R**ange Format can be used to override global format in specified ranges. This command will change the numeric display format for any range or reset the format to global settings. When / **RF** is selected, the menu will provide the same format choices as in / **Worksheet Global Format,**

> Fixed
> Scientific
> Currency
> ,
> General
> +/-
> Percent
> Date
> Text

as well as **R**eset. For a description of the types of formats, refer to the discussion on **W**orksheet **G**lobal **F**ormat commands in chapter 3. Selecting **R**eset will return the specified range to the global format.

After the format has been selected, the user will be prompted to specify a range. All values entered into cells within the range prior to / **RF** execution as well as all values entered after the execution of / **RF** will be displayed in the format selected for that range. Cells formatted using / **RF** will not be affected by changes in global format unless the cells are **R**eset to global format.

The format of a cell will be indicated on the control panel for the cell that is currently indicated by the cell pointer, as in the example that follows:

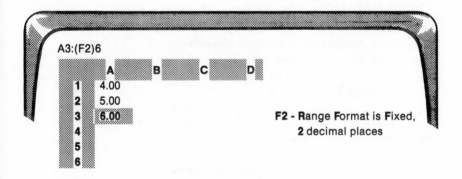

A3:(F2)6

	A	B	C	D
1	4.00			
2	5.00			
3	6.00			
4				
5				
6				

F2 - Range Format is Fixed,
2 decimal places

Cells formatted with / **Range** Format that are erased with / **Range** Erase will not return to the global format unless the worksheet is saved on diskette and then retrieved. Cells can be returned to a global format using / **R**ange **F**ormat **R**eset. If cells formatted with / **R**ange **F**ormat are moved with / **M**ove, the format will be retained by the cells that are moved. The area that the cells were moved from will be assigned the global format.

If a formatted cell is copied to other cells, the format will also be copied even if the cell does not contain a value.

/RANGE LABEL-PREFIX

/ **R**ange **L**abel-Prefix is used to change the alignment of labels that are currently on the worksheet. This command does not affect value entries or labels entered after the execution of / **RL**. 1-2-3 allows three alignment choices:

Left	Labels are left justified within the cell.
Right	Labels are right justified within the cell.
Centered	Labels are centered within the cell

If a label is longer than the cell it occupies, the label will start at the left edge of the cell and continue over any empty cells to the right of the cell it occupies.

The steps for using / **RL** are as follows:

User Step 1:	Select /**RL**
1-2-3 response:	Left Right Center
User Step 2:	Point to desired alignment and press ↵, or type the first letter of the choice (**L**, **R**, or **C**).
1-2-3 response:	Enter range of labels: A1..A1
User Step 3:	Specify the range to be affected by pointing or typing
User Step 4:	Press ↵

Label alignment for a cell will be indicated in the control panel by one of the following symbols:

'	Indicates left alignment
"	Indicates right alignment
^	Indicates centered

These symbols will not, however, be displayed with the label on the worksheet.

/RANGE ERASE

The /Range Erase command deletes the contents of cells within a specified range unless protection is enabled. Once /RE has been executed, the contents of the cells within the specified range will be lost. Cells formatted with /Range Format will retain the same format unless the worksheet is saved and retrieved before subsequent entries are made. The user may wish to save the worksheet before executing this command to prevent accidental loss of information.

User steps for executing /Range Erase are as follows:

User Step 1:	Select /RE
1-2-3 Response:	Enter range to erase: A1..A1 (The range indicated will correspond to the cell pointer position.)
User Step 2:	Specify the range to be erased and press ↵.
1-2-3 Response:	Contents of cells within the range will be erased followed by a return to the Ready mode unless protection has been enabled. If protection has been enabled, 1-2-3 will beep, enter the Error mode, and the message "Protected cell" will appear in the lower left corner.

To erase the contents of a range when protection is enabled, the user must first disable the protection for the range by using /Range Unprotect.

/RANGE NAME

The /Range Name command allows the user to assign a name to a range of cells. A range name can consist of 1 to 15 characters and spaces. If the user tries to enter more than 15 characters, 1-2-3 will beep and enter the Edit mode.

A range name can be used in lieu of cell addresses to specify a range in formulas and commands. For example, if the range A1..A6 was named Numbers, that range name could be used in the following formula,

@SUM (A1..A6)

to replace A1..A6 as follows with the same results:

@SUM (Numbers)

If the user is prompted by 1-2-3 to enter a range, the range name can be entered. The range name will generate the same results as that range's cell addresses. Pressing the F3 key (Name) while in the point mode will display a menu of the current range names in the control panel.

When / **RN** is selected, the user will be provided with four options:

> **Create**
>
> **Delete**
>
> **Labels**
>
> **Reset**

A discussion of these options is included in table 4-1.

Table 4-1. / **R**ange Name Command Options

/RN Option	Description
Create	This option is used to assign or change a range name. A range name can be 1 to 15 characters in length. This command is also used to name macros. To create a name: User Step 1: Select /**RNC**. 1-2-3 Response: Enter name: Previously entered range names will be displayed. User Step 2: Enter a name. User Step 3: Press ↵ 1-2-3 Response: Enter range: A1..A1 User Step 4: Specify the range of cells to be named. This can be accomplished by pointing or typing. User Step 5: Press ↵ To change a range indicated by a name: User Step 1: Select /**RNC** 1-2-3 Response: Enter name: User Step 2: Type or point to the range name to be changed. User Step 3: Press ↵ 1-2-3 Response: Enter range: A1..A6

Table 4-1 (cont). / Range Name Command Options

/RN Option	Description
	User Step 4: Enter the new range to be symbolized by the range name by using the arrow keys or by typing.
	User Step 5: Press ↵
	To change a range name:
	User Step 1: Select /**RNC**
	1-2-3 Response: Enter name:
	User Step 2: Type in new name.
	User Step 3: Press ↵
	1-2-3 Response: Enter range: A1..A1
	User Step 4: Specify range.
	User Step 5: Press ↵
	User Step 6: Delete old range name with /**R**ange **N**ame Delete
Delete	This option will delete a range name. All formulas referencing the deleted range name will reference the cell addresses of the deleted range after /**RND** execution. The range name will no longer appear in the range name menu once it has been deleted.
	User Step 1: Select /**RND**.
	1-2-3 Response: Enter name to delete: The range names for the current worksheet will be displayed.
	User Step 2: Type of point to the name to be deleted.
	User Step 3: Press ↵
	1-2-3 Response: Returns to Ready mode unless range name does not exist. If range name does exist, 1-2-3 will beep, and the Error mode will be indicated. The error message "Range name does not exist" will appear in the screen's lower left area. If an error occurs, press the ESC key to return to the Ready mode.

Table 4-1. /Range Name Command Options (cont.)

/RN Option	Description
Labels	This option allows creation of range names for one-cell ranges using existing cell label entries. The label cells must be immediately above, below, to the right, or to the left of the cells to be named. An example of /**RL** is shown in figure 4-2.
Reset	The **R**eset option deletes all range names from the current worksheet. Exercise caution when using this option, as when it is executed, all names will be immediately deleted. Any formula that referred to range names will now refer to the same ranges by cell address.
	Since macros are assigned names using the **R**ange **N**ame **C**reate command and /**R**ange **N**ame **R**eset deletes all range names including macro names, it is necessary to reassign names to macros before they can be used.

USING RANGE NAMES

Using the /**R**ange **L**abels example in figure 4-2, the user can calculate ratios by entering the following formulas:

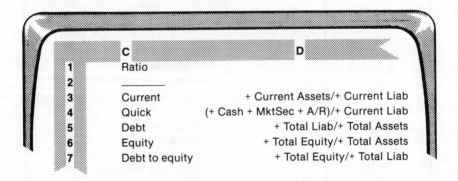

	C	D
1	Ratio	
2	———	
3	Current	+ Current Assets/+ Current Liab
4	Quick	(+ Cash + MktSec + A/R)/+ Current Liab
5	Debt	+ Total Liab/+ Total Assets
6	Equity	+ Total Equity/+ Total Assets
7	Debt to equity	+ Total Equity/+ Total Liab

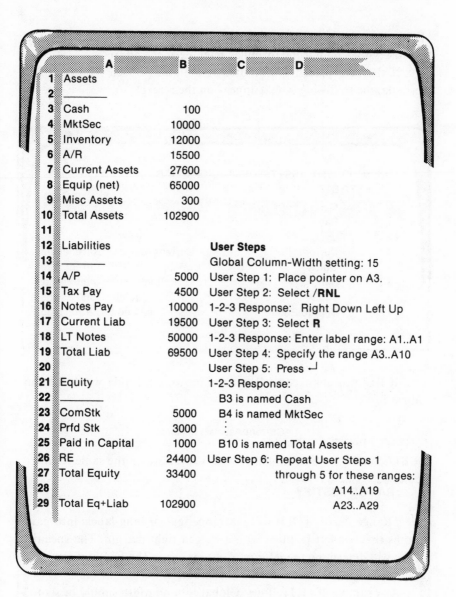

	A	B	C	D
1	Assets			
2	_____			
3	Cash	100		
4	MktSec	10000		
5	Inventory	12000		
6	A/R	15500		
7	Current Assets	27600		
8	Equip (net)	65000		
9	Misc Assets	300		
10	Total Assets	102900		
11				
12	Liabilities		**User Steps**	
13	_____		Global Column-Width setting: 15	
14	A/P	5000	User Step 1: Place pointer on A3.	
15	Tax Pay	4500	User Step 2: Select /**RNL**	
16	Notes Pay	10000	1-2-3 Response: Right Down Left Up	
17	Current Liab	19500	User Step 3: Select **R**	
18	LT Notes	50000	1-2-3 Response: Enter label range: A1..A1	
19	Total Liab	69500	User Step 4: Specify the range A3..A10	
20			User Step 5: Press ↵	
21	Equity		1-2-3 Response:	
22	_____		B3 is named Cash	
23	ComStk	5000	B4 is named MktSec	
24	Prfd Stk	3000	⋮	
25	Paid in Capital	1000	B10 is named Total Assets	
26	RE	24400	User Step 6: Repeat User Steps 1	
27	Total Equity	33400	through 5 for these ranges:	
28			A14..A19	
29	Total Eq+Liab	102900	A23..A29	

FIGURE 4-2. /Range Labels Example

Formulas referenced by range names will be more meaningful in subsequent sessions than if the formulas referenced cell addresses.

If the user placed the pointer at D3 and pressed F2 to edit the formula, the following would appear on the screen:

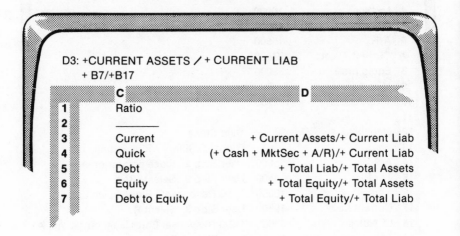

```
D3: +CURRENT ASSETS / + CURRENT LIAB
    + B7/+B17
```

	C	D
1	Ratio	
2	————	
3	Current	+ Current Assets/+ Current Liab
4	Quick	(+ Cash + MktSec + A/R)/+ Current Liab
5	Debt	+ Total Liab/+ Total Assets
6	Equity	+ Total Equity/+ Total Assets
7	Debt to Equity	+ Total Equity/+ Total Liab

If B17 was changed to B18, the following formula would be contained in D3:

+Current Assets/+LTNotes

or B17 could have been edited to read LTNotes with the same results.

/RANGE JUSTIFY

/ **R**ange Justify (/ **RJ**) will rearrange text or long-labels into paragraphs that are left-justified with a ragged right margin. The specified range will determine the left and right margins. The width of the paragraph can be not be more than 240 characters.

An example of / **RJ** follows. Global column width should be set to 9 (initial setting).

User Step 1:   Place the cell pointer on A1 and type:

The following schedule summarizes net profit by month for each division during 1983.

User Step 2:	Press ↵
User Step 3:	Select /**RJ**
1-2-3 Response:	Enter justify range: A1..A1
User Step 4:	Specify the range A1..E3
User Step 5:	Press ↵
1-2-3 Response:	

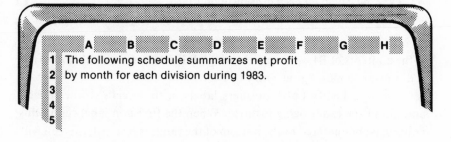

	A	B	C	D	E	F	G	H
1	The following schedule summarizes net profit
2	by month for each division during 1983.
3	
4	
5	

The text to be justified can either be entered into one cell or into a column of cells. If the range specified is too small for the amount of text to be justified, 1-2-3 will beep and enter the Error mode. The error message, "Justify range is full or line too long" will appear.

If enter is pressed again at this point, 1-2-3 will position as much of the text as it can in the space provided. To remedy this situation, select / **RJ** again and specify a larger range.

If global protection is enabled, an error will occur if the range specified for / **RJ** has not been unprotected (using / **RU**).

Even though the text appears to occupy a range of cells once / **RJ** has been executed in 1-2-3's memory, the text will only occupy the left column of cells in that range. In the preceeding example, A1 would contain the following text:

'The following schedule summarizes net profit

And A2 would contain:

'by month for each division during 1983.

If a 2 was entered into B1, the screen would appear as follows:

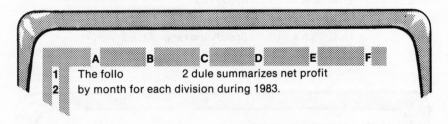

If the contents of B1 were erased (using / **RE**), the screen would appear as it did prior to making the entry to B1.

/ **R**ange **J**ustify only considers labels in those cells in the far left column of the range being justified. When the first non-label cell in this column is encountered or the bottom of the range is reached, this cell will be considered the end of the text to be justified. Blank cells are considered to be label cells.

/ **RJ** can cause cell contents to be moved elsewhere on the worksheet. It can also cause labels to be combined with entries already present on the screen.

The 1-2-3 manual states that if a Range Justified label is rejustified to fit in a thinner range, cells contents below the range may be shifted down. However, if the paragraph is "widened", the cell contents will shift up to their original position. This writer could find no predictability in the movement of cells or in justification if an error resulted and the user pressed Enter. For example, suppose the screen appeared as follows:

	A	B	C	D	E	F
1						
2						
3						
4	($000)	Div.A	Div.B	Div.C		
5	Income	2000	4000	3000		
6	Prod.Exp	2008	2040	1999		
7	Net Profi	.8	1960	1001		

And the following entries were made,

User Step 1:	Enter the following text into A1:
	The following schedule summarizes net profit by month for each division during 1983. ↵
User Step 2:	Select /**RJ**
1-2-3 Response:	Enter range to justify: A1..A1
User Step 3:	Specify the range A1..C8
1-2-3 Response:	Error
User Step 4:	Press ↵
1-2-3 Response:	

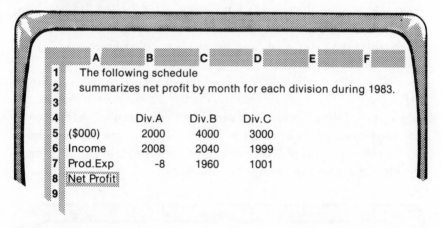

	A	B	C	D	E	F
1	The following schedule					
2	summarizes net profit by month for each division during 1983.					
3						
4		Div.A	Div.B	Div.C		
5	($000)	2000	4000	3000		
6	Income	2008	2040	1999		
7	Prod.Exp	-8	1960	1001		
8	Net Profit					
9						

Even when the justification range was "widened" as suggested in the manual, the cell entries in column A did not move back to their original positions as the manual indicated.

The results of this command were unpredictable if worksheet entries other than the text to be justified were present. It is suggested that the user save the worksheet on diskette prior to executing this command.

/RANGE PROTECT
/RANGE UNPROTECT

The **R**ange Unprotect command is used to allow changes to cell contents when the global protection is enabled. To use / **R**ange Unprotect, select the command from the menu, specify the range of cells for which protection is to be disabled and press ↵. The contents of the cells in the range specified can then be changed.

To protect cells that have been unprotected with / **R**ange Unprotect, use the **R**ange **P**rotect command. This command reverses the effects of / **R**ange Unprotect so that when global protection is enabled, no changes will be allowed to the cells.

/RANGE INPUT

/ **R**ange Input allows entry of data only into specified cells by limiting the area of movement with the cell pointer. This is extremely useful when a form for data entry is being created. The **R**ange **I**nput command can only be used if there are cells in the range specified that are not protected. If there are no unprotected cells in the range selected, 1-2-3 will beep, enter the Error mode and the message, "No unprotected cells in range" will be displayed.

When / **RI** is selected, the user will be prompted to specify a range. After the range has been entered and the Enter key has been pressed, the top left cell of the range specified will be located in the upper left corner of the worksheet. The cell pointer will be positioned at the top left unprotected cell in that range. Title rows and columns will, of course, remain visible. An example of / **R**ange Input follows:

	A	B	C	D	E	F	G
1	Inventory						
2			Qty	Qty			
3	Item	Unit	Beg	End	Purch	Used	Loc.
4	Screws		500	450			A-1
5	Nuts		200	250			A-1
6	Bolts		250	250			A-1

User Step 1:	Place pointer on D4.
User Step 2:	Select /**RU**
1-2-3 Response:	Enter range to unprotect: D4..D4

User Step 3:	Press ↓↓
1-2-3 Response:	Enter range to unprotect: D4..D6
User Step 4:	Press ↵
User Step 5:	Select /**RI**
1-2-3 Response:	Enter data input range: D4..D4
User Step 6:	↓↓
1-2-3 Response:	Enter data input range: D4..D6
User Step 7:	↵
1-2-3 Response:	

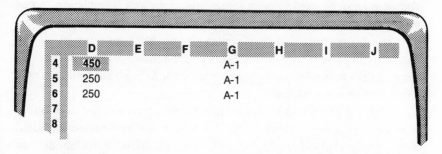

The pointer will only move to D1, D2, D3. The user will not be able to enter any command. Pressing the left and right arrow keys will cause the pointer to move up and down.

/RANGE INPUT WITH /WORKSHEET TITLES

If the Worksheet Titles command was in effect for Rows 1 through 3 and column A in the preceeding example and User Steps 1 through 7 were executed, the worksheet would appear as follows:

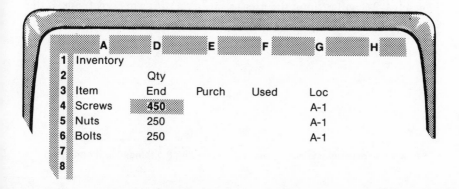

The pointer will still only move to D1, D2, and D3, but the title rows and column make input easier by providing a guide.

While the **Range Input** command is in effect, the only function keys that can be used are F1 (Help), F2 (Edit) and *F9 (Calc). To end / **Range Input**, press Esc or Enter (↵) while in the Ready mode.

COPY COMMAND

The **Copy** command is a very useful and time saving command. This command can be used to copy labels, numbers, and formulas from one cell or range to others thereby saving keystrokes.

The **Copy** command itself is very simple, but predicting its results can sometimes be difficult. The **Copy** command will overwrite the contents of cells being copied to unless protection is enabled. Cell contents could be lost if overwritten.

If global protection is enabled and the user tries to copy to cells that have protected status (that is, cells that have not had protection lifted with / **Range** Unprotect), 1-2-3 will beep, enter the Error mode and display "Protected cell" in the screen's lower left corner. Pressing Esc will return the user to the Ready mode.

To avoid losing information entirely, save the worksheet before making any changes. If an error is made or the results are not as anticipated, the original worksheet can be retrieved allowing the user to try again.

/COPY FROM ONE CELL TO ANOTHER

To copy an entry in a single cell to another cell, select / **Copy** from the menu. 1-2-3 will prompt the user to specify a range to copy from. If the cell pointer is on A1, the control panel will read as follows:

---

* This writer experienced difficulties in using F9 with the **Range Input** command.

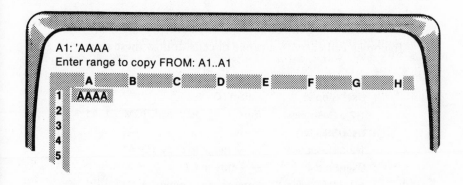

A1: 'AAAA
Enter range to copy FROM: A1..A1

If the range indicated is correct, press ←. If the pointer is not on the correct cell, type in the cell address and press ←. Alternatively, press Esc, point to the correct cell, and press ←. After ← has been pressed, 1-2-3 will respond:

Enter range to copy TO: A1

The indicated cell address will be that of the cell pointer. Denote the cell to copy to by typing or pointing. In this case the user would type C1 or press → twice.

Pressing the ← key at this point will execute the Copy command. The display will then resemble the following:

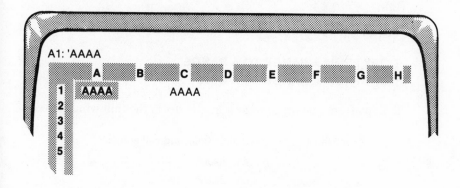

A1: 'AAAA

/COPY FROM A SINGLE CELL TO A RANGE

To copy a cell entry to a range of cells, follow these steps:

User Step 1:	Enter AAAA in A1.
User Step 2:	Select /**C**
1-2-3 Response:	Enter range to copy FROM: A1..A1
User Step 3:	Press ⏎
1-2-3 Response:	Enter range to copy TO: A1
User Step 4:	→ → or type C1
1-2-3 Response:	Enter range to copy TO: C1
User Step 5:	→ → →
1-2-3 Response:	Enter range to copy TO C1..F1
User Step 6:	Press ⏎

After these steps have been executed, the screen will appear as follows:

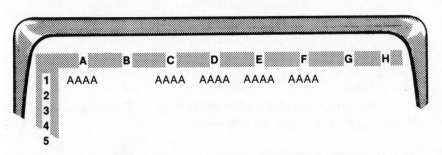

/COPY FROM A RANGE TO A RANGE
/COPY FROM A RANGE TO A CELL

To copy from one range to another, perform the following steps:

User Step 1:	Make the following cell entries:

> A1: AAAA
> B1: BBBB
> C1: CCCC
> D1: DDDD

1-2-3 Response:

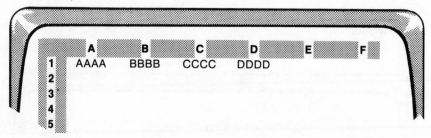

User Step 2:	Press Home and select /**C**
1-2-3 Response:	Enter range to copy FROM: A1..A1
User Step 3:	Type A1..D1 or; press → three times. Press ↵
1-2-3 Response:	Enter range to copy FROM: A1..D1
	If the pointing method was used, each cell in the range will be highlighted.
User Step 4:	Press ↵
1-2-3 Response:	Enter range to copy TO: A1
User Step 5:	Type A2..D2. Alternatively, point to A2, press the period key, and point to D2.
1-2-3 Response:	Enter range to copy TO: A2..D2
	If pointing was used, A2..D2 will be highlighted.
User Step 6:	Press ↵

1-2-3 Response:

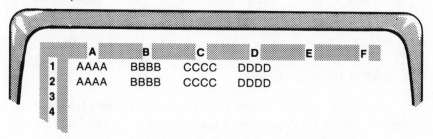

When a range is copied to a single cell as in the following example:

Enter range to copy FROM: A1..D1
Enter range to copy TO: A2

1-2-3 will overwrite enough cells to the right of the indicated cell, A2 to accommodate the range. In this case, B2, C2 and D2 would be overwritten.

In the next example, we will use the following worksheet:

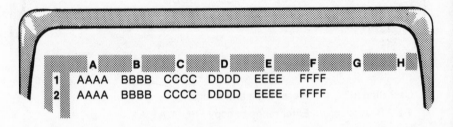

	A	B	C	D	E	F	G	H
1	AAAA	BBBB	CCCC	DDDD	EEEE	FFFF		
2	AAAA	BBBB	CCCC	DDDD	EEEE	FFFF		

If the following ranges were used for / Copy,

    Enter range to copy FROM: A1..F1
    Enter range to copy TO: C2

the results would be:

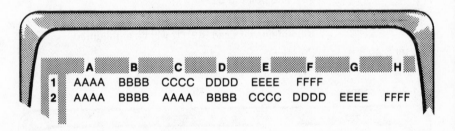

	A	B	C	D	E	F	G	H
1	AAAA	BBBB	CCCC	DDDD	EEEE	FFFF		
2	AAAA	BBBB	AAAA	BBBB	CCCC	DDDD	EEEE	FFFF

OVERLAPPING RANGES

If overlapping FROM and TO ranges are indicated, 1-2-3 will restrict the copy FROM portion of the range to those cells that do not overlap. The following example will illustrate this:

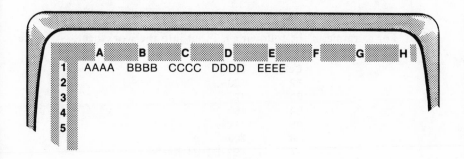

/Copy Range Entries
Enter range to copy FROM: A1..E1
Enter range to copy TO: C1..G1

These entries result in the following display:

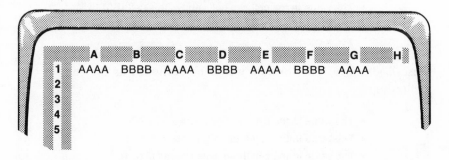

This restriction would not be observed if the upper left hand corner of the FROM and TO ranges were identical as in the following:

Enter range to copy FROM: A1..E1
Enter range to copy TO: A1..G1

COPYING FORMULAS

Copying formulas that contain cell addresses is somewhat more complicated than copying labels and numbers. Whether relative or absolute cell addresses are used will determine the means by which 1-2-3 will copy formulas.

In order to fully appreciate the following discussion on relative and absolute cell addresses, we must first explain how 1-2-3's memory functions. For example, if the following is input into the worksheet,

Cell	Entry
B2	100
B3	123
B4	160
B5	111
B6	200
B7	+B2+B3+B4+B5+B6

Lotus 1-2-3 would remember the formula in B7 as the sum of the following:

- The value in the cell five cells above this cell (B2).
- The value in the cell four cells above this cell (B3).
- The value in the cell three cells above this cell (B4).
- The value in the cell two cells above this cell (B5).
- The value in the cell immediately above this cell (B6).

If the same formula was copied to C7, 1-2-3 would copy it as described above. The formula would be evaluated as the sum of the following:

- The value in the cell five cells above C7 (C2).
- The value in the cell four cells above C7 (C3).
- The value in the cell three cells above C7 (C4).
- The value in the cell two cells above C7 (C5).
- The value in the cell above C7 (C6).

This formula would appear as follows in C7:

+C2+C3+C4+C5+C6

The following example will further illustrate how relative addresses are copied. To calculate salesmen's commissions for the current month, the first step would be to enter the net sales for each salesman by week. Refer to figure 4-3, and enter the corresponding data into a 1-2-3 worksheet.

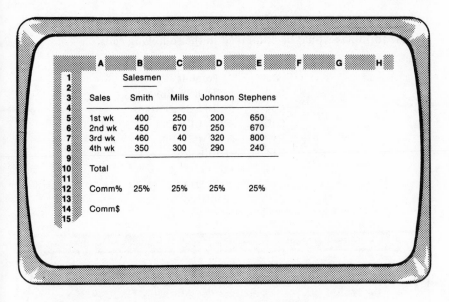

FIGURE 4-3. Initial Sales Commission Worksheet Entries

To total the sales and calculate commission, enter the following formulas and copy to the appropriate cells:

User Step 1:	Place pointer on B10
User Step 2:	Type @SUM(B5..B8) ↵
User Step 3:	Select /**C**
1-2-3 Response:	Enter range to copy FROM:B10..B10
User Step 4:	Press ↵
1-2-3 Response:	Enter range to copy TO:B10
User Step 5:	Type C10..E10↵
User Step 6:	Place pointer on B14
User Step 7:	Type +B10*B12 ↵
User Step 8:	Select /**C**
1-2-3 Response:	Enter range to copy FROM:B14..B14
User Step 9:	Press ↵
1-2-3 Response:	Enter range to copy TO:B14
User Step 10:	Type C14..E14↵

The worksheet should now resemble that depicted in figure 4-4. These formulas would be contained in the following cells:

Cell	Formula
B10	@SUM(B5..B8)
C10	@SUM(C5..C8)
D10	@SUM(D5..D8)
E10	@SUM(E5..E8)
B14	+B10*B12
C14	+C10*C12
D14	+D10*D12
E14	+E10*E12

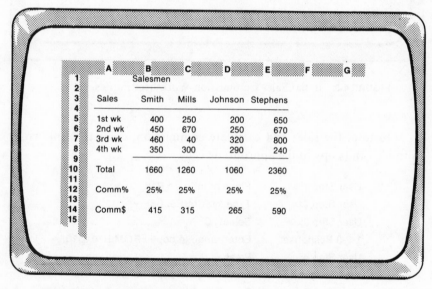

FIGURE 4-4. Copying Formulas

MOVE COMMAND

The **Move** command allows the user to rearrange the worksheet without retyping and erasing. Formulas will automatically be adusted so they will function after / **Move** as they did before / **Move**. This is shown in the following example. Suppose the worksheet resembles figure 4-5.

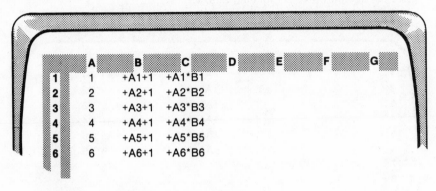

FIGURE 4-5. Worksheet Prior to / Move*

To move column C to column F, the user would follow these steps:

User Step 1:	Place pointer on C1
User Step 2:	Select /**M**
1-2-3 Response:	Enter range to move FROM C1..C1
User Step 3:	Type C1..C6 ↵
1-2-3 Response:	Enter range to move TO:
User Step 4:	Type F1..F6 ↵
1-2-3 Response:	

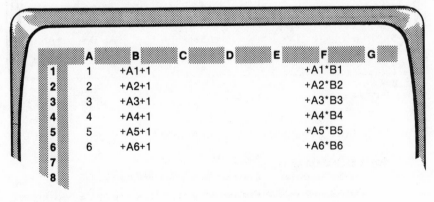

* Global format is **Text**

Suppose we moved the formulas in column B to column D. The effect of such a move is depicted below:

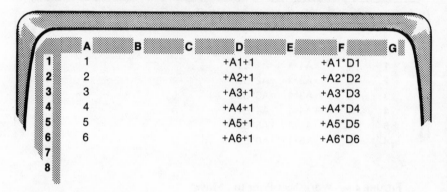

	A	B	C	D	E	F	G
1	1			+A1+1		+A1*D1	
2	2			+A2+1		+A2*D2	
3	3			+A3+1		+A3*D3	
4	4			+A4+1		+A4*D4	
5	5			+A5+1		+A5*D5	
6	6			+A6+1		+A6*D6	
7							
8							

Note that the formulas in column F that referred to the cells that were moved have been adjusted to reflect the move.

What happens if we move the cells that are used in formulas? If our worksheet appeared as follows,

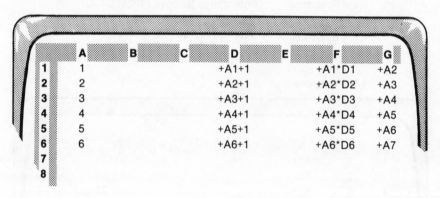

	A	B	C	D	E	F	G
1	1			+A1+1		+A1*D1	+A2
2	2			+A2+1		+A2*D2	+A3
3	3			+A3+1		+A3*D3	+A4
4	4			+A4+1		+A4*D4	+A5
5	5			+A5+1		+A5*D5	+A6
6	6			+A6+1		+A6*D6	+A7
7							
8							

and the following command entries were made,

User Step 1:	Select /**M**
1-2-3 Response:	Enter range to move FROM: G1..G6
User Step 2:	Press ↵
1-2-3 Response:	Enter range to move TO: D1..D6
User Step 3:	Press ↵

the worksheet would appear as follows:

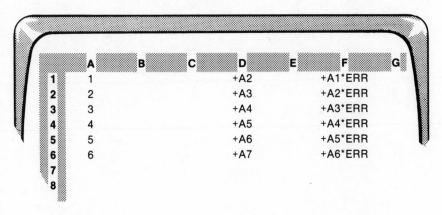

	A	B	C	D	E	F	G
1	1			+A2		+A1*ERR	
2	2			+A3		+A2*ERR	
3	3			+A4		+A3*ERR	
4	4			+A5		+A4*ERR	
5	5			+A6		+A5*ERR	
6	6			+A7		+A6*ERR	
7							
8							

Since the contents of the cells used in the formulas in column F were overwritten by the cell contents moved from column G, the formulas in column F will become invalid.

5

File Commands

Introduction

The File commands enable the user to store and retrieve information on diskettes. Once the user has executed the **Q**uit command or / Worksheet **E**rase, information on the current worksheet will be lost. The File commands will save information for future sessions. File commands allow the user to copy information from one worksheet to another. This saves time since duplicate keyboard entries can be eliminated.

In order to use the File commands, it is necessary to have several formatted diskettes. If these were not formatted prior to using the File commands, a disk error will occur if the user tries to execute a File command.

DOS

The Disk Operating System (or DOS) controls information storage on diskettes. An **operating system** can be defined as a group of programs that manage the computer's operation. A **disk operating system** (DOS) can be defined as the group of programs that manage the transfer of data to and from a storage device such as a diskette.

FILES & FILENAMES

The information stored on diskettes is stored in files. A file can be defined as a collection of related data. Every file that is stored on the same diskette must have a unique filename that identifies that file. In other words, no two files on the same diskette can have the same filename. With 1-2-3, a filename can contain as many as 8 characters. These characters can be letters of the alphabet (A...Z), integer numbers (0...9) or __. A filename cannot have any blank spaces between characters. All alphabetic characters are interpreted as uppercase. Example of valid and invalid filenames follow:

Valid	Invalid	Reason
AR1	A/R1	Invalid character (/)
CASHDISB	CASHDISBURSEMENTS	Too long
JAN1983	JAN 1983	Space not allowed
STORE__12	STORE 12	Space not allowed

If an illegal filename is entered, 1-2-3 will beep, enter the Error mode, and display the message "Illegal character in filename." If the filename entered is too long, 1-2-3 will crop it to 8 characters.

FILENAME EXTENSIONS

1-2-3 automatically assigns a filename extension to each file created. There are three types of files.

Type	Extension
Worksheet files	.WKS
Print files	.PRN
Graph (picture) files	.PIC

BACKING UP DISKETTES

Back-up copies of important diskettes should be maintained. If a working diskette becomes damaged or a file is erased or overwritten, the original information will still be available on the back-up diskette. To make back-up copies of diskettes, use the DiskCopy command of the Disk Manager program. To make copies of individual files, use File Manager's Copy command.

The standard configuration for 1-2-3 is drive B as the data drive. For instructions on changing this configuration, see chapter 3.

FILE COMMAND BASICS

In DOS, the various filenames for those files stored on a disk are stored in a **directory**. A directory is a file which contains information pertaining to other files contained on a disk drive.

In DOS versions 1.0 and 1.1, a directory structure was used whereby each diskette contained a single directory that could hold up to 64 files (112 files for dual-sided diskettes). However, such a directory system was not adequate for a fixed disk system as a fixed disk can store thousands of files. If a single directory attempted to store several hundred files, the time required to find that file in the directory would be greatly increased. With DOS 2.0, groups of related files can have their own directories, and all of these directories can exist on the same disk.

In DOS 2.0, as in DOS 1.0 and 1.1, a single directory is created on each disk when it is formatted. This directory is known as the **root** or **system directory**. The root directory can hold either 64 or 112 files. The maximum size of a fixed drive's root directory is contingent upon the size of the DOS partition.

The root directory can contain the names of other directories as well as filenames. These other directories, known as **sub-directories**, are actually files. Sub-directories are not limited in size, and can contain any number of files. In fact, sub-directories can include other sub-directories as well as files. Sub-directories follow the same naming conventions as filenames — a primary name of 1 to 8 characters and an optional extension of 1 to 3 characters.

Different directories can contain identical filenames or directory names. In other words, each directory can contain file and directory names that appear in other directories as well.

DOS can identify a default directory just as it can a default drive. This default directory is known as the current directory. When a filename is entered without specifying a directory, DOS will search the current directory.

Upon start-up, DOS will use the root directory as the current directory. The current directory can be either changed or identified via the DOS command, CHDIR. 1-2-3 uses the current directory when generating a directory listing with the File List command.

1-2-3's File Directory command can also be used to change the current directory. With DOS 2.0, this command will specify the current directory in the disk's tree structure. With DOS 1.1, the current directory would be set to one of the disk drives — generally A or B.

When one of the file commands is executed*, the current directory will be accessed. The current directory is set upon startup by the Worksheet Global Default Directory command. The current directory can later be displayed and/or changed using the File Directory command.

Generally, the initial current directory setting will be B: \ . This indicates the second diskette drive on a two diskette system or the diskette drive on a single-diskette, single fixed disk system**. In such cases, a File command will search the diskette in drive B for 1-2-3 files with filename extensions of .WKS (worksheet), .PRN (print), or .PIC (picture). 1-2-3 will then display a menu of the available filenames of the appropriate type in the control panel. If the control panel is filled with filenames, any additional existing filenames can be displayed by pressing → repeatedly, until the cell pointer moves from the screen's right-hand corner to its left.

---

* The File Directory command is an exception.
** In such systems, the system drive (A) is redefined as B when 1-2-3 is configured.

File Directory can be used to change the current directory. For instance, suppose our system contained one diskette drive (configured as drive B) and one fixed drive (configured as drive C). By specifying C: \ TEMP as the current directory, we could access files stored in the sub-directory named TEMP on the fixed drive. If a File command was subsequently issued, 1-2-3 would search drive C for files created under TEMP with filename extensions of .WKS, .PRN or .PIC. These would then be displayed on the control panel.

/FILE RETRIEVE

The File Retrieve command (/ FR) retrieves Worksheet files that have been stored on diskette. A retrieved file will replace the currently displayed worksheet. The information on the replaced worksheet will be lost unless it has been stored on diskette using / File Save.

To use / File Retrieve, place the data diskette in drive B* and type:

/FR

1-2-3 will respond:

Enter name of file to retrieve:

A menu of all current files will also be located on the next line. All filenames may not appear on the screen simultaneously. However, by using the pointer, the user will be able to survey all of the filename choices.

The file to be retrieved can be selected by pointing or by typing. The filename, if typed, must match a filename in the filename menu. Otherwise, an error will result. After the selection has been made and Enter has been pressed, the current worksheet will disappear. The selected worksheet file becomes the current worksheet and will appear exactly as it did when saved along with all of the saved settings. This may take from a few seconds to several minutes depending on the file's size. While 1-2-3 is reading the file, it will be in the Wait mode. The user should not touch the keyboard during the file retrieval process. Since the keyboard is still

---

* or whichever drive is the data drive.

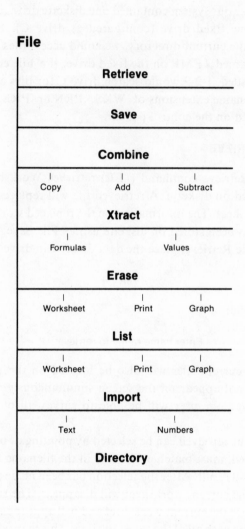

FIGURE 5-1. File Command Tree

active, unpredictable results may be experienced as a result of pressing a key.

/FILE SAVE

/ File Save (/ **FS**) stores the current worksheet on diskette. The worksheet is stored along with all the settings. Each file is automatically assigned the filename extension, .WKS. This command should be used often as the user progresses with his or her work. It can save time if a portion of the worksheet is overwritten or erased with undesired results. Several versions of the same worksheet can be saved under different filenames if the user wants to experiment.

To save a worksheet, place a formatted diskette into drive B* and type:

/FS

1-2-3 will respond:

Enter save file name:

If the current worksheet has been stored previously, the current filename will appear next to 1-2-3's response and the Edit mode will be entered. The existing filename as it appears can be used by pressing ↵ or type a new filename and press ↵. To examine a menu of all existing filenames on the current data diskette, press Esc. The filename menu will appear below the filename prompt.

If an existing filename is selected, 1-2-3 provides two choices:

Cancel   Replace

If Cancel is selected, the file stored under the selected filename will remain intact and 1-2-3 will return to the Ready mode. The current

---

* or whichever drive is the data drive.

worksheet will be displayed as it appeared before / **FS** was selected.

If **R**eplace is selected, the existing file stored under that name will be replaced with the new file. This is known as **overwriting** a file. Overwriting a file is the usual practice when updating files. However, the results of accidentally overwriting a file can be disastrous, since the old file's contents will be completely erased.

It may take from a few seconds to several minutes for 1-2-3 to complete / **FS** depending on the size of the worksheet. Do not touch the keys while the disk drive is operating. If the current diskette does not contain sufficient available space for storing a file, 1-2-3 will enter the Error mode and will display the error message, "Disk full". If this occurs, press Esc to return to the Ready mode. Replace the diskette in the data drive with another formatted diskette and repeat the procedure for / **FS**.

If the current worksheet will not fit on one diskette, use / File **X**tract to save it in parts on several diskettes. To retrieve a file saved with / File Extract, use / File **C**ombine in conjunction with / File **R**etrieve.

/FILE COMBINE

/ File **C**ombine allows the user to combine either worksheet or data from different worksheets.

> Note: To avoid possible loss of information by overwriting,
> it is a good practice to first /File **S**ave the current
> worksheet before executing /**FC**.

For / **FC** to execute properly, before execution, the cell pointer must be positioned to the top left hand cell of the area in which the combined worksheet is to be located.

When / **FC** is selected, the following menu will appear in the control panel:

Copy   **A**dd   **S**ubtract

These options are discussed in table 5-1.

The incoming file can be either an entire file or a named range. If Entire File is selected, the user will be prompted to enter the filename. Current filenames will appear underneath the prompt. The filename can be selected by pointing or typing. After ⏎ has been pressed, the incoming file will be combined with the current worksheet. If Named Range is selected, 1-2-3 will prompt the user to enter a range name. After the range name has been entered, 1-2-3 will prompt the user to enter the name of the file in which the range can be found. After the Enter key has been pressed, the incoming range will be combined with the current worksheet.

The incoming file or range will be positioned on the current worksheet so that its upper left cell resides at the point where the cell pointer was positioned on the worksheet before / FC was executed.

Only the contents of the incoming cells will be transferred to the current worksheet. Current worksheet settings will not be affected by / FC.

Table 5-1. / File Combine Options

/FC Option	Description
Copy	The cells in the current worksheet will be replaced by those of the file or range being combined.
Add	The cells containing values in the incoming file or named range will be added to the overlapped cells in the current worksheet. Cells on the current worksheet that contain formulas or labels will not be affected. The results of formulas may change if values of cells referenced in the formulas were affected by Add.
Subtract	Works like Add except values contained in the incoming file or range will be subtracted from overlapping cells in the current worksheet.

The following example will serve to illustrate / FC. Suppose the following worksheets had been created with NUMBERS1 being the current worksheet.

NUMBERS1

	A	B	C	D		CELL	TEXT FORMAT
1	A	B	A+B				
2	1	5	6			C2	+A2+B2
3	2	6	8			C3	+A3+B3
4	3	7	10			C4	+A4+B4
5	4	8	12			C5	+A5+B5

NUMBERS2

	A	B	C	D		CELL	TEXT FORMAT
1	D	E		E-D			
2	1	2		1		D2	+B2-A2
3	1	2		1		D3	+B3-A3
4	1	2		1		D4	+B4-A4
5	1	2		1		D5	+B5-A5

User Step 1:	Place pointer on A2 of NUMBERS1.
User Step 2:	Select /**FC**.
1-2-3 Response:	Copy Add Subtract
User Step 3:	Select **C**.
1-2-3 Response:	Entire File Named Range
User Step 4:	Select **E**.
1-2-3 Response:	Enter name of file to combine: NUMBERS1 NUMBERS2
User Step 5:	Point to NUMBERS2 and press ↵.
1-2-3 Response:	

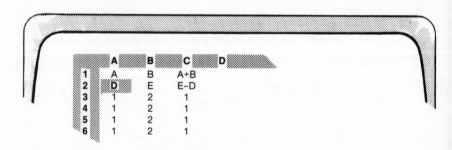

	A	B	C	D
1	A	B	A+B	
2	D	E	E-D	
3	1	2	1	
4	1	2	1	
5	1	2	1	
6	1	2	1	

If **Add** was selected instead of Copy in User Step 3, the following would result:

	A	B	C	D		
1	A	B	A+B		CELL	TEXT FORMAT
2	1	5	6		C2	+A2+B2
3	3	8	11		C3	+A3+B3
4	4	9	13		C4	+A4+B4
5	5	10	15		C5	+A5+B5
6	1	2	1		C6	1

As indicated by the text format of C6, only the values in the incoming cells were considered, not the formulas.

/FILE XTRACT

/ File Xtract saves a designated portion of a worksheet in a Worksheet file on a diskette. This command can be used when a worksheet is too large to be stored on one diskette and must be saved in portions. / **FX** can be used when portions of the worksheet are to be stored in separate files such as macros to be copied to other worksheets. If the entire worksheet is not needed, / **FX** allows the user to store only values instead of formulas.

When / **FX** is selected, 1-2-3 will prompt the user to specify whether formulas are to be saved or whether their values are to be saved. After the selection has been made, 1-2-3 will prompt the user to input a filename for the Xtract file. After the filename has been entered, the user must enter the range address or range name of the portion of the worksheet that is to be saved.

Files stored using / **FX** are stored with worksheet settings as Worksheet files. A file saved with / **FX** can be retrieved by using / File Retrieve or / File Combine.

When retrieving an entire worksheet that was stored in portions on different files, the first file must be retrieved using / File Retrieve. This is necessary since / **FR** will also retrieve the worksheet settings. / File Combine does not retrieve worksheet settings. Once / **FR** has been executed, the remainder of the worksheet can then be retrieved using / **FC**.

To store a worksheet in two files, the following steps should be followed:

Assumptions:	The worksheet contains a customer file which is to be divided into two separate files. CUSTA_M will store those customers with names beginning with A through M. CUSTN_Z will store customers with names beginning with N through Z. The customers on the worksheet have been alphabetized. The first customer with a name beginning with the letter N is located at row 1000. The worksheet ends at row 2000. Each customer row extends from column A through column N.
User Step 1:	Place pointer on A1.
User Step 2:	Place a formatted diskette (diskette A) into the data drive*.
User Step 3:	Select /**FX**.
1-2-3 Response:	Formulas Values
User Step 4:	Select **F**.
1-2-3 Response:	Enter xtract filename:
User Step 5:	Type CUSTA_M and press ↵.
1-2-3 Response:	Enter xtract range: A1..A1
User Step 6:	Specify range A1..N999 and press ↵.
1-2-3 Response:	Stores file named CUSTA_M and returns to Ready mode.
User Step 7:	Remove diskette A from data drive. Replace it with a new formatted diskette (diskette B). Place pointer on A1000.
User Step 8:	Select /**FX**.
1-2-3 Response:	Formulas Values
User Step 9:	Select **F**.
1-2-3 Response:	Enter xtract filename:
User Step 10:	Type CUSTN_Z and press ↵.
1-2-3 Response:	Enter xtract range: A1000..A1000

---

* usually drive B.

User Step 11:	Specify range A1000..N2000 and press ↵.
1-2-3 Response:	Stores file named CUSTN_Z and returns to Ready mode.

The following steps will retrieve the entire worksheet:

User Step 1:	Press Home.
User Step 2:	Insert diskette A into the data drive.
User Step 3:	Select /FR.
1-2-3 Response:	Enter name of file to retrieve:
User Step 4:	Select CUSTA_M and press ↵.
1-2-3 Response:	The selected file will appear on the screen with all worksheet settings as they were when it was saved.
User Step 5:	Replace diskette A with diskette B.
User Step 6:	Place pointer on A1000.
User Step 7:	Select /FC.
1-2-3 Response:	Copy Add Subtract
User Step 8:	Select C.
1-2-3 Response:	Entire File Named Range
User Step 9:	Select E.
1-2-3 Response:	Enter name of file to combine:
User Step 10:	Type CUSTN_Z and press ↵.
1-2-3 Response:	Retrieves CUSTN_Z so that its top left corner resides at A1000 as it did on the original worksheet.

/FILE ERASE

/ File Erase (/ FE) is used to erase diskette files. When / FE is selected, 1-2-3 will display the following:

      Worksheet   Print   Graph

The user must select which file type is to be erased. As mentioned previously, 1-2-3 indentifies file types by their filename extensions. After the file type selection has been made, the following prompt will appear:

      Enter name of file to erase:

The filename menu for the selected file type will appear beneath the prompt. The user can either type or point to the name of the file to be erased. After Enter has been pressed, the following choices will appear in the control panel:

No   Yes

Selecting **No** will cancel the command and will return 1-2-3 to the Ready mode. Selecting **Yes** will delete the selected file.

If a filename is entered that does not exist, 1-2-3 will enter the Error mode and display the error message, "Cannot delete file".

FILENAME MATCH CHARACTERS

Filename Match Characters can be used with / **F**ile **E**rase to erase more than one file at a time. Lotus 1-2-3 allows the use of two filename match characters, the asterisk (*) and the question mark (?). A ? will match any single character in the same position. For example, suppose the following files were stored on the current data diskette:

FILE1
FILE2
FILE3
FILE4
FILECUST
FILES

An entry of FILE? would match each of the above except FILECUST.

An * will match all characters to the end of the filename. Using the previous example's filenames, if FILE* was entered, it would match all of the files. If only * was entered, all filenames would be matched and deleted.

/FILE LIST

/ **F**ile **L**ist will display a list of all filenames of a specified file type as well as the available disk space (in bytes).

When / **FL** is selected, the user will be prompted to select the type of files to be displayed — **W**orksheet, **P**rint or **G**raph. Once the file type has been selected, 1-2-3 will display a list of the files stored on the current data diskette. The display will resemble that depicted in figure 5-2.

A1:
Available disk space (bytes): 282624
PERS   ACCT1   SALES1   CUST

MENU

FIGURE 5-2. / File List Display

When Esc is pressed, 1-2-3 will return to the Ready mode. If no files of the type chosen exist on the diskette, an error will occur. Pressing Esc will return 1-2-3 to the Ready mode.

/FILE IMPORT

/ File Import (/ **FI**) enables the user to retrieve print files from other programs and incorporate these in the current worksheet. This command will generally work with **standard text files** generated by other programs as long as the filename extension has been changed to .PRN.

If a word processor **document file** is read with / **FI**, unexpected results may occur. This is because document files contain special characters. Most word processors allow the user to generate standard text files that can be used with / **FI**. / File Import provides two options for importing files — Text and Numbers. A discussion of each is included in table 5-2.

Data imported with / **FI** will overwrite existing cell contents. Blank lines in a data file will cause rows to be skipped on the worksheet. The cell contents of any skipped rows will be unaffected.

When importing data with / File Import, the user will generally use / **FIText** unless the other program can configure its output so it can be imported with / **FINumbers** (see table 5-2).

For example, when importing data from PFS®, the user would execute / **FIT** for text files and / **FIN** for numeric files. Text data and numeric data cannot be imported simultaneously with / **FIN** since PFS does not enclose text in quotes.

Table 5-2. / File Import Options

/FI Option	Description
Text	With this option in effect, each line of data being imported will be treated as a label and will be given a left justification label-prefix. The first line will be entered into the cell where the cell pointer was positioned before /**FIT** was initiated. The following line of data will be entered into the next cell in the same row. This process will continue until the end of the data file has been reached.
Numbers	This option will import numbers and character strings. The character strings must be enclosed in quotation marks (" "). Otherwise, they will be ignored. Character strings will be left-justified. When 1-2-3 reads the first line of data, it enters the first numeric string or valid character string in that cell that contained the cell pointer before /**FIN** was executed. The next valid string will be entered in the next cell in the same row. This will continue until the end of the data line is encountered. The next line will be placed in cells in subsequent rows until the end of the data file has been reached. For example, if the cell pointer was on A1 when /**FIN** was executed, the following file:

754, "Joe Brown" 165.25,6

153, "Joan Smith" 91.30,4

would be imported to the current worksheet as:

754	JoeBrown	165.25	6
153	JoanSmith	91.30	4

/FILE DIRECTORY

The File Directory command can be used to display and then change the current directory. When / **FD** is executed, 1-2-3 will display the current directory. In DOS 1.1, this will be a single letter indicating one of the diskette drives (e.g. A:, B:, C:). In DOS 2.0, the current directory will be indicated by a directory path (e.g. B:\ ).

To retain the current directory, press the Enter key. In DOS 1.1, the current directory can be changed by entering a new drive letter. In DOS 2.0, a full or partial path must be entered. If a partial path is indicated, 1-2-3 will assume that the path begins at the current directory.

When indicating a file that is not located in the current directory, / **FD** should first be issued to change the current directory as desired. When a filename is prefixed with a drive letter, 1-2-3 will search that drive's current directory for the file rather than the current directory indicated by / **FD**.

For instance, if B:STKMKT was specified and the current directory was C:\ TEMP, 1-2-3 would search for a file named STKMKT on the current directory in drive B rather than in the directory named TEMP in drive C.

The **W**orksheet **G**lobal **D**efault **D**irectory command can also be used to specify or change the current directory. Note that changes made with / **WGDD** will be displayed when / **FD** is subsequently executed.

6

Print Commands

Introduction

The **P**rint command is used to output worksheet data to the printer. The user has the option of either outputting data directly to the printer or of storing data in a **print file** for subsequent output.

/ **P**rint includes a number of options which allow the user to accomplish the following tasks:

- Format the page being output
- Advance the paper in the printer
- Specify what portion of the worksheet is to be printed
- Clear printer format settings

Figure 6-1 depicts the tree structure of the **P**rint command.

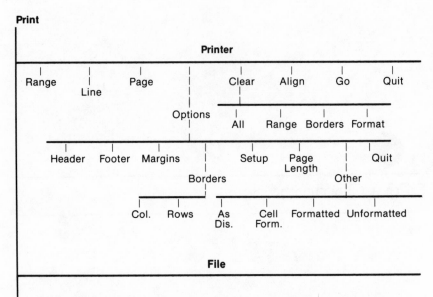

(Prompt for filename will appear followed by same structure as Printer)

FIGURE 6-1. Print Command Tree Structure

Notice that once **P**rinter or File has been selected under / **P**rint, an identical set of options is available. These are known as the / **P**rint menu and include the following:

Range   **L**ine   **P**age   **O**ptions   **C**lear   **A**lign   **G**o   **Q**uit

Each of these will be discussed in the following sections.

---

* Print files can be interpreted by most word processing programs. DOS's TYPE command can be used to output a print file.

When Printer is selected, output will subsequently be directed to the printer. The Go command causes output indicated by the Range command to be output to the printer. The Print menu will be displayed after the specified data has been output.

When File is selected, output will be directed to a print file. Print files are assigned the suffix .PRN. The Range command specifies the data that will be output to the Print file when the Go command is executed.

/Print (Printer or File) Range

The / PPRange command allows the user to specify a portion of the worksheet for output to the printer. If a new range is not indicated, the most recently specified range will be used.

Once / PPR or / PFR has been selected from the menu, the user will be prompted as follows:

Enter print range:

The range last specified will be indicated to the right of this prompt. That range will also be highlighted. This range can be specified by pressing Enter. A new range can be chosen by entering the addresses of the new range's free and anchor cells, by highlighting the new range with the expanded cell pointer, or by indicating the desired range name from the range name menu (displayed by pressing F3 — Name).

Regardless of the specified range, / Print will never output characters that would extend beyond the printer margins set in / Print Options Borders or in / Worksheet Global Default Printer. If the specified range does extend beyond the allowed borders, the areas extending beyond the margin will be printed as a separate page as illustrated in figure 6-2.

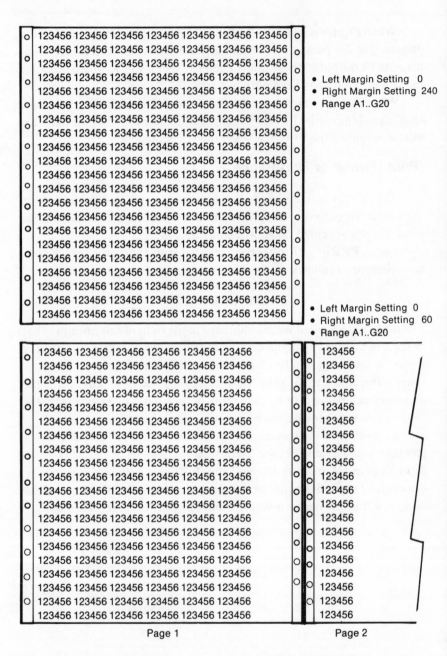

FIGURE 6-2. /Print when Range Extends Beyond Borders

/Print (Printer or File) Line

Each time / **PPL** or / **PFL** is chosen, a blank line will be inserted in the output. When the bottom of the page is reached, this command causes the printer to advance to the top of the next page.

/Print (Printer or File) Page

/ **PPP** and / **PFP** cause the printer to advance to the top of a new page.

/Print (Printer or File) Options

When **Options** is chosen from the / **Print** menu, the **Options** menu will be displayed. The **Options** menu selections allow the user to format the printer output. These are described in the following sections.

HEADER

The **Header** command allows the user to specify up to 240 characters to be output just below the top margin. This command can be especially useful in outputting report titles and dates. The current date will be output by entering @. Sequential page numbers beginning with 1 can be output by specifying #.

Headers (and footers) can be divided into three separate segments by dividing the text with the split vertical bar character (¦). Suppose the following was entered in response to the **Header** prompt:

Enter header line: Sales Report ¦ Page # ¦ @

The output would resemble that depicted in figure 6-3.

FOOTER

The **Footer** command functions exactly as **Header**, except that copy is output just above the page's bottom margin.

MARGINS

The **Margins** command allows the user to specify new margin settings. These do not alter the **Global Default Printer Margins**. However, they will affect /Print output until they have been changed or cleared.

Upon start-up, 1-2-3 reads a default file that includes various printer default values. The defaults include the margin settings. These defaults can be changed using /Worksheet Global Default Printer. Once altered, the Margin command settings can be returned to the defaults by selecting the Clear command (explained later) under Option. 1-2-3's initial default settings are as follows:

Left	4 spaces from paper's left edge
Right	76 spaces from paper's left edge
Top	2 lines from top of page
Bottom	2 lines from bottom of page

	Sales Report 1983		Page 1	01-Jan-84
	January	11234.00		
	February	14564.00		
	March	12394.00		
	April	15640.00		
	May	9829.00		
	June	8945.00		
	July	10980.00		
	August	12387.00		
	September	14970.00		
	October	18970.00		
	November	21348.00		
	December	16829.00		

FIGURE 6-3. Printer Output Utilizing Headers

BORDERS

The Borders commands allows the user to indicate the following:

- One or more columns as the printed range's left border
- One or more rows as the printer range's top margin.

The Borders command is especially useful in outputting column and/or row headers. Borders can also be used to output two disconnected areas of the worksheet side by side.

When Borders is selected for the Options menu, the user will initially be prompted to either specify columns or rows. This can be accomplished by either entering a range name or by expanding the cell pointer.

When a row is specified, the contents of that row lying in columns corresponding to those indicated in the print range will be printed as the top border on every page of output. When a column is specified, the contents of that column corresponding to those indicated in the print range will be printed as the left margin on every page of output.

The usage of the Borders command can be illustrated in the following example. Suppose that our worksheet appeared as depicted in figure 6-4. With a range specification of A1..C3, the output indicated in figure 6-4 would be generated once Go was executed. Suppose we then executed the Borders command followed by Columns, moved the cell pointer to E1, and pressed the Enter key. Then, suppose we executed Borders again followed by Rows, moved the cell pointer to A8, and pressed the Enter key. Subsequent execution of the Go command would produce output similar to that depicted in figure 6-4.

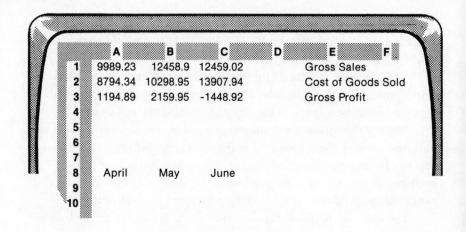

	A	B	C	D	E	F
1	9989.23	12458.9	12459.02		Gross Sales	
2	8794.34	10298.95	13907.94		Cost of Goods Sold	
3	1194.89	2159.95	-1448.92		Gross Profit	
4						
5						
6						
7						
8	April	May	June			
9						
10						

Output Prior to Borders Execution

```
        9989.23    12458.9   12459.02
        8794.34   10298.95   13907.94
        1194.89    2159.95   -1448.92
```

```
                    April       May      June
Gross Sales        9989.23    12458.9   12459.02
Cost of Goods Sold 8794.34   10298.95   13907.94
Gross Profit       1194.89    2159.95   -1448.92
```

FIGURE 6-4. Using the Borders Command

SETUP

The Setup command allows the user to temporarily specify a printer control string other than that specified in the global default settings.

PAGE-LENGTH

The Page-Length command allows the user to temporarily specify a page length in lines other than that specified in the global default settings.

OTHER

When the Other command is specified, the following menu will appear:

As-Displayed   Cell-Formulas   Formatted   Unformatted

As-Displayed is the default setting. This causes output to be printed as it appears on the worksheet. Cell-Formulas causes the contents of each cell in the print range to be output with each cell's contents appearing on a separate print line. The cell's contents as displayed on the first line of the control panel will be displayed. These contents include:

- Cell address
- Format
- Protection status (if unprotected)
- Cell contents

Range A1..C3 from our example in figure 6-4 was output in figure 6-5 with Cell-Formulas active.

The Unformatted command causes data to be output without headers, footers, and top of page breaks. The Formatted command restores these.

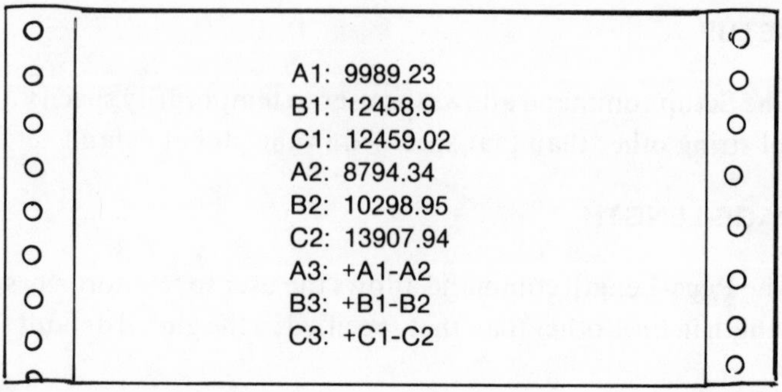

```
A1:  9989.23
B1:  12458.9
C1:  12459.02
A2:  8794.34
B2:  10298.95
C2:  13907.94
A3:  +A1-A2
B3:  +B1-B2
C3:  +C1-C2
```

FIGURE 6-5. Effect of Cell-Formula

/Print (Printer or File) Clear

This command allows the user to clear the borders, print range, headers/footers, and printer format settings* to their default values.

/Print (Printer or File) Align

This command should be selected after having manually reset top of page, to inform 1-2-3 of the new top of page position.

/Print (Printer or File) Go

This command causes the specified print range to be output either to the printer or to the indicated print file. Printing can be stopped by issuing a Control-Break.

---

* Page-Length, Setup string, Margins.

7

Graph Commands

Introduction

In this chapter, we will discuss 1-2-3's **Graph** command. / **Graph** allows data to be represented as several different types of graphs. The **Graph** command includes several options which allow the user to:

- Draw graphs in color as well as B & W
- Add labels, titles and/or legends to graphs
- Store graph setting with worksheet files
- Assign names to graphs

This chapter will be divided into two sections. The first section will contain an overview of the graph generation process using 1-2-3. The following topics will be discussed:

- Types of graphs
- Defining a graph
- Graph (F10) key
- Generating color graphs
- Adding labels to graphs
- Printing graphs
- Naming graphs
- Resetting graphs

The second section will contain a description of the selections available under the Graph command. The Graph command's tree structure is depicted in figure 7-1. Obviously, some discussion of the Graph command menu selections will be necessary in the first section. The discussion of these selections in the second section will be more comprehensive. This discussion will proceed in the order in which the menu selections are displayed when / Graph is executed.

Generating Graphs — An Overview

DEFINING A GRAPH

Creating a graph with 1-2-3 is a simple process requiring only three steps. These are:

- Specify the type of graph to be drawn (Line, Bar, Stacked-Bar, Pie, XY)
- Indicate the cell range whose values are to be displayed
- Specify View to display the graph

The following simple graphing example will illustrate how these three steps can be implemented to display a graph. First, suppose that the worksheet appeared as follows:

	A	B	C	D	E	F	G	H
1	1000		3000		5000			
2	2000		4000		6000			
3								
4								
5								

Graph

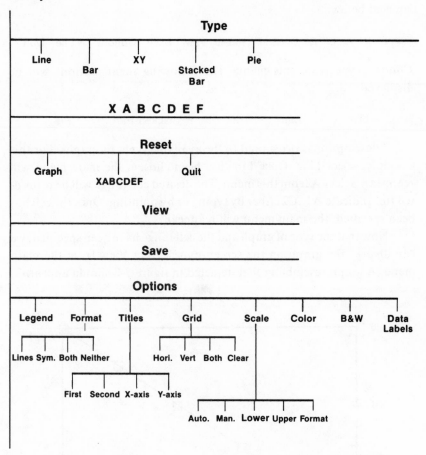

FIGURE 7-1. Graph Command Tree Structure

Next, issue /G to display the Graph command's main menu. This menu is depicted below:

Type X A B C D E F Reset View Save Options Name Quit

Choose Type from this menu. The following menu options will be displayed:

Line   Bar   XY   Stacked-Bar   Pie

These options correspond to the available types of graphs. For this example, select Line. Once Line has been chosen, the main menu will reappear. Select A from this menu. The desired cell range will be prompted for. Indicate A1..C2 either by typing or by pointing. Once the cell has been specified, the main menu will reappear.

Now that the type of graph and the cell range have been specified, we can display the graph on the screen by selecting View from the main menu. A graph resembling that depicted in figure 7-2 should appear.

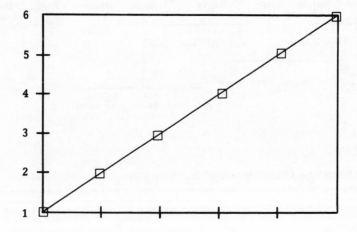

FIGURE 7-2. Line Graph Example

If your computer system only contains a graphics video screen, 1-2-3 will replace the worksheet with the graph. To display the worksheet and control panel once again, press any key.

If your computer system has both a monochrome and a graphics monitor, the former will be used to display the worksheet and the latter will be used to display the graph. The graph will remain on the graphics monitor until one of the following occurs:

- /Worksheet Erase is executed
- /File Retrieve is executed
- /Graph Reset is executed
- 1-2-3 Session is ended

F10 (Graph) Key

The F10 key can be used to display a graph while 1-2-3 is in the Ready mode. The graph settings last specified will be used to draw the graph. The F10 key is especially useful in drawing a graph several times using data that has been modified.

For instance, suppose that we continued with our elementary graphing example by pressing the Esc key until 1-2-3's Ready mode was active. If the contents of cell C2 were changed to 4000 and F10 was pressed, our revised graph could be displayed by pressing F10.

LINE GRAPHS

With line graphs, the values in a range can be represented with symbols, symbols connected with a line, a line without symbols, or a Data-Label*. Examples of each of these line graph options are included in figure 7-3.

Up to six ranges can be indicated for a line graph (A-F). Each range will be assigned a unique symbol, and if a color monitor is in use, a unique color as well.

---

* Data-Labels are discussed on page 173.

If **Data**-Labels had been specified using the / **Graph O**ptions **D**ata-Labels command, these will appear in place of the standard symbols.

The **Graph O**ptions **F**ormat command can be used to indicate whether a line only, symbols only, or line with symbols line graph will be displayed.

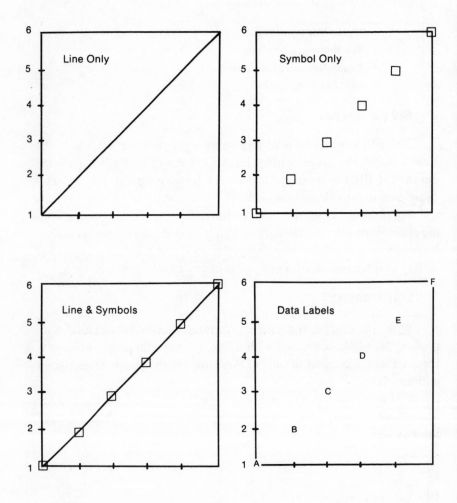

FIGURE 7-3. Line Graphs

BAR GRAPHS

In our preceding example, we defined the settings for a line graph. In this section, we will use the same initial worksheet to define a bar graph. First of all, execute the Type command and specify **B**ar. Next, choose **A** to specify the range and enter A1..E2. When View is selected, the graph in figure 7-4 will appear on the screen.

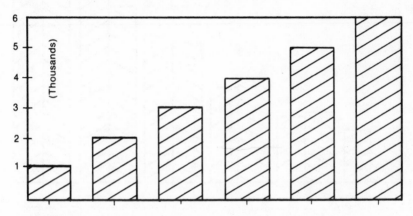

FIGURE 7-4. Bar Graph Example

Two different sets of data can be specified next to each other, by specifying a second range of values for **B**. Suppose we had revised our worksheet as follows:

	A	B	C	D	E	F	G	H
1	1000		3000		5000			
2	2000		4000		6000			
3								
4	1500		2790		5250			
5	1900		4200		6390			
6								
7								
8								
9								
10								
11								
12								
13								
14								
15								
16								
17								
18								

If we specified **B** as A4..E5 and indicated **View**, the graph would appear as depicted in figure 7-5.

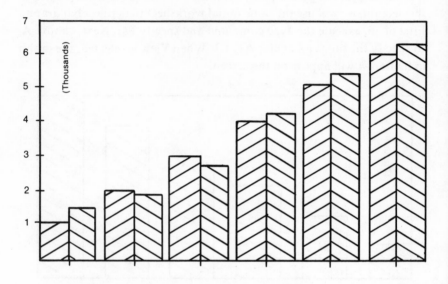

FIGURE 7-5. Bar Graph with Two Ranges Specified

XY GRAPH

XY graphs are based upon the Cartesian coordinate system. An example of an XY graph appears in figure 7-6. As you might recall from algebra, a value is plotted in the graph using its x and y values. The junction of these two coordinates is used to indicate the value on the graph.

To specify an XY graph, two ranges must be specified. The **X** range will correspond to the x-axis. The **A** range will correspond to the y-axis. Suppose we were using the same worksheet data as in the bar graph example, and we indicated A1..E2 for **X** and A4..E5 for **A**. Upon pressing **View**, our graph would resemble the one depicted in figure 7-6.

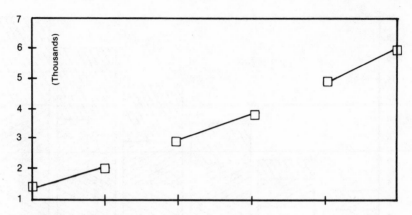

FIGURE 7-6. XY Graph

STACKED-BAR GRAPH

With a stacked bar graph, the values specified for ranges A through F are stacked one on top of the other in a bar graph. The A value is the bottom of the bar followed by B, C, etc.

Suppose the worksheet appeared as follows:

	A	B	C	D	E	F	G	H
1	1000		3000		5000			
2	2000		4000		6000			
3								
4	1500		2790		5250			
5	1900		4200		6390			
6								
7	1200		3780		5780			
8	2300		3980		6784			
9								
10								
11								
12								
13								
14								
15								
16								
17								
18								
19								
20								

If Stacked-Bar was selected for **Type**, and A1..E2 was selected for **A**, A4..E5 for **B**, and A7..E8 for **C**, the stacked bar graph would resemble that depicted in figure 7-7.

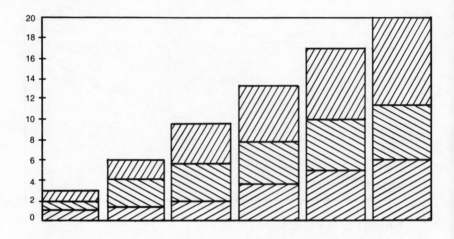

PIE GRAPH

A Pie graph is pictured in figure 7-8. The graph in figure 7-8 would be output when A1..E2 was specified for **A**. Notice that individual percentage values for each of the quantities making up the graph are displayed.

FIGURE 7-7. Stacked Bar Graph

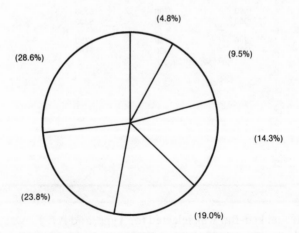

FIGURE 7-8. Pie Graph

COLOR AND B&W

As we have already seen, when graphs are displayed in B&W, different cross-hatching patterns are used to distinguish bar graphs for each range, and different symbols are used to distinguish line and XY graphs. If a color monitor is connected to your system, graphs can be displayed in color by indicating the Graph Options Color command. Notice that different colors will be used to distinguish different ranges in bar, stacked-bar, line, and XY graphs.

ADDING LABELS

1-2-3 allows the user to add labels to graphs in a number of different ways. One of the most useful of these is adding x-axis labels. Suppose the worksheet appeared as follows:

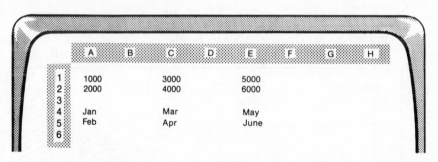

	A	B	C	D	E	F	G	H
1	1000		3000		5000			
2	2000		4000		6000			
3								
4	Jan		Mar		May			
5	Feb		Apr		June			
6								

If we defined the Type as Bar, the X range as A4..E5 and the A range as A1..E2 a graph similar to that depicted in figure 7-9 would appear. Notice that if we changed the Type to Line, x-axis labels will be displayed on the line graph. X-axis labels will also be displayed for pie and stacked bar graphs.

1-2-3's Graph Option Titles command allows the user to specify graph titles. Two separate title lines can be defined as well as the x-axis and y-axis titles.

1-2-3's Graph Options Legend command allows the user to define a legend which will be used to reference a cross-hatching pattern or a color. The legend will appear at the bottom of the graph display. Figure 7-10 illustrates a bar graph drawn with titles and legends included.

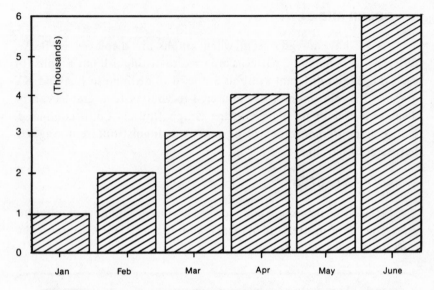

FIGURE 7-9. Bar Graph with X-axis Labels

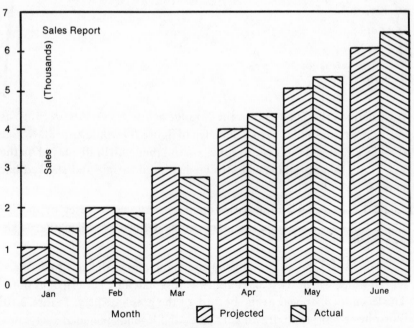

FIGURE 7-10. Bar Graph with Titles and Legends

PRINTING GRAPHS

1-2-3 does not include a command which allows the user to print a graph. However, a graph can still be output to the printer using the PrintGraph program. Before a graph can be output using PrintGraph, it must first be saved. Refer to chapter 8 for a discussion of PrintGraph.

NAMING GRAPHS

When the File Save or File Xtract commands are used to save a worksheet, the graph settings will also be stored. When this worksheet is later redisplayed using / File Retrieve, its graph can be displayed by pressing the F10 key.

A problem arises, however, when the user wishes to display a worksheet as a number of different graphs, as 1-2-3 can only store one group of graph settings. This problem can be solved by indicating **graph names** using 1-2-3's Graph Name Create command.

This command allows the user to assign a name consisting of up to 15 characters to the current group of graph settings. When a Graph Name Use command is issued, those settings will be retrieved, and the graph automatically drawn.

RESETTING GRAPHS

1-2-3's Graph Reset command allows the user to either erase the entire current graph setting (by indicating Graph), or one or more of the data ranges (A-F,X). The Graph Reset command will not cancel graph names. This can be accomplished by executing either the Graph Name Delete or Graph Name Reset commands.

Graph Command Selections

Now that we have gained an overview of the graphing process, we will describe each of the individual Graph commands.

/GRAPH TYPE

The Graph Type commands allows the user to indicate which kind of graph will be created. 1-2-3 allows for **Line**, **Bar**, **XY**, Stacked-Bar, and **Pie** graphs.

/GRAPH X(A B C D E or F)

These commands allow the user to specify the individual data ranges.

/GRAPH RESET

This command allows the user to cancel the current graph setting by indicating **Graph**. Also, / Graph **Reset** can be used to cancel any one of the individual data ranges.

/GRAPH VIEW

This command causes the graph to be displayed on the monitor.

/GRAPH SAVE

This command can be used to save the current graph as a graph file. The user will be prompted to enter a filename. The graph file will be assigned that name with the extension .PIC. The graph file will be stored in the current directory.

/GRAPH OPTIONS LEGEND

When the Graph **O**ptions command is executed, the menu depicted in figure 7-11 will be displayed. The first menu choice, Legend, can be used to define a legend for each of the various data ranges. With Bar and Stacked-Bar graphs, the legend will define the color or cross-hatching pattern used to represent that range. With XY and Line graphs, the legend will identify the symbol used to represent that range. The legend will be displayed at the bottom of the video screen when the graph is drawn.

/GRAPH OPTIONS FORMAT

The Graph **O**ptions Format command is used to determine whether Line and XY graphs are to be drawn using Lines or Symbols. If Symbols is chosen, each point in the data range will be represented with one of the following symbols:

□ ———▶ A range data points
+ ———▶ B range data points
◇ ———▶ C range data points
△ ———▶ D range data points
x ———▶ E range data points
▽ ———▶ F range data points

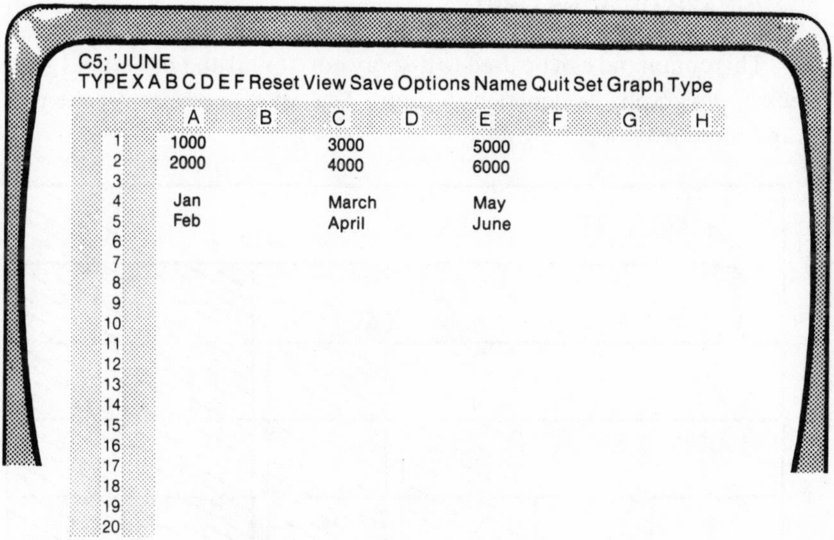

```
C5; 'JUNE
TYPE X A B C D E F Reset View Save Options Name Quit Set Graph Type
            A      B      C      D      E      F      G      H
 1        1000          3000          5000
 2        2000          4000          6000
 3
 4        Jan           March         May
 5        Feb           April         June
 6
 7
 8
 9
10
11
12
13
14
15
16
17
18
19
20
```

FIGURE 7-11. Graph Options Command Menu

If Line is selected, each point will be connected with a straight line. If Both is selected, both lines and points will be plotted. If Neither is selected, neither lines nor points will be plotted.

/GRAPH OPTIONS TITLES

This command allows the user to specify a title for the following portions of the graph:

First line in graph display
Second line in graph display
x-axis
y-axis

As many as 39 characters can be specified for each title. Notice that when a Titles selection is made, 1-2-3 will enter the Edit mode in order to facilitate data entry. A cell's contents can be specified for a title by prefixing the cell address with the backslash character (\ ).

/GRAPH OPTIONS GRID

This command can be used to display horizontal and or vertical grid lines in the graph. As depicted in figure 7-12, grid lines often make the graph more readable.

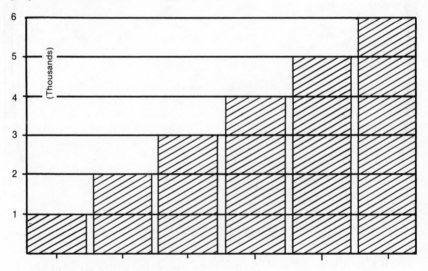

FIGURE 7-12. Bar Graph with Horizontal Grid Lines

/GRAPH OPTIONS SCALE

This command allows the user to specify a numeric range for the x and y axis. The graph will be output using these ranges as upper and lower limits. This command is generally used to expand an area of the graph that warrants close examination. The Scale command must be used with an axis whose value is numeric. For Line, Bar, and Stack-Bar graphs, Scale can only be used with the numeric y-axis. For **XY** graphs, Scale can be used with either axis.

We will use a practical example to illustrate **/GOS** usage. Suppose the worksheet appeared as follows:

	A	B	C	D	E	F	G	H
1	1000		3000		5000			
2	2000		4000		6000			
3								
4								
5								
6								

If we selected Scale from the Options menu, the following menu would appear:

Y Scale   X Scale   Skip

Since we are drawing a bar graph, only the y-axis would be numeric. Therefore, select Y Scale from the menu. The following menu will appear:

Automatic   Manual   Lower   Upper   Format   Quit

Automatic causes the graph to be drawn so that all data points are displayed. Manual causes 1-2-3 to draw the graph using the defined scale limits. These limits are defined by Lower and Upper. Format allows the user to specify how the numeric values will be represented.

Continuing our example, suppose that we wished to display our worksheet data as a bar graph with a lower limit of 2000 and an upper limit of 5000. Our first step would be to indicate Manual. Next, we would establish our limits using Lower and Upper. Now that we have established our scale limits, we can display the graph by indicating Quit twice and then indicating View. Our graph would resemble that depicted in figure 7-13. Note the lower limit of 2000 is ignored and the graph is scaled from 0 to 5000. For a Bar or Stack-Bar graph, 1-2-3 ignores a positive lower limit so the scale always includes zero (0).

/ GOS can also be used to set the **skip** factor for the x-axis. The skip factor dictates which elements of the x data range will be used as labels.

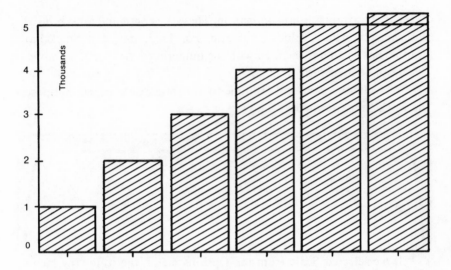

FIGURE 7-13. Bar Graph Using Upper and Lower Scale Limits

For example, suppose we revised our worksheet as follows,

	A	B	C	D	E	F	G	H
1	1000		3000		5000			
2	2000		4000		6000			
3								
4	Jan		Mar		May			
5	Feb		Apr		June			
6								
7								
8								
9								
10								
11								
12								
13								
14								
15								
16								
17								
18								
19								
20								

and indicated the x-data range as A4..E5. The graph depicted in figure 7-13 would resemble that in figure 7-14 if a Skip factor of 2 was specified.

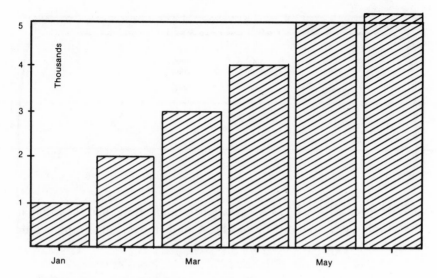

FIGURE 7-14. Bar Graph with X-axis Skip Factor

/GRAPH OPTIONS COLOR
/GRAPH OPTIONS B&W

Color causes graph bars and lines to be displayed in the following colors:

White ⟶ A&D data ranges
Red ⟶ B&E data ranges
Blue ⟶ C&F data ranges

B&W returns 1-2-3 to the initial black and white setting.

/GRAPH OPTIONS DATA-LABELS

Data-Labels is used to indicate a range of cells which will be used to label the data points of a graph. Each data range (A-F) can have its own set of labels.

The following example will illustrate **Data-Labels**. Suppose our worksheet appeared as follows,

	A	B	C	D	E	F	G	H
1	1000		3000		5000			
2	2000		4000		6000			
3								
4	Jan		Mar		May			
5	Feb		Apr		June			
6								
7								

and we specified A4..E5 as A's data-labels range. If we then chose **Bar** as the graph **Type** and A1..E2 as the **A** data range, our graph would resemble that depicted in figure 7-15.

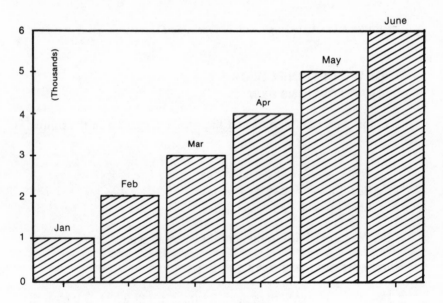

FIGURE 7-15. Bar Graph with Data-Labels

/GRAPH NAME

The **Graph Name** command is used to assign names to and store graph settings so they can be later recalled. When / **GN** is executed, the following menu will be displayed:

Use   Create   Delete   Reset

If **U**se is selected, a prompt will appear asking for the graph name to be made current. The existing graph names will be displayed in line 3 of the control panel. When one of these is specified, that graph will be displayed on the screen.

Create allows the user to save the current graph settings under a graph name of up to 14 characters. **D**elete allows the user to delete a graph name. **R**eset will erase all named graphs.

8

PrintGraph

Introduction

The PrintGraph program is used to output graphs saved as .PIC files to the printer or plotter. PrintGraph includes a number of different options which allow the user to control the way in which the individual graphs are printed. For example, PrintGraph allows the user to specify whether colors are to be used in the graph, what character styles are to be used, as well as how the output should be positioned on the page. The various PrintGraph options will be discussed in this chapter.

Before beginning our discussion of these options, we will detail the configuration procedure for PrintGraph. Like 1-2-3, PrintGraph requires information regarding the hardware upon which it is installed in order to function properly. This information is included in PrintGraph's configuration file.

Starting PrintGraph

In order to start PrintGraph from 1-2-3, it will be necessary to exit 1-2-3 first. Before exiting 1-2-3, be certain that the current worksheet, current graph settings and graph names have been saved using the **Graph Save** command. The Lotus Access System menu will be displayed once 1-2-3 has been exited. Select PrintGraph from the menu. Lotus will then prompt for a disk change. The 1-2-3 System disk should be replaced with the PrintGraph program disk. Press any key, and the PrintGraph menu will appear.

If both 1-2-3 and PrintGraph have been installed on the fixed disk in a single diskette, fixed drive system, the disk swapping step will be eliminated.

PrintGraph can also be started from DOS by inserting the Print-Graph diskette in drive A and entering the following:

GRAPH ◄┘

The PrintGraph menu includes the following options:

Select	Allows the user to choose one or more graphs for output to the printer.
Options	Allows the user to choose among available output options (character style, color, page position).
Go	Output indicated graph to the printer.
Configure	Set PrintGraph's configuration.
Align	Sets the current paper position in the printer as top of page.
Page	Advances the paper in the printer to the top of the next page.
Quit	Allows the user to return to the Lotus Access System menu.

PrintGraph's Configuration

PrintGraph's current configuration settings are displayed in the area of the screen normally occupied by the worksheet. This display is depicted in figure 8-1. If changes are made to the configuration settings, these will be updated on the screen.

The first time PrintGraph is started up, the default configuration parameters will be as follows:

DRIVES	GRAPHICS DEVICE	INTERFACE
Pictures: B:\	Epson FX-80/1™	Parallel
Fonts: A: \		

PAGE SIZE
Length: 11.000
Width: 8.000

The default configuration parameters can be interpreted as follows:

- PrintGraph will search for graph files on drive B.
- Typeface style files are stored on drive A (on the PrintGraph diskette).
- The Epson FX-80/1 in the single density mode is installed as the printer device.
- The printer is connected to the system via its parallel port.
- The page size is 8″ by 11″.

Copyright 1982,1983 Lotus Development Corp. All Rights reserved   MENU

Select Options   Go   Configure   Align   Page   Quit
Select pictures

SELECTED	COLORS	SIZE	HALF	DIRECTORIES
GRAPHS	Grid: Black	Left Margin:	.750	Pictures
	A Range: Black	Top Margin:	.395	B: \
	B Range: Black	Width:	6.500	Fonts
	C Range: Black	Height	4.691	A:\
	D Range: Black	Rotation	.000	
	E Range: Black			GRAPHICS DEVICE
	F Range: Black	MODES		Epson FX-80/1
		Eject: Yes		Parallel
	FONTS	Pause: Yes		PAGE SIZE
	1: SCRIPT2			Length 11.000
				Height 8.000

FIGURE 8-1. PrintGraph Initial Display Example

CHANGING THE CONFIGURATION SETTINGS

To change PrintGraph's configuration settings, choose Configure from the PrintGraph menu. Once Configure has been selected, the following menu will be displayed:

Files   Device   Page   Interface   Save   Reset   Quit

Each of these will be discussed in the following sections.

FILES

Files allows the user to indicate the drive (in DOS 1.1) or the directory (in DOS 2.0) where PrintGraph will look for graph and font files. The following selections will be displayed:

Pictures	Indicates drive or directory which is to be searched for graph files.
Fonts	Indicates drive or directory to be searched for font files.
Quit	Returns PrintGraph to Configure menu.

If the user wanted to specify drive A as the drive to be examined for graph files, he or she could do so by selecting Pictures and then entering "A: \ " .

DEVICE

PrintGraph includes a file known as a **device library**, which includes device drivers for the following printers and plotters*:

Anadex 9620A Silent Scribe Printer™

Epson FX80 Printer; Single, Double, Triple, Quad Density Modes

HP 7470A Plotter™

IBM Graphics Printer™, Single, Double, Triple, Quad Density Modes

* These may differ on your PrintGraph disk.

Epson MX-80™ or MX-100™, Single, Double, Triple
Density Modes

NEC 8023™ Printer

Okidata 82A™ or 83A™ Printer

A number sign (#) will indicate the current device. The current device can be changed by moving the pointer to the desired cell using the ↓ and ↑ keys. When the space bar key is pressed, the number sign will move to the indicated device. When the Enter key is pressed, the new device will be made current, and the Configure menu will be displayed. The configuration settings display will be updated to reflect the new device.

Several of the Device choices allow the user to specify the following modes:

Single density

Double density

Triple density

Quad density

Density refers to the resolution with which the graph will be output. Double density offers more precision than single density. Triple density offers more precision than double density, and quad density offers more precision than triple density. Generally, with a higher density specification, a greater amount of time will be required to output the graph.

PAGE

The Page option allows the user to specify the length and width of the output page. The defaults are 11″ and 8″ respectively.

INTERFACE

Printers generally use one of two means of communication with the computer; **parallel** and **serial**. In parallel communications, the 8 bits representing a character or byte are sent simultaneously from the computer to the printer. In serial communications, these 8 bits are sent one at a time. PrintGraph must be configured for the current communications method in order to function properly.

When Interface is selected from the Configure menu, the following choices will be available:

1	Parallel Port
2	Serial Port
3	Second Parallel Port
4	Second Serial Port

Select 1 if the IBM Monochrome Display and Printer Adapter or a similar device is installed. Select 2 if an IBM Asynchronous Communications Adapter or similar device is installed. Select 3 if an optional second parallel interface is installed. Select 4 if an optional second serial interface is installed.

If a serial device is chosen, 2 or 4, PrintGraph will prompt the user for the **baud** rate. Baud rate can be defined as the speed, measured in characters per second, at which the serial device will transmit characters. The following choices are available:

1	110 baud
2	150 baud
3	300 baud
4	600 baud
5	1200 baud
6	2300 baud
7	4800 baud
8	9600 baud
9	19,200 baud

Printers generally operate most efficiently at 1200 baud. Refer to your printer's manual to determine the optimum baud rate.

SAVE

Any changes made to the configuration setting will take effect immediately and will affect the current PrintGraph session. However, these changes will not be made permanent until they have been saved on the PrintGraph disk. Save allows the configuration setting changes to be saved on the PrintGraph disk.

When Save is indicated from the Configure menu, the following choices will be available:

Cancel

Replace

Cancel ends Save and returns PrintGraph to the Configure menu. Replace saves the current configuration on the PrintGraph disk.

RESET

Reset allows the user to cancel any changes made to the configuration settings during the current PrintGraph session. When Reset is chosen from the Configure menu, the following options will be displayed:

Yes   No

Yes results in the configuration settings being reset to those current when PrintGraph was started or to those current when a Save was effected.

Outputting Graphs

The selections other than Configure on the PrintGraph main menu pertain to outputting 1-2-3 graph files on the printer. These will be discussed individually in the following sections.

SELECT

Select allows the user to select one or more graph files for output. When Select is indicated, the diskette in the device specified in the Pictures configuration setting will be read. Any 1-2-3 graph files residing on this diskette will be displayed on the screen in the following format:

PICTURE	DATE	TIME	SIZE
# FCST1	08-24-83	6:18	4352
TEST1	09-05-83	4:21	1664
TEST2	09-05-83	4:22	640
TEST3	09-05-83	4:23	1024

The ↑ and ↓ keys can be used to move the pointer to the desired file. When this file is highlighted, press the space bar key to select it. The selected file will be denoted with the number sign character (#). The # indicator can be removed by pressing the space bar a second time.

When the Enter key is pressed, the selected files will be noted for output by PrintGraph. PrintGraph's main menu will reappear, and the selected graph files will be listed underneath "Selected Graphs" on the display screen in the order in which they were chosen.

OPTIONS

The Options menu selection allows the user to indicate characteristics used to output graphs. The Options setting will affect all graphs indicated by Select. Therefore, if the Options settings are to be changed, only Select those graph files which are to be output under a single setting. The Options settings are as follows:

Color	Pause
Font	Eject
Size	Quit

These will be described in the following sections.

COLOR OPTION

The Color option has no effect unless a color output device is being used. The Color option allows the user to indicate colors for the following portions of the graph:

Grid	D-range
A-range	E-range
B-range	F-range
C-range	

Once the portion of the graph to be colored has been selected, PrintGraph will display a list of colors in the control panel. The selected color will be assigned to that portion of the graph. The configuration settings will be updated to reflect this change.

FONT OPTION

The Font option allows the user to select the fonts which will be used in printing the text portions of the graph. The font files will be loaded from the PrintGraph diskette when Go is specified.

Two fonts can be indicated — font1 and font2. If both are indicated, font1 will be used for the first line of the graph title, and font2 will be used for the remainder of the graph. If font2 is not specified, font1 will be used for the entire graph.

When the Font Option and font number have been specified, the available fonts will be read from the PrintGraph diskette and listed on the screen. These include:

BLOCK1	ROMAN1
BLOCK2	ROMAN2
ITALIC1	SCRIPT1
ITALIC2	SCRIPT2

Fonts are selected exactly as graph filenames are in Select.

SIZE OPTION

The Size option allows the user to specify how the graph should be placed on the paper. When Size is indicated, the following menu will appear:

Full	Half	Manual	Quit

Full indicates that the graph will take up an entire page. Half indicates that the graph will only occupy half of a page. Manual allows the user to place the graph on the page using the following settings:

Height	Top
Width	Rotation
Left	

These are displayed as menu selections when Manual is indicated.

Height specifies the graph's vertical length in inches. Width indicates the graph's width in inches. Left specifies the size of the left margin in inches. Top specifies the top margin in inches.

Rotation adjusts the rotation of the graph on the page in a clockwise direction. A setting of zero causes the graph's x-axis to be output parallel to the page width. A setting of 90° will cause the graph's x-axis to be printed perpendicular to the page width.

PAUSE OPTION

If the Pause option is indicated, PrintGraph will pause after each graph has been output. The pause will be indicated with a steady beeping.

EJECT OPTION

The Eject option allows the user to specify whether or not Print-Graph will advance to the top of the next page before outputting a new graph.

ALIGN & PAGE

Align and Page appear on PrintGraph's main menu. These are used to align the printer before beginning output. Align sets the printer's current position as top of page. Use the printer controls to position the paper as desired before indicating Align. Page is used to advance the paper to the top of the next page.

GO

The Go option is used to instruct PrintGraph to actually begin outputting the graphs.

System Information and PrintGraph

When PrintGraph is run on a two diskette system, the standard configuration is as follows:

PrintGraph	Installed in drive A
Data diskette	Installed in drive B
Pictures	Set to drive B
Fonts	Set to drive A

When graph files have been selected and Go indicated, PrintGraph will read the indicated font files from the PrintGraph diskette and the graph files from the data diskette. After these have been read, PrintGraph will output the graph files to the printer.

When PrintGraph is run on a single-diskette, fixed disk system, and the directories are set as follows:

Pictures	C:\ *directory**
Fonts	C:\ *directory*

PrintGraph will read the font and graph files from the indicated directories. After Go has been selected, PrintGraph will then display the following prompt:

Pausing, press space to continue

The selected graph file will be output after the space bar has been pressed.

PrintGraph Example

In this section, we will use a simple example to illustrate the procedures involved in outputting a graph using PrintGraph. This example will assume that a simple bar graph had been created and saved as FIG5.PIC, and that a dual diskette system with DOS 2.0 is in use.

Our first step is to exit 1-2-3 to the Access System Menu. Replace the System disk with the PrintGraph diskette. Select PrintGraph to load that program. After PrintGraph has been loaded, the main menu will be displayed along with the configuration settings.

Before attempting to print the graph, we should check the configuration settings to ascertain that they have been set as desired. Be sure to check the directories settings for pictures and fonts. For our example, these should be set as follows:

Pictures	B:\
Fonts	A:\

---

* *directory* denotes the directory name

The PrintGraph diskette should be installed in drive A, and the data diskette containing FIG5.PIC should be installed in drive B.

Our next step is to select FIG5. First, indicate Select from the main menu. Use the space bar key to indicate FIG5 and press Enter. FIG5 will be noted in the screen underneath Selected Graphs, and the main Print-Graph menu will be displayed.

Check to be sure that the desired fonts have been selected. Indicate Go on the main menu. PrintGraph will read the selected font files from the PrintGraph diskette drive A, followed by FIG5.PIC from the data diskette on drive B. PrintGraph will pause and omit a stream of beeps before printing the graph. After the user presses a key, the printing process will begin. Once FIG5.PIC has been output, the main Print-Graph menu will reappear.

9

DataBase Commands and Functions

Introduction

A database is a collection of related information. A database is divided into segments referred to as **records** and **fields**. A field is a single piece of data. Fields which are related are grouped together as a record. These records, in turn, make up the database.

A simple illustration may help you understand the concepts of a database, record, and field. Take an address book as an example of a database. This file would contain name, address, and telephone number data for the individuals appearing in the address book. Each individual's name, address, and phone number would represent one record. For example, the following data would make up one record:

Jay Gatsby
1 Shore Lane
West Egg, NY 10565
516-787-2122

Each individual data item within the record (ie. name, street address, city, state, zip code, telephone number) could be thought of as a field.

With 1-2-3, databases are made up of cells that are organized in rows and columns in the familiar worksheet form. A field can be defined as a single cell containing information. A record can be defined as a row of cells (or fields) within the database.

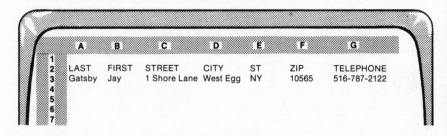

In this example, A3..G3 would make up a record and A3 would constitute a field. The term **field column** will refer to an entire column of similar information.

The first row of a 1-2-3 database, in this case A2 through G2, is reserved for **field names**. Field names provide a brief description of the type of information to be found in the column below. Field names are used to perform a number of data commands.

One of the convenient features of 1-2-3 databases is that the same spreadsheet form and commands are used for database input and design as are used with the worksheet. Only a few special commands and functions must be learned in order to manipulate the database to its full advantage.

Since 1-2-3 uses only RAM to process database information, it is best suited to small and medium size databases. The user is limited to a maximum of 2000 records. He or she is even further restricted by the amount of RAM available.

Despite these size limitations, the 1-2-3 **Data** commands and functions are extremely useful in all types of recordkeeping including:

Sales

Inventory

Personnel

Expenses

Mailing Lists

There are a few basic rules to remember when constructing a database. The first row is reserved for field names. These names are required so 1-2-3 will be able to locate information. No two field names in the same database can be identical. Moreover, these should not be preceded or ended with a space. All 256 columns can be used for the database. However, 32 is the maximum number of field columns that will be recognized by the **D**ata commands. The / **D**ata command tree is shown in figure 9-1.

Data

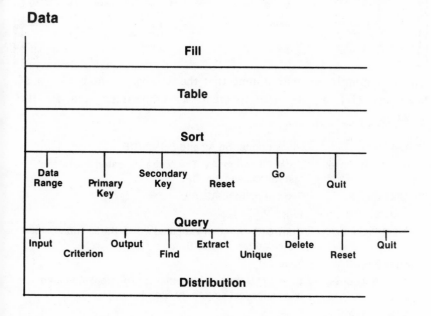

FIGURE 9-1. /**D**ata Command Tree

/Data Fill

The **Data** **Fill** command (/**DF**) will fill a specified range with a sequence of numbers. The user can specify the starting number, the ending number, and the increment (or decrement). Upon execution of /**DF**, the contents of the range specified for /**DF** will be erased entirely even if they are not replaced by numbers.

The following database will be used in our /**Data** **Fill** example:

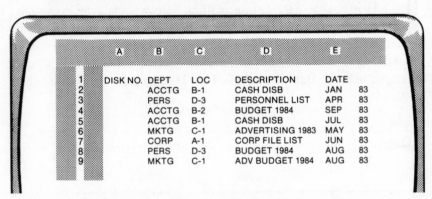

	A	B	C	D	E
1	DISK NO.	DEPT	LOC	DESCRIPTION	DATE
2		ACCTG	B-1	CASH DISB	JAN 83
3		PERS	D-3	PERSONNEL LIST	APR 83
4		ACCTG	B-2	BUDGET 1984	SEP 83
5		ACCTG	B-1	CASH DISB	JUL 83
6		MKTG	C-1	ADVERTISING 1983	MAY 83
7		CORP	A-1	CORP FILE LIST	JUN 83
8		PERS	D-3	BUDGET 1984	AUG 83
9		MKTG	C-1	ADV BUDGET 1984	AUG 83

In this example, we will assume that the database contains a list of diskettes. /**DF** will be used to create a numbering system for the diskettes.

User Step 1:	Place pointer on A2 and Select /**DF**.
1-2-3 Response:	Enter Fill range: A2. The range indicated will be the last range used for /**DF**.
User Step 2:	Type or point to A2..A9.
User Step 3:	Press ↵.
1-2-3 Response:	Start: 0 (the number indicated will be the last number indicated for /**DF** start)
User Step 4:	Type 101 ↵.
1-2-3 Response:	Step: 1 (1 is the default setting, the number indicated will be the last setting for Step.)
User Step 5:	Press ↵.
1-2-3 Response:	Stop: 2047 (2047 is the default setting, the number indicated will be the last setting for Stop.
User Step 6:	Press ↵.
1-2-3 Response:	Fills the range A2..A9 as depicted below:

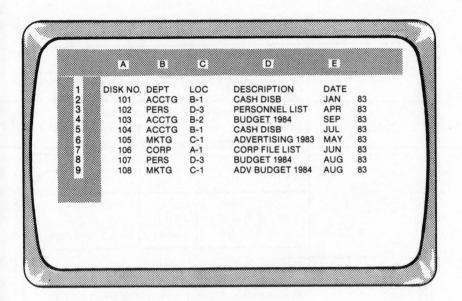

	A	B	C	D	E	
1	DISK NO.	DEPT	LOC	DESCRIPTION	DATE	
2	101	ACCTG	B-1	CASH DISB	JAN	83
3	102	PERS	D-3	PERSONNEL LIST	APR	83
4	103	ACCTG	B-2	BUDGET 1984	SEP	83
5	104	ACCTG	B-1	CASH DISB	JUL	83
6	105	MKTG	C-1	ADVERTISING 1983	MAY	83
7	106	CORP	A-1	CORP FILE LIST	JUN	83
8	107	PERS	D-3	BUDGET 1984	AUG	83
9	108	MKTG	C-1	ADV BUDGET 1984	AUG	83

To fill a range with numbers in descending order, indicate a negative number for Step and a number less than the Start number for Stop.

/DATA TABLE

The **Data Table** command (/ **DT**) enables the user to see the results of a "what if" situation in table form. / **Data Table** includes the following three options:

1   2   Reset

These options are discussed in table 9-1.

Table 9-1. / Data Table Options

/DT Option	Description
1	This option enables the user to vary the input of one cell (referred to as the input cell) and output the results of one or more formulas that are dependent on the input cell. /**DT1** has a matrix effect as depicted in the following table:

	then			
if X is:	a(X)=	b(X)=	c(X)=	d(X)=
a	a(a)	b(a)	c(a)	d(a)
b	a(b)	b(b)	c(b)	d(b)
c	a(c)	b(c)	c(c)	d(c)

/DT Option	Description
2	This option allows the user to vary two input cells and output the results of one formula that is dependent on these input cells. The effect of /**DT2** is depicted below:

If x = x+y

		and y =		
x=	a	b	c	d
a	then z=a+a	z=a+b	z=a+c	z=a+d
b	z=b+a	z=b+b	z=b+c	z=b+d
c	z=c+a	z=c+b	z=c+c	z=c+d
d	z=d+a	z=d+b	z=d+c	z=d+d
e	z=e+a	z=e+b	z=e+c	z=e+d

/DT Option	Description
Reset	This option resets the following /**Data Table** settings to their default settings:

Table range
Input Cell 1
Input Cell 2

/DATA TABLE 1 EXAMPLES

In the following examples, we will illustrate the use of / Data Table 1.

Example 1

This example calculates the monthly payment amount for a loan of a given amount at varying interest rates. We will begin with the following worksheet:

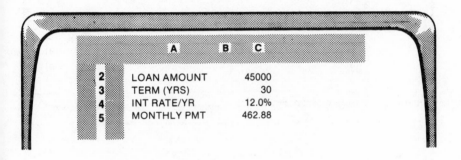

	A	B	C
2	LOAN AMOUNT		45000
3	TERM (YRS)		30
4	INT RATE/YR		12.0%
5	MONTHLY PMT		462.88

The formula contained in C5 is:

@PMT(C2,C4/12,C3*12)

The format for C4 is **P**ercent - 1 decimal place.
The format for C5 is **F**ixed - 2 decimal places.

To enter the table, make the following cell entries:

Cell	Entry	Meaning
C8	+C5	◄——— This is the input cell
B9	.11	
B10	.115	
B11	.12	
B12	.125	
B13	.13	
B14	.135	Variables to be substituted
B15	.14	for the input cell
B16	.145	
B17	.15	
B18	.155	
B19	.16	
B20	.165	

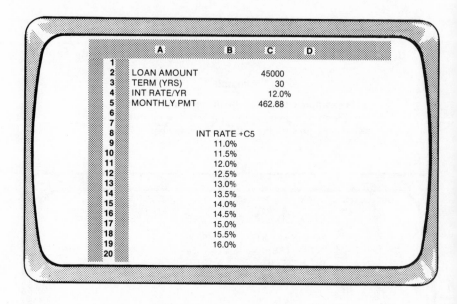

To execute /**DT1**, use the following steps:

User Step 1:	Select /**DT**
1-2-3 Response:	1 2 Reset
User Step 2:	Select **1**
1-2-3 Response:	Enter Table range: *A1
User Step 3:	Specify B8..C19 and press ↵
1-2-3 Response:	Enter Input Cell: *A1
User Step 4:	Specify C4 and press ↵
1-2-3 Response:	

* Displays last input for /**DT1**, or if **R**eset, the cell address of the cell pointer.

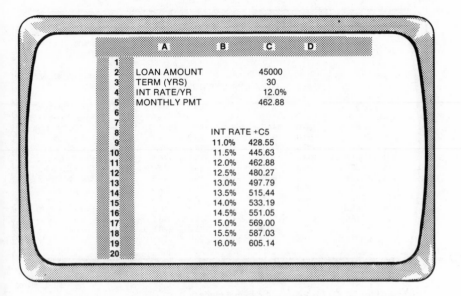

The F8 or Table function key can be used to recalculate the payment amounts in the data table after changing either the LOAN AMOUNT (C2) or TERM (C3). 1-2-3 will remember the last settings for the Data Table commands unless / Data Table Reset has been executed.

Example 2

In this example, we will begin with the worksheet in figure 9-2. This example asks "What will be the effect on projected profits for 1984 through 1988 if the quantity for 1984 is the 1983 quantity plus *x* percent".

	A	B	C	D	E	F	G	H
1								
2								PROJECTION
3	$(000)	EST.		PROJECTION				ASSUMPTIONS
4	YEAR	1983	1984	1985	1986	1987	1988	
5	QTY	45.0	49.5	54.5	59.9	65.9	72.5	PREV YR+10%
6	PRICE	10.0	11.0	12.1	13.3	14.6	16.1	PREV YR+10%
7	SALES$	450.0	544.5	658.8	797.2	964.6	1167.2	PRICE*QTY
8	COST	150.0	190.6	230.6	279.0	337.6	408.5	SALES*35%
9	V.M.	300.0	353.9	428.2	518.2	627.0	758.7	SALES-COST
10	SALARIES	100.0	110.0	121.0	133.1	146.4	161.1	PREV YR+10%
11	SALES EXP	35.0	40.8	49.4	59.8	72.3	87.5	SALES*7.5%
12	ADVERT	70.0	81.7	98.8	119.6	144.7	175.1	SALES*15%
13	RENT	10.0	10.0	10.0	10.0	12.5	12.5	
14	DEPR	2.5	2.5	2.5	2.5	2.5	2.5	
15	OFFICE	5.5	6.1	6.7	7.3	8.1	8.9	PREV YR+10%
16	TOTAL EXP	223.0	251.1	288.4	332.3	386.5	447.5	
17	PROFIT	77.0	102.9	129.9	185.9	240.5	311.1	
18	%SALES	17%	19%	21%	23%	25%	27%	
19								

The format for B8..G17 is **F**ixed -- 1 decimal place
The format for B18..G18 is **P**ercent -- 0 decimal places

FIGURE 9-2. / **D**ata **T**able 1 Example 2

Table 9-2. Example 2 Cell Entries

H2: 'PROJECTION	G8: +C7*0.35	E13: 10
A3: '$(000)	D8: +D7*0.35	F13: 12.5
B3: "EST.	E8: +E7*0.35	G13: 12.5
C3: -	F8: +F7*0.35	A14: 'DEPR
D3: 'PROJECTIO	G8: +G7*0.35	B14: 2.5
E3: 'N-------	H8: 'SALES*35%	C14: 2.5
F3: -	A9: 'V.M.	D14: 2.5
G3: -	B9: +B7-B8	E14: 2.5
H3: 'ASSUMPTIONS	C9: +C7-C8	F14: 2.5
A4: (F0) "YEAR	D9: +D7-D8	G14: 2.5
B4: (R0) 1983	E9: +E7-E8	A15: 'OFFICE
C4: (F0) 1984	F9: +F7-F8	B15: 5.5
D4: (F0) 1985	G9: +G7-G8	C15: +B15*1.1

Table 9-2. Example 2 Cell Entries (cont.)

E4: (F0) 1986	H9: 'SALES-COST	D15: +C15*1.1
F4: (F0) 1987	A10: 'SALARIES	E15: +D15*1.1
F4: (F0) 1988	B10: 100	E15: +E15*1.1
A5: 'QTY	C10: +B10*1.1	G15: +F15*1.1
B5: 45	D10: +C10*1.1	H15: 'PREV YR+10%
C5: +B5*1.1	E10: +D10*1.1	A16: 'TOTAL EXP
D5: +C5*1.1	F10: +E10*1.1	B16: @SUM(B10..B15)
E5: +D5*1.1	G10: +F10*1.1	C16: @SUM(C10..C15)
F5: +E5*1.1	H10: 'PREV YR+10%	D16: @SUM(D10..D15
G5: +F5*1.1	A11: 'SALES EXP	E16: @SUM(E10..E15)
H5: 'PREV YR+10%	B11: 35	F16: @SUM(F10..F15)
A6: 'PRICE	C11: +C7*0.075	G16: @SUM(G10..G15)
B6: 10	D11: +D7*0.075	A17: PROFIT
C6: +B6*1.1	E11: +E7*0.075	B17: +B9-B16
D6: +C6*1.1	F11: +F7*0.075	C17: +C9-C16
E6: +D6*1.1	G11: +G7*0.075	D17: +D9-D16
F6: +E6*1.1	H11: 'SALES*7.5%	E17: +E9-E16
G6: +F6*1.1	A12: 'ADVERT	F17: +F9-F16
H6: 'PREV YR+10%	B12: 70	G17: +G9-G16
A7: 'SALES	C12: +C7*0.15	H17: 'VM-TOTAL EXP
B7: +B5*B6	D12: +D7*0.15	A18: '%SALES
C7: +C5*C6	E12: +E7*0.15	B18: (P0) +B17/+B7
D7: +D5*D6	F12: +F7*0.15	C18: (P0) +C17/+C7
E7: +E5*E6	G12: +G7*0.15	D18: (P0) +D17/+D7
F7: +F5*F6	H12: 'SALES*15%	E18: (P0) +E17/+E7
G7: +G5*G6	A13: 'RENT	F18: (P0) +F17/+F7
H7: 'PRICE*QTY	B13: 10	G18: (P0) +G17/+G7
A8: 'COST	C13: 10	H18: 'PROFIT/SALES
B8: 150	D13: 10	

To enter the data table, make the following cell entries:

Cell	Entry	Meaning
C21	+C17	Profit for 1984
*D21	+D17	Profit for 1985
*E21	+E17	Profit for 1986
*F21	+F17	Profit for 1987
*G21	+G17	Profit for 1988
B21	+B5*1.05	1983 Qty+5%
B22	+B5*1.1	1983 Qty+10%
B23	+B5*1.15	1983 Qty+15%
B24	+B5*1.2	1983 Qty,20%

The table will appear as follows:

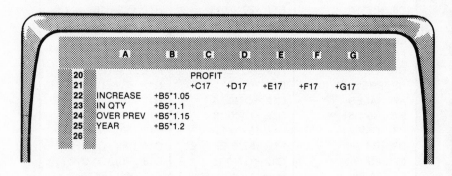

C21..G21 and B22..B25 formatted in
Text using /RF

The following steps are used to execute / **DT1:**

User Step 1:	Select /**DT1**
1-2-3 Response:	Enter Table range:*A1
User Step 2:	Specify B21..G25 and press ⏎
1-2-3 Response:	Enter Input Cell 1:*A1
User Step 3:	Specify C5 and press ⏎
1-2-3 Response:	

* or use /**C**opy from C21 to D21..G21

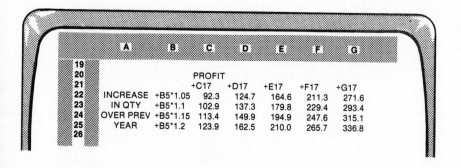

	A	B	C	D	E	F	G
19							
20			PROFIT				
21			+C17	+D17	+E17	+F17	+G17
22	INCREASE	+B5*1.05	92.3	124.7	164.6	211.3	271.6
23	IN QTY	+B5*1.1	102.9	137.3	179.8	229.4	293.4
24	OVER PREV	+B5*1.15	113.4	149.9	194.9	247.6	315.1
25	YEAR	+B5*1.2	123.9	162.5	210.0	265.7	336.8
26							

/DATA TABLE 2 EXAMPLES

Example 1

In this example, monthly payments are calculated for a
given loan amount for varying interest rates and terms.
We begin with the following worksheet:

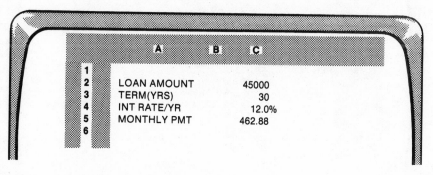

	A	B	C
1			
2	LOAN AMOUNT		45000
3	TERM(YRS)		30
4	INT RATE/YR		12.0%
5	MONTHLY PMT		462.88
6			

The formula in C5 is:

@PMT (C2,C4/12,C3*12)

To create the data table, make the following cell entries:

Cell	Entry	Meaning
B8	+C5	Output formula
B9	.11	
B10	.115	
B11	.12	Interest rates
B12	.125	

B13	.13	⎫
B14	.135	⎪
B15	.14	⎪
B16	.145	⎬ Interest rates
B17	.15	⎪
B18	.155	⎪
B19	.16	⎭
C8	30	⎫
D8	25	⎬ term of
E8	20	⎪ loan
F8	15	⎭

The table should appear as follows:

	A	B	C	D	E	F
6						
7		NO. OF YEARS				
8	+C5		30	25	20	15
9		11.0%				
10	INTEREST	11.5%				
11	RATE	12.0%				
12	PER YEAR	12.5%				
13		13.0%				
14		13.5%	B1 formatted Text			
15		14.0%	B9..B19 formatted Percent -1 decimal			
16		14.5%				
17		15.0%				
18		15.5%				
19		16.0%				

To execute /**DT2**, follow these steps:

User Step 1:	Select /**DT2**
1-2-3 Response:	Enter Table range: A1
User Step 2:	Type B8..F19 ⏎
1-2-3 Response:	Enter Input Cell1: A1
User Step 3:	Type C4 ⏎
1-2-3 Response:	Enter Input Cell2: A1
User Step 4:	Type C3 ⏎
1-2-3 Response:	

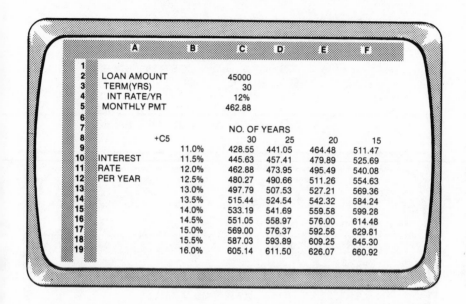

	A	B	C	D	E	F
1						
2	LOAN AMOUNT		45000			
3	TERM(YRS)		30			
4	INT RATE/YR		12%			
5	MONTHLY PMT		462.88			
6						
7			NO. OF YEARS			
8		+C5	30	25	20	15
9		11.0%	428.55	441.05	464.48	511.47
10	INTEREST	11.5%	445.63	457.41	479.89	525.69
11	RATE	12.0%	462.88	473.95	495.49	540.08
12	PER YEAR	12.5%	480.27	490.66	511.26	554.63
13		13.0%	497.79	507.53	527.21	569.36
14		13.5%	515.44	524.54	542.32	584.24
15		14.0%	533.19	541.69	559.58	599.28
16		14.5%	551.05	558.97	576.00	614.48
17		15.0%	569.00	576.37	592.56	629.81
18		15.5%	587.03	593.89	609.25	645.30
19		16.0%	605.14	611.50	626.07	660.92

If the loan amount was changed, the data table could be recalculated by simply pressing the F8 (Table) key. 1-2-3 will remember / **Data Table** settings until / **DTR**eset has been executed.

Example 2

This example uses the worksheet depicted in figure 9-2 with the same cell entries as listed in table 9-2. In this example, we will calculate the effects of changing the percentage increase of quantities over the base year (1983) and also the effects of different costs (as a percent of sales) on 1984 profits. To set up the table:

User Step 1: Place the cell pointer on C23 and type +C17↵. This is the cell that will be dependent on the two input cells.

User Step 2: Type the variables for Input Cell 1 (1984 INCREASE IN QUANTITY OVER 1983).

Cell	Variable	Meaning
C24	+B5*1.05	QTY=1983 QTY+5%
C25	+B5*1.1	QTY=1983 QTY+10%
C26	+B5*1.15	QTY=1983 QTY+15%
C27	+B5*1.2	QTY=1983 QTY+20%

User Step 3:		Type the variables for Input Cell 2 (COST AS A PERCENT OF SALES$).

Cell	Variable	Meaning
D23	0.3*C7	COST=30%*SALES$
E23	0.325*C7	COST=32.5%*SALES$
F23	0.35*C7	COST=35%*SALES$
G23	0.375*C7	COST=37.5%*SALES$
H23	0.4*C7	COST=40%*SALES$

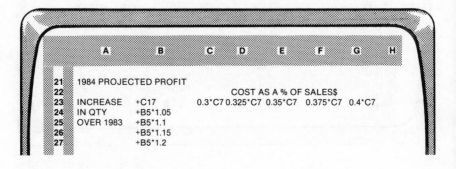

	A	B	C	D	E	F	G	H
21	1984 PROJECTED PROFIT							
22				COST AS A % OF SALES$				
23	INCREASE	+C17		0.3*C7	0.325*C7	0.35*C7	0.375*C7	0.4*C7
24	IN QTY	+B5*1.05						
25	OVER 1983	+B5*1.1						
26		+B5*1.15						
27		+B5*1.2						

C23..C26 and D23..H23 formatted **Text** with **/RF**
D24..H27 formatted **Fixed** -1 decimal place with **/RF**

To execute / **DT2**:

User Step 1:	Select /**DT**
1-2-3 Response:	1 2 Reset
User Step 2:	Select **2**
1-2-3 Response:	Enter Table range:*A1
User Step 3:	Specify C23..H27 and press ↵
1-2-3 Response:	Enter Input cell 1:*A1
User Step 4:	Specify C5 and press ↵
1-2-3 Response:	Enter Input cell 2:*A1
User Step 5:	Specify C8 and press ↵
1-2-3 Response:	

* Displays last input for /**DT2** or if **Reset**, the cell pointer address

	A	B	C	D	E	F	G	H
21	1984 PROJECTED PROFIT							
22					COST AS A % OF SALES$			
23	INCREASE		+C17	0.3*C7	0.325*C7	0.35*C7	0.375*C7	0.4*C7
24	IN QTY		+B5*1.05	110.9	81.2	66.4	51.5	36.7
25	OVER 1983		+B5*1.1	137.5	124.5	111.5	98.5	85.5
26			+B5*1.15	149.3	135.7	122.0	108.4	94.8
27			+B5*1.2	161.0	146.8	132.6	118.3	104.1

/DATA SORT

The **Data Sort** command (/ **DS**) sorts a database's records. When / **DS** has been selected, the following menu choices will appear:

> **D**ata-Range
>
> **R**ange-Key
>
> **S**econdary-Key
>
> **R**eset
>
> **G**o
>
> **Q**uit

These options are discussed in table 9-3.

The field column that is used to determine the sort order is called a **key**. 1-2-3 allows the user to select a primary and secondary key. The user has the choice of ascending and descending order which is exclusive to each key.

Table 9-3. / Data Sort Options

/DS Option	Description
Data-Range	Indicates the range to be sorted.
Primary-Key	This option is used to indicate the field name cell of the column that will determine the sort order of the records. The order can be ascending or descending. For example, in a residential telephone book, the primary key would be the last names of the listed subscribers.

Table 9-3. / Data Sort Options (cont.)

Secondary-Key	This option is optional and is used to indicate the field name cell of the field column to be used as a secondary sort key after the primary sort. An example of a secondary sort would be first names in a residential telephone book. If last names were the **P**rimary-Key and if identical last names were encountered, 1-2-3 would then sort by first names (the secondary key). The user is given a choice of ascending or descending order for the **S**econdary-Key. This is exclusive of the **P**rimary-Key sort order.
Reset	**/DS** stores the sort specifications. The **R**eset option deletes previous sort specifications.
Go	Selection of this option causes the database to be sorted.
Quit	Returns 1-2-3 to the Ready mode

SORT ORDER

1-2-3 sorts records according to the following order:

- Ascending
    1. Blank cells
    2. Label cells according to ASCII code (label-prefixes will be ignored). An ASCII code is a standard code assigned to each character. A list of ASCII codes is included in appendix A.
    3. Numbers and values of formulas in numeric order from the smallest to the largest number.
- Descending

    Records are sorted in the reverse of ascending order.

SORT EXAMPLE

To sort the following database according to department, follow these User Steps:

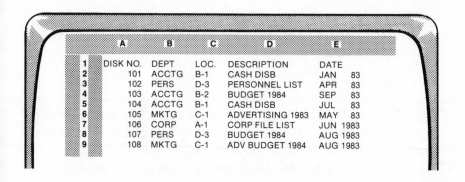

	A	B	C	D	E
1	DISK NO.	DEPT	LOC.	DESCRIPTION	DATE
2	101	ACCTG	B-1	CASH DISB	JAN 83
3	102	PERS	D-3	PERSONNEL LIST	APR 83
4	103	ACCTG	B-2	BUDGET 1984	SEP 83
5	104	ACCTG	B-1	CASH DISB	JUL 83
6	105	MKTG	C-1	ADVERTISING 1983	MAY 83
7	106	CORP	A-1	CORP FILE LIST	JUN 1983
8	107	PERS	D-3	BUDGET 1984	AUG 1983
9	108	MKTG	C-1	ADV BUDGET 1984	AUG 1983

User Step 1:	Select /**DS**
1-2-3 Response:	Data-Range Primary-Key Secondary-Key Reset Go Quit
User Step 2:	Select **D**
1-2-3 Response:	Enter Data range:A1
User Step 3:	Type or point to A2..E9 and press ⏎
1-2-3 Response:	Returns to /**DS** menu.
User Step 4:	Select **P**
1-2-3 Response:	Enter Primary sort key address:A1
User Step 5:	Indicate B1 and press ⏎
1-2-3 Response:	Enter Sort order (A or D):A
User Step 6:	Press ⏎
1-2-3 Response:	Returns to /**DS** menu
User Step 7:	Select **G**
1-2-3 Response:	

	A	B	C	D	E
1	DISK NO.	DEPT	LOC.	DESCRIPTION	DATE
2	103	ACCTG	B-2	BUDGET 1984	SEP 83
3	104	ACCTG	B-1	CASH DISB	JUL 83
4	101	ACCTG	B-1	CASH DISB	JAN 83
5	106	CORP	A-1	CORP FILE LIST	JUN 83
6	105	MKTG	C-1	ADVERTISING 1983	MAY 83
7	108	MKTG	C-1	ADV BUDGET 1984	AUG 83
8	102	PERS	D-3	PERSONNEL LIST	APR 83
9	107	PERS	D-3	BUDGET 1984	AUG 83

To sort by location, the user would select **P** (Primary-Key) and indicate C1, by disk number, A1, etc. **Q**uit would be selected in order to return to the Ready mode.

DATA QUERY

The **D**ata **Q**uery command enables the user to find, select, and delete records in a database according to user-supplied criteria. The database must be a range whose first row contains field names.

When /**DQ** is selected, the following menu options will appear:

> Input
> Criterion
> Output
> Find
> Extract
> Unique
> Delete
> Reset
> Quit

The **I**nput, **C**riterion, and **O**utput options define the database, the criteria to be used and where to put any records satisfying these criteria. The input, criterion, and output ranges are depicted in figure 9-3. The ranges that are referred to in these options must be prepared before initiating /**DQ**. The input range and criterion ranges are also used in the database statistical functions. All of these options are discussed in detail in table 9-4.

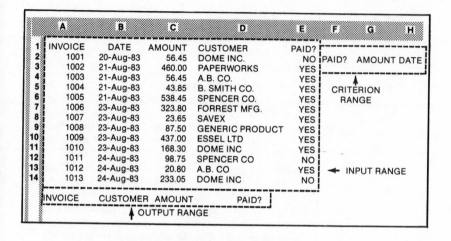

FIGURE 9-3. Input, Criterion and Output Ranges

Table 9-4. /Data Query Options

/DQ Option	Description
Input	This option defines the database (in terms of location in the worksheet) to be used in the **D**ata **Q**uery command. The first row of the range specified is assumed to contain the field names.
Criterion	This option defines the range containing the criteria to be used in execution of /**DQ**. The first row of the criterion range contains field names. These can either be some of the field names in the database or all, in any order. The criteria for each field name is contained in the other rows. Criteria match characters may be used. The criterion range should be placed away from the database.
Output	This option defines the location to which selected fields are to be copied when using /**DQ E**xtract or /**DQ U**nique. The first row of the output range will contain the field names of the fields to be output according to the criterion range. Place the output range away from the database to make sure there will be enough room for the output. The user need only specify the cell addresses of the first row, and

Table 9-4. / Data Query Options (cont.)

	the output range will extend to the bottom of the worksheet.
Find	This option initially highlights the first record in the database that satisfies the criteria defined with Criterion. The user can use the ↓ key to locate subsequent records in the database that meet the criteria. The ↑ key will move the cursor back up the database to previously highlighted records. The → and ← keys will move the flashing bar from the left to right to each cell within the highlighted area. The Home key will highlight the first record within the input range even if it does not meet the criteria. The End key will highlight the last record. While using this command, the mode indicator will read "FIND". To return to the /DQ menu, press Esc.
Extract	The Extract option copies the fields of the records that match the criteria specified in the criterion range to the output range. The fields copied depend on the field names specified in the output range. If there is not enough space in the output range, 1-2-3 will enter the Error mode. When /DQE is executed, the output range will be erased except for the field names. It is suggested that the user save the worksheet before using this command.
Unique	This option performs as does Extract except that duplicate records will not appear in the output range.
Delete	This option will delete all records matching the criteria specified in the criterion range. The range specified for the input range will be adjusted to correspond to the new dimensions of the database.
Reset	This option clears the Input, Criterion, and Output settings.
Quit	Selection of Quit returns the user to the Ready mode.

Criteria Matches

How 1-2-3 matches criteria in the criterion range to fields in the input range (the database) depends on whether the criteria is a label, a number or a formula. If the criteria is a label, then 1-2-3 will search the fields in the input range under the same field name as the criteria. The field names must match exactly. Criteria label-match characters can be used. Empty cells do not match any criteria labels.

CRITERIA LABEL-MATCH CHARACTERS

There are three characters that can be used in label criteria to match fields:

? * ~

A ? in a label will match any single character. For example, D?VE would match the following:

DOVE
DIVE
DAVE
but not DIVER

* matches all characters from that point to the end of the label. DON* would match the following:

DONE
DONKEY
DONATE
DONUT
but not DINER

A ~ (tilde) placed at the beginning of a label will match every field except those that match the label. For the following fields:

JOHN
JENNIFER
GEORGE
DAVE

~JOHN would match every field but JOHN. ~J* would match GEORGE and DAVE.

NUMBERS

1-2-3 will search fields under the appropriate field name for fields that match the criteria number exactly. Using a zero (0) will result in a match of all blank cells and labels.

FORMULAS

Formulas in the criterion range are used to test fields for selection of records as a match. If the test returns a TRUE value (that is, ≠ zero), it is considered a match. The criteria formula is set up to test the first field under that field name in the input range. As 1-2-3 tests each field, it will adjust the cell references in the criteria formula so that the test is the same for each field. In criteria formulas, references to cell addresses within the input range must be relative and references to cell addresses outside the input range must be absolute.

Using the following worksheet, we will discuss the results of using various criteria formulas:

	A	B	C	D	E	F	G	H
1	INVOICE	DATE	AMOUNT	CUSTOMER	PAID?			
2	1001	20-Aug-83	56.45	DOME INC	NO	PAID?	AMOUNT	DATE
3	1002	21-Aug-83	460.00	PAPERWORKS	YES			
4	1003	21-Aug-83	56.45	A.B. CO	YES			
5	1004	21-Aug-83	43.85	B. SMITH CO	YES		Criterion Range	
6	1005	21-Aug-83	538.45	SPENCER CO	YES			
7	1006	23-Aug-83	323.80	FORREST MFG	YES			
8	1007	23-Aug-83	23.65	SAVEX	YES			
9	1008	23-Aug-83	87.50	GENERIC PRODUCT	YES			
10	1009	23-Aug-83	437.00	ESSEL LTD	YES			
11	1010	23-Aug-83	168.30	DOME INC	YES			
12	1011	24-Aug-83	98.75	SPENCER CO	NO			
13	1012	24-Aug-83	20.80	A.B. CO	YES			
14	1013	24-Aug-83	233.05	DOME INC	NO			

↑ Input Range

To match all invoices that are greater than $500.00, +C2>500 would be entered in G3. The record A6..E6 would be matched.

To match all invoices over 90 days old and unpaid, No would be entered in F3 and +B2<(@TODAY-90) would be entered in H3. Assuming today is December 31, 1983, the following records would be matched:

```
1001  20-Aug-83      56.45   DOME INC          NO
1011  24-Aug-83      98.75   SPENCER CO        NO
1013  24-Aug-83     233.05   DOME INC          NO
```

/Data Query Examples

The database in figure 9-4 will be used with the /**Data Query**
examples.

	A	B	C	D	E	F	G
1	NAME	ADDRESS	CITY	STATE	STATUS	LIMIT	TELEPHONE
2	JOHN	21 NORTH ST	CLEVELAND	OH	OK	1050	123-2345
3	SUE	23789 EAST AVE	MANCHESTER	WA	BAD	500	345-8674
4	JOHN	1234 LEXINGTON AVE	HUNTINGTON	NJ	OK	4000	456-2344
5	JACK	23458 KENNEDY LN	LEWISTOWN	OH	BAD	3000	687-8966
6	LISA	432 ADENA AVE	PORTLAND	OR	OK	950	784-9901
7	TED	943 DOVER ST	CERRITOS	CA	OK	1000	897-1234
8	JANE	9834 ELLINGTON AVE	BURLINGTON	LA	BAD	250	986-6733
9							

FIGURE 9-4. /Data Query Examples

Sorting the Database

* Defining the Data Range

User Step 1:	Select /**DS**
1-2-3 Response:	Displays /**D**ata **S**ort menu
User Step 2:	Select **D**ata-Range
1-2-3 Response:	Enter Data range:A1
User Step 3:	Specify the range A2..H8 and press ↵
1-2-3 Response:	Returns to the /**DS**

* Selecting the Primary Sort Key

User Step 1:	Select **P**rimary-Key
1-2-3 Response:	Enter Primary sort key address:A1
User Step 2:	Specify A1 and press ↵
1-2-3 Response:	Enter Sort order (A or D):D

User Step 3:   Type A and press ↵
1-2-3 Response: Returns to the /**DS** menu

● Defining the Secondary Sort Key

User Step 1:   Select **S**econdary-Key.
1-2-3 Response: Enter Secondary sort key address:A1
User Step 2:   Specify B1 and press ↵
1-2-3 Response: Enter sort order (A or D):A
User Step 3:   Select **A**
1-2-3 Response: Returns to /**DS** menu

● Sorting the Data

User Step 1:   Select **Go**
1-2-3 Response:

```
A1: 'NAME                                           READY
        A              B              C         D    E      F       G
1  NAME  ADDRESS                  CITY       STATE STATUS LIMIT TELEPHONE
2  JACK  23458 KENNEDY LN         LEWISTOWN   OH   BAD     300  687-8966
3  JANE  9834 ELLINGTON AVE       BURLINGTON  LA   BAD     250  986-6733
4  JOHN  1234 LEXINGTON AVE       HUNTINGTON  NJ   OK     4000  456-2344
5  JOHN  21 NORTH ST              CLEVELAND   OH   OK     1050  123-2345
6  LISA  432 ADENA AVE            PORTLAND    OR   OK      950  784-9901
7  SUE   23789 EAST AVE           MANCHESTER  WA   BAD     500  345-8674
8  TED   943 DOVER ST             CERRITOS    CA   OK     1000  897-1234
9
                                                          CAPS
```

/Data Query — Finding & Outputting all Records with LIMITS > 1000.

● Setting up the Criterion Range

User Step 1:   Make the following cell entries:

        Cell   Entry
        J1   LIMIT
        J2   +F2 > 1000

● Setting up the Output Range

User Step 1:   Select /**C**opy
1-2-3 Response: Enter range to copy FROM:A1..A1

User Step 2:	Type A1..H1 and press ↵
1-2-3 Response:	Enter range to copy TO:A1
User Step 3:	Type A100↵
1-2-3 Response:	Returns to the Ready mode

- Specifying the Input Range

User Step 1:	Select /**DQ**
1-2-3 Response:	Displays the /**DQ** menu
User Step 2:	Select Input
1-2-3 Response:	Enter Input range:A1
User Step 3:	Type A1..H8↵
1-2-3 Response:	Returns to the /**DQ** menu

- Specifying the Criterion Range

User Step 1:	Select **C**riterion
1-2-3 Response:	Enter Criterion range:J2
User Step 2:	Type J1..J2↵
1-2-3 Response:	Returns to /**DQ** menu

- Specifying the Output Range

User Step 1:	Select **O**
1-2-3 Response:	Enter Output range:J2
User Step 2:	Type A100..H100↵
1-2-3 Response:	Output range is defined as the range A100..H2048. Returns to **DQ** menu

- Finding records that fit the criteria

User Step 1:	Select **F**ind
1-2-3 Response:	Highlights the following record:

      John 1234 Lexington Ave Huntington NJ OK 4000 456-2344

User Step 2:	Press ↓
1-2-3 Response:	Highlights:

      John 21 North St Cleveland OH OK 1050 123-2345

User Step 3:	Pressing ↑ ↓ keys will highlight records that meet criteria. Pressing Esc will return to the /**DQ** menu.

• Extracting records and viewing extracted records with /**W**orksheet **W**indows

User Step 1:	While in the Ready mode, press the home key, place pointer on A11 and select /**WW**
1-2-3 Response:	Displays /**WW** menu
User Step 2:	Select **H**
1-2-3 Response:	The worksheet will be horizontally split at A11
User Step 3:	Press the F6 (Window) key to move the pointer to the lower screen. Then, press the F5 (Goto) key and type A100↵
1-2-3 Response:	

```
A100: 'NAME                                                    READY
       A           B                 C          D     E      F      G
 1 NAME   ADDRESS              CITY          STATE STATUS LIMIT TELEPHONE
 2 JACK   23458 KENNEDY LN     LEWISTOWN     OH    BAD      300  687-8966
 3 JANE   9834 ELLINGTON AVE   BURLINGTON    LA    BAD      250  986-6733
 4 JOHN   1234 LEXINGTON AVE   HUNTINGTON    NJ    OK      4000  456-2344
 5 JOHN   21 NORTH ST          CLEVELAND     OH    OK      1050  123-2345
 6 LISA   432 ADENA AVE        PORTLAND      OR    OK       950  784-9901
 7 SUE    23789 EAST AVE       MANCHESTER    WA    BAD      500  345-8674
 8 TED    943 DOVER ST         CERRITOS      CA    OK      1000  897-1234
 9
10
       A           B                 C          D     E      F      G
100 NAME  ADDRESS              CITY          STATE STATUS LIMIT TELEPHONE
101
102
103
104
105
106
107
108
```

User Step 4:	Select /**DQ**
1-2-3 Response:	Displays /**DQ** menu
User Step 5:	Select **E**xtract
1-2-3 Response:	Returns to the /**DQ** menu. The screen will appear as depicted on the next page:

```
A100: 'NAME                                                    MENU
Input   Criterion   Output   Find   Extract   Unique   Delete   Reset   Quit
Copy all records that match criteria to Output range
       A              B                C          D     E       F       G
  1 NAME  ADDRESS              CITY          STATE STATUS  LIMIT TELEPHONE
  2 JACK  23458 KENNEDY LN     LEWISTOWN     OH    BAD      300  687-8966
  3 JANE  9834 ELLINGTON AVE   BURLINGTON    LA    BAD      250  986-6733
  4 JOHN  1234 LEXINGTON AVE   HUNTINGTON    NJ    OK      4000  456-2344
  5 JOHN  21 NORTH ST          CLEVELAND     OH    OK      1050  123-2345
  6 LISA  432 ADENA AVE        PORTLAND      OR    OK       950  784-9901
  7 SUE   23789 EAST AVE       MANCHESTER    WA    BAD      500  345-8674
  8 TED   943 DOVER ST         CERRITOS      CA    OK      1000  897-1234
  9
 10
       A              B                C          D     E       F       G
100 NAME  ADDRESS              CITY          STATE STATUS  LIMIT TELEPHONE
101 JOHN  1234 LEXINGTON AVE   HUNTINGTON    NJ    OK      4000  456-2344
102 JOHN  21 NORTH ST          CLEVELAND     OH    OK      1050  123-2345
103
104
105
106
107
108
```

User Step 6:   Select **Q**

1-2-3 Response: Returns to Ready mode

- Using more than one criteria to **E**xtract the records of all customers with LIMITS>1000 and located in Ohio.

User Step 1:   Make the following cell entries:

Cell	Entry
K1	STATE
K2	OH

User Step 2:   Press home and select /**DQC** to redefine the criterion range to J1..K2

1-2-3 Response: Returns to /**DQ** menu

User Step 3:   Select **E**xtract

1-2-3 Response:

```
A1: 'NAME                                                    MENU
Input   Criterion   Output   Find   Extract   Unique   Delete   Reset   Quit
Copy all records that match criteria to Output range
```

	A	B	C	D	E	F	G
1	NAME	ADDRESS	CITY	STATE	STATUS	LIMIT	TELEPHONE
2	JACK	23458 KENNEDY LN	LEWISTOWN	OH	BAD	300	687-8966
3	JANE	9834 ELLINGTON AVE	BURLINGTON	LA	BAD	250	986-6733
4	JOHN	1234 LEXINGTON AVE	HUNTINGTON	NJ	OK	4000	456-2344
5	JOHN	21 NORTH ST	CLEVELAND	OH	OK	1050	123-2345
6	LISA	432 ADENA AVE	PORTLAND	OR	OK	950	784-9901
7	SUE	23789 EAST AVE	MANCHESTER	WA	BAD	500	345-8674
8	TED	943 DOVER ST	CERRITOS	CA	OK	1000	897-1234
9							
10							

	A	B	C	D	E	F	G
100	NAME	ADDRESS	CITY	STATE	STATUS	LIMIT	TELEPHONE
101	JOHN	21 NORTH ST	CLEVELAND	OH	OK	1050	123-2345
102							
103							
104							
105							
106							
107							
108							

- Using the F7 (Query) key

Pressing the F7 key causes the most recent /**D**ata **Q**uery command to be repeated. If the cell entry in D4 was changed to OH and F7 was pressed, the previous /**D**ata **Q**uery **E**xtract example would be repeated with the following results:

```
D4: 'NAME                                                    READY
```

	A	B	C	D	E	F	G
1	NAME	ADDRESS	CITY	STATE	STATUS	LIMIT	TELEPHONE
2	JACK	23458 KENNEDY LN	LEWISTOWN	OH	BAD	300	687-8966
3	JANE	9834 ELLINGTON AVE	BURLINGTON	LA	BAD	250	986-6733
4	JOHN	1234 LEXINGTON AVE	HUNTINGTON	NJ	OK	4000	456-2344
5	JOHN	21 NORTH ST	CLEVELAND	OH	OK	1050	123-2345
6	LISA	432 ADENA AVE	PORTLAND	OR	OK	950	784-9901
7	SUE	23789 EAST AVE	MANCHESTER	WA	BAD	500	345-8674
8	TED	943 DOVER ST	CERRITOS	CA	OK	1000	897-1234
9							
10							

	A	B	C	D	E	F	G
100	NAME	ADDRESS	CITY	STATE	STATUS	LIMIT	TELEPHONE
101	JOHN	1234 LEXINGTON AVE	HUNTINGTON	OH	OK	4000	456-2344
102	JOHN	21 NORTH ST	CLEVELAND	OH	OK	1050	123-2345
103							
104							
105							
106							
107							
108							

/Data Distribution

The **Data Distribution** command provides a frequency distribution of values in a range. In order to use / **DD**, a **bin range** must be prepared. The values in the bin range are used to test the values in the Values range and determine where they belong in the distribution.

The bin range must be positioned in a column on the worksheet so that there is a blank column to the right of it. This blank column will contain the results of / **DD**. It must extend one cell below the last cell of the bin range. This cell will contain all values greater than the last value in the bin range. The values in the bin range must be in increasing order from top to bottom.

/ **Data Distribution** tests each value in the bin range. If a value is less than or equal to a value in the bin range, it is included in that interval of the distribution. Blank and label cells are interpreted as the value zero.

/DATA DISTRIBUTION EXAMPLE

To find the distribution of invoice amounts for the database in figure 9-5, use the following steps:

	A	B	C	D	E
1	INVOICE	DATE	AMOUNT	CUSTOMER	PAID?
2	1001	20-Aug-83	56.45	DOME INC	NO
3	1002	21-Aug-83	460.00	PAPERWORKS	YES
4	1003	21-Aug-83	56.45	A.B. CO	YES
5	1004	21-Aug-83	43.85	B. SMITH CO	YES
6	1005	21-Aug-83	538.45	SPENCER CO	YES
7	1006	23-Aug-83	323.80	FORREST MFG	YES
8	1007	23-Aug-83	23.65	SAVEX	YES
9	1008	23-Aug-83	87.50	GENERIC PRODUCT	YES
10	1009	23-Aug-83	437.00	ESSEL LTD	YES
11	1010	23-Aug-83	168.30	DOME INC	YES
12	1011	24-Aug-83	98.75	SPENCER CO	NO
13	1012	24-Aug-83	20.80	A.B. CO	YES
14	1013	24-Aug-83	233.05	DOME INC	NO

FIGURE 9-5. / Data Distribution Example

User Step 1:	Enter the bin range by making the following cell entries:

```
*D16  RESULTS
*C16  BIN RANGE
 C17  50
 C18  100
 C19  250
 C20  500
 C21  1000
```

User Step 2:	Select /**DD**
1-2-3 Response:	Enter Values range:A1 (The last entered range will be displayed)
User Step 3:	Specify C2..C14 and press ↵
1-2-3 Response:	Enter Bin range:A1 (The last entered range will be displayed.)
User Step 4:	Specify C17..C21 and press ↵
1-2-3 Response:	

	A	B	C	D
16			BIN RANGE	RESULTS
17			50	4
18			100	3
19			250	2
20			500	3
21			1000	1
22				0

Graphing with /DD

Graphing the results of /**DD** is simple. Use the bin range for the X-axis and the results column as the **A** range of the graph. Using the example of /**DD**, the graphs depicted in figures 9-5 and 9-6 would result from the following entries:

---

* This label entry is optional

User Step 1:	Press Home and select /**G**
1-2-3 Response:	Displays /**G**raph menu
User Step 2:	Select **X**
1-2-3 Response:	Enter X-axis range:A1
User Step 3:	Specify C17..C21 and press ↵
1-2-3 Response:	Returns to /**G**raph menu
User Step 4:	Select **A**
1-2-3 Response:	Enter first data range:A1
User Step 5:	Type D17..D21 and press ↵
1-2-3 Response:	Returns to /**G**raph menu
User Step 6:	Select **T**ype
1-2-3 Response:	Displays **T**ype menu
User Step 7:	Select **P**ie
1-2-3 Response:	Returns to /**G**raph menu
User Step 8:	Select **V**iew
1-2-3 Response:	Displays a graph similar to figure 9-6
User Step 9:	Press Esc to return to /**G**raph menu
User Step 10:	Select **T**ype
1-2-3 Response:	Displays **T**ype menu
User Step 11:	Select **B**ar
1-2-3 Response:	Returns to /**G**raph menu
User Step 12:	Select **V**iew
1-2-3 Response:	Displays a graph similar to figure 9-7
User Step 13:	Press Esc, then **Q** to return to the Ready mode.

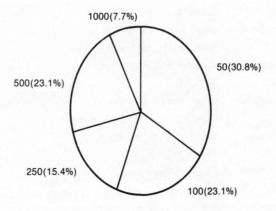

FIGURE 9-6. Pie Graph using /**DD** Example

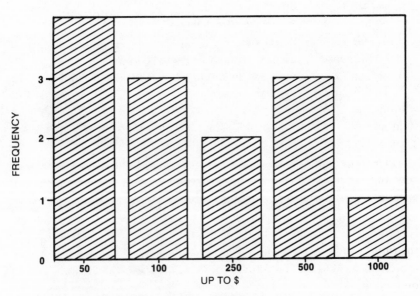

FIGURE 9-7. Bar Graph using /**DD** Example

Database Functions

1-2-3 has seven Database functions.

Function	Description
@DAVG	This function returns the average of those values meeting criteria.
@DCOUNT	This function counts those records that meet the criteria.
@DMAX	This function returns the maximum value that meets the criteria.
@DMIN	This function returns the minimum value that meets the criteria
@DSTD	This function returns the standard deviation of those values meeting the criteria.
@DSUM	This function returns the sum of those values meeting the criteria.
@DVAR	This function returns the variance of those values meeting criteria.

All of the database functions have the same configuration.

Configuration

@D*function*, (*input range, a, criterion range*)

The *input range* is the location of a database that is to be used in finding records to match specified criteria. The *input range* includes the field names of the database. It is similar to the input range used in the **D**ata commands.

The *criterion range* is a range consisting of field names in the first row and criteria pertaining to the field names in the second row. The criteria is used in finding matching records in the input range.

a indicates which field column in the *input range* is to be used in the function. The value of *a* indicates a column relative to the first column of the *input range*. A zero would represent the first column, a one would represent the column one column to the right of the first column, and so on.

In the figure depicted below, *input range* would be A1..D6 and the *criterion range* would be E2..E3. If the values to be used in the functions were prices, the value of *a* would be 2. If average life values were to be used in the function, then *a* would be 3.

	A	B	C	D	E
1	CAR	ORIGIN	PRICE	AVG LIFE	
2	A	foreign	9000	11	ORIGIN
3	B	foreign	8000	7	Domestic
4	C	domestic	8500	9	
5	D	domestic	7600	6	
6	E	foreign	8700	8	

DATABASE FUNCTION EXAMPLE

The worksheet to be used in this example is depicted in figure 9-8.

	A	B	C	D	E
1	NAME	SCHOOL HISTORY	GRADE		
2	BILL	PRIVATE	88		
3	BOB	PUBLIC	72.5		
4	JANE	PUBLIC	91		
5	JACKIE	PRIVATE	85		
6	LORI	PUBLIC	78		
7	CARL	PUBLIC	82		
8					
9					
10					
	D	E	F		
12		SCHOOL HISTORY	SCHOOL HISTORY		
13		PRIVATE	PUBLIC		
14	COUNT				
15	AVERAGE				
16	VARIANCE				
17	STANDARD DEV				
18	MAXIMUM				
19	MINIMUM				
20	SUM				

FIGURE 9-8. Database Functions Example

In this example, the number of students of each type of school history will be counted. Then the average grade, variance, standard deviation, highest and lowest grade and sum of grades for each group will be calculated. The results are shown in figure 9-9. The *criterion range* for students with a private school history is E12..E13. The *criterion range* for students with a public school history is F12..F13. The *input range* is A1..C7.

The field column labeled GRADE contains the values to be used in the functions. Since this column is two columns to the right of the first column in the *input range*, *a* is 2.

- Finding the number of students from each type of school

  Entering @DCOUNT (A1..C7,2,E12..E13) in cell E14 will return the number of students that went to private schools.
  Entering @DCOUNT (A1..C7,2, F12..F13) in F14 will return the number of students that went to public schools.

- Calculating the average grade

Type	Cell	Entry
PRIVATE	E15	@DAVG(A1..C7,2,E12..E13)
PUBLIC	F15	@DAVG(A1..C7,2,F12..F13)

- Calculating the variance

Type	Cell	Entry
PRIVATE	E16	@DVAR(A1..C7,2,E12..E13)
PUBLIC	F16	@DVAR(A1..C7,2,F12..F13)

- Calculating the standard deviation

Type	Cell	Entry
PRIVATE	E17	@DSTD(A1..C7,2,E12..E13)
PUBLIC	F17	@DSTD(A1..C7,2,F12..F13)

- Finding the highest grade

Type	Cell	Entry
PRIVATE	E18	@DMAX(A1..C7,2,E12..E13)
PUBLIC	F18	@DMAX(A1..C7,2,F12..F13)

- Finding the lowest grade

Type	Cell	Entry
PRIVATE	E19	@DMIN(A1..C7,2,E12..E13)
PUBLIC	F18	@DMIN(A1..C7,2,F12..F13)

- Calculating the sum of the grades

Type	Cell	Entry
PRIVATE	E20	@DSUM(A1..C7,2,E12..E13)
PUBLIC	F20	@DSUM(A1..C7,2,F12..F13)

	A	B	C	D	E
1	NAME	SCHOOL HISTORY	GRADE		
2	BILL	PRIVATE	88		
3	BOB	PUBLIC	72.5		
4	JANE	PUBLIC	91		
5	JACKIE	PRIVATE	85		
6	LORI	PUBLIC	78		
7	CARL	PUBLIC	82		
8					
9					
10					

	D	E	F
12		SCHOOL HISTORY	SCHOOL HISTORY
13		PRIVATE	PUBLIC
14	COUNT	2	4
15	AVERAGE	86.5	80.875
16	VARIANCE	2.25	45.546875
17	STANDARD DEV	1.5	6.7488424933
18	MAXIMUM	88	91
19	MINIMUM	85	72.5
20	SUM	173	323.5

FIGURE 9-9. Database Function Example — Results

10

1-2-3 Functions

Introduction

This chapter describes in detail each of 1-2-3's functions. There are seven types of 1-2-3 functions:

- Mathematical
- Statistical
- Logical
- Financial
- Database
- Date
- Special

The functions are grouped by type in table 10-1.

The following rules and abbreviations will be used in this chapter in our configuration descriptions of the 1-2-3 functions:

1. All functions must begin with an @.
2. Any capitalized words are keywords. Keywords may be input in either uppercase, lowercase or both. Keywords are converted automatically to uppercase letters.
3. Any words, phrases, or letters shown in lowercase italics enclosed in parentheses ( ) indicate that an argument is to be entered by the user.
4. Allowable arguments for functions that require a single value as an argument are:

   number
   cell address
   function
   one-cell range name
   formula

5. Allowable arguments for functions that require a range as an argument are:

   cell address..cell address
   range name

6. Any punctuation marks (example: , ( )) must be included where they are shown.
7. An ellipsis (...) indicates that an item may be repeated as often as necessary.

Table 10-1. 1-2-3 Functions

Function	Configuration	Description
Mathematical		
@ABS	@ABS(*a*)	absolute value
@ACOS	@ACOS(*a*)	arc cosine
@ASIN	@ASIN(*a*)	arc sine
@ATAN	@ATAN(*a*)	2-quadrant arctangent
@ATAN2	@ATAN(*a*,*b*)	4-quadrant arctangent
@COS	@COS(*a*)	cosine
@EXP	@EXP(*a*)	exponential
@INT	@INT(*a*)	integer
@LN	@LN(*a*)	natural log
@LOG	@LOG(*a*)	log base 10

Table 10-2. 1-2-3 Functions (cont.)

Function	Configuration	Description
@MOD	@MOD(*a*,*b*)	modulus of *a*/*b*
@PI	@PI	π (pi)
@RAND	@RAND	random number (0 to 1)
@ROUND	@ROUND(*a*,*b*)	round *a* to *b* decimal places
@SIN	@SIN(*a*)	sine
@SQRT	@SQRT(*a*)	square root
@TAN	@TAN(*a*)	tangent
Statistical		
@AVG	@AVG(*list*)	average of values in a list
@COUNT	@COUNT(*list*)	counts items in a list
@MAX	@MAX(*list*)	maximum value in a list
@MIN	@MIN(*list*)	minimum value in a list
@STD	@STD(*list*)	standard deviation of a population
@SUM	@SUM(*list*)	sum of values in a list
@VAR	@VAR(*list*)	variance of a population
Logical		
@IF	@IF(*expression, true clause, false clause*)	if *expression*=true, *true clause* if *expression*≠true, *false clause*
@ISERR	@ISERR(*a*)	1, if *a*=ERR 0, if *a*≠ERR
@ISNA	@ISNA(*a*)	1, if *a*=NA 0, if *a*≠NA
@FALSE	@FALSE	0
@TRUE	@TRUE	1
Financial		
@FV	@FV(*payment, interest, periods*)	future value
@IRR	@IRR(*guess, range*)	internal rate of return
@NPV	@NPV(*interest rate, range*)	present value of a series of unequal payments
@PV	@PV(*periodic payment, periodic interest rate, no. of periods*)	present value
@PMT	@PMT(*principal, periodic interest rate, no. of periods*)	periodic payment amount
Database		
@DAVG	@DAVG(*input range , a, criterion range*)	average of values meeting criteria
@DCOUNT	@DCOUNT(*input range, a, criterion range*)	counts records that meet criteria

Table 10-2. 1-2-3 Functions (cont.)

Function	Configuration	Description
@DMAX	@DMAX(*input range, a, criterion range*)	maximum value that meets criteria
@DMIN	@DMIN(*input range, a, criterion range*)	minimum value that meets criteria
@DSTD	@STD(*input range, a, criterion range*)	standard deviation of values meeting criteria
@DSUM	@DSUM(*input range, a, criterion range*)	sum of values meeting criteria
@DVAR	@DVAR(*input range, a, criterion range*)	variance of values meeting criteria
Date		
@DATE	@DATE(*year, month, day*)	returns a date serial number
@DAY	@DAY(*a*)	day number of a date serial number
@MONTH	@MONTH(*a*)	month number of a date serial number
@TODAY	@TODAY	returns the last date input when 1-2-3 was loaded
@YEAR	@YEAR(*a*)	year number of a date serial number
Special		
@CHOOSE	@CHOOSE(*test, response$_0$, response$_1$, response$_2$,...*)	selects an argument
@ERR	@ERR	ERR
@HLOOKUP	@HLOOKUP(*test, table, a*)	horizontal look-up
@NA	@NA	NA
@VLOOKUP	@VLOOKUP(*test, table, a*)	vertical look-up

@ABS

The @ABS function returns the absolute value of the argument.

Configuration

@ABS(*a*)

Examples	Results
@ABS(-81)	81
@ABS(2.3)	2.3

@ACOS

The @ACOS function returns the arc cosine of the argument. The arc cosine is the angle in radians whose cosine is the argument. If the value of the argument is between -1 and +1, the value of the @ACOS function will always lie between 0 and π. If the value of the argument is not between -1 and +1, the value of the function will be ERR.

Configuration

@ACOS(a)

Examples	Results
@ACOS(.5)	1.047197
@ACOS(D14)	arc cosine of the value of cell D14

@ASIN

The @ASIN function returns the arc sine of the argument. The arc sine is the angle (in radians) whose sine is the argument. The value of the @ASIN function is always between $-\pi/2$ and $+\pi/2$. If the argument is not between -1 and +1, then the value returned is ERR.

Configuration

@ASIN(a)

Examples	Results
@ASIN(-.5)	-0.52359
@ASIN(D14)	arc sine of the value of cell D14

@ATAN

The @ATAN function returns the arctangent of the argument or the angle in radians whose tangent is the argument. This is a value that corresponds to the angle between a leg and the hypotenuse of a right triangle. This value is always between $-\pi/2$ and $+\pi/2$.

Configuration
@ATAN(*a*)

The angle of the function represents the ratio of the lengths of the triangle's two legs. For example, in the figure depicted below, the value of the angle can be represented as @ATAN(2/3).

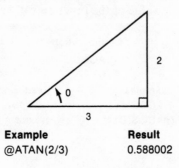

Example	Result
@ATAN(2/3)	0.588002

@ATAN2

The @ATAN2 function is a generalized version of the @ATAN function. This function uses Cartesian coordinates for arguments instead of lengths of sides. The value returned is the angle between the vector (*x,y*) and the positive X axis.

Configuration
@ATAN2(*x,y*)

For example, in the figure below, the value of the angle (0) could be represented as @ATAN2(-3,-2,).

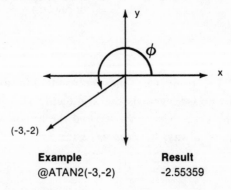

Example	Result
@ATAN2(-3,-2)	-2.55359

@AVG

The @AVG function returns the value which is the average of all items in a list. The sum of the items in the list is divided by the number of items in the list. If the argument is a range, blank cells will be ignored unless all cells are blank. If all cells are blank, then ERR will be returned. If the argument references cells addresses, then cells that are blank will be included in the average.

Configuration
@AVG(*list*)

list is a list of values, cell addresses, ranges or a combination of the three.

Examples	Results
@AVG(A1..A5)	1001
@AVG(A1,A2.A3,A4,A5)	600.6
@AVG(A2..C2)	ERR
@AVG(A2,B2,C2)	0

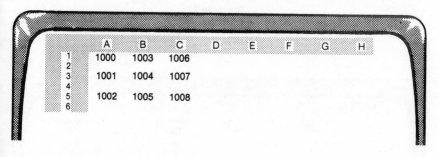

	A	B	C	D	E	F	G	H
1	1000	1003	1006					
2								
3	1001	1004	1007					
4								
5	1002	1005	1008					
6								

FIGURE 10-1. @AVG Example

@CHOOSE

The @CHOOSE function evaluates the test argument and converts it to an integer. It then selects the response argument in the position equal to the value of the integer value of the test argument. If the integer value of the test argument is less than zero or greater than the number of response arguments, ERR will be returned. The examples that follow will clarify this function.

Configuration

@CHOOSE(*test, response$_0$,response$_1$,response$_2$,response$_3$,...*)

Example 1

If @CHOOSE(D1,2,3,4,5,6) was entered in A1 of the worksheet in figure 10-2, the value returned would be 4. This is because the integer value of D1 was 2 and value of *response$_2$* was 4.

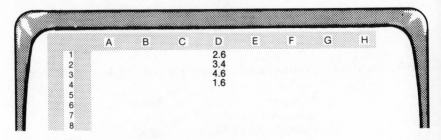

FIGURE 10-2. @CHOOSE Example 1

Example 2

The @CHOOSE function can be used to calculate depreciation for assets of different ages. Figure 10-3 will be used in this example.

	A	B	C	D	E
1	ASSET NO.	LIFE	AGE	BASIS	DEPRECIATION
2	101	5	1	1000	
3	102	3	3	1500	
4	103	5	4	5600	
5	104	5	2	2300	
6	105	5	5	4800	
7					
8	5 year	3 year			
9	.15	.25			
10	.22	.38			
11	.21	.37			
12	.21				
13	.21				
14					
15					

FIGURE 10-3. @CHOOSE Example 2

Since Asset No. 101 has a life of 5 years, the following formula could be entered in E2 to calculate the depreciation:

+D2*(@CHOOSE(C2,@ERR,A$9,A$10,A$11,A$12,A$13))

The result would be 150 or 1000*.15.

The following formula could be entered for the 3 year life asset:

+D3*(@CHOOSE(C3,@ERR,B$9,B$10,B$11))

As an alternative, one formula could be used that would differentiate between 3 and 5 year assets. For example, the formula that would be entered in E2 would be:

+D2*(@CHOOSE(B2,@ERR,@ERR,@ERR,@CHOOSE
(C2,@ERR,B$9,B$10,B$11,),@ERR,@CHOOSE
(C2,@ERR,A$9,A$10,A$11,A$12,A$13)))

The formula could be copied to E3, E4, E5, and E6 with the following results:

	A	B	C	D	E
1	ASSET NO.	LIFE	AGE	BASIS	DEPRECIATION
2	101	5	1	1000	150
3	102	3	3	1500	555
4	103	5	4	5600	1176
5	104	5	2	2300	506
6	105	5	5	4800	1008
7					
8	5 year	3 year			
9	.15	.25			
10	.22	.38			
11	.21	.37			
12	.21				
13	.21				
14					
15					

@COS

The @COS function returns the cosine of its argument. The argument is interpreted as an angle in radians.

Configuration
@COS(*a*)

Examples	Results
@COS(B3)	returns the cosine of the value in B3
@COS(6)	0.960170

@COUNT

The @COUNT function returns the number of items in a given list. The list can include ranges, cell addresses, values or a combination of all three. If the argument is a range, then all non-blank cells within the range will be counted. If a cell address is referenced, it will count as 1 even if it is blank.

Configuration
@COUNT(*list*)

Examples	Results
@COUNT(A1..C5)	9
@COUNT(A2)	1
@COUNT(10,A1,A2,A3,A4,A5)	6

	A	B	C	D	E	F	G	H
1	1000	1003	1006					
2								
3	1001	1004	1007					
4								
5	1002	1005	1008					
6								
7								
8								
9								
10								
11								
12								
13								
14								

FIGURE 10-4. @COUNT Example

@DATE

The @DATE function returns a date serial number which corresponds to the date specified in the argument. The date serial number represents number of days since December 31,1899.

Configuration
@DATE(*year,month,day*)

If the arguments entered do not constitute a valid date, ERR will be returned. *year* must be a value from 0 (the year 1900) to 199 (the year 2099). *month* can be a value between 1 and 12 (January=1,February=2...). *day* can be a value from 1 to 31. If a non-integer value is entered, 1-2-3 will consider only the integer portion.

Example	Results General format	Results Date 1 format
@DATE(08,3,18)	3000	18-Mar-08
@DATE(55,1,15)	20104	15-Jan-55
@DATE(83,2,29)	ERR February only had 28 days in 1983	ERR
@DATE(84,2,29)	30741	29-FEB-84

@DAY

The @DAY function returns the day of the month of a given date serial number.

Configuration
@DAY(*a*)

Example	Results General format	Results Date 1 format
@DAY(20104)	15	15-Jan-00
@DAY(A1);where A1=3000	18	18-Jan-00

a must be a number respresenting the date serial number of a day between January 1,1900 and December 31,2099. If @DAY is used with Date Format Options, the month and year will appear as Jan and 00 respectively.

@DAVG

The @DAVG function returns the average of the values that fit the criteria specified in the *criterion range*. *a* specifies the field column location of the values within the *input range*.*

Configuration

@DAVG(*input range, a, criterion range*)

@DCOUNT

The @DCOUNT function returns an integer equal to the number of records in the *input range* that fit the criteria in the *criterion range**.

Configuration

@DCOUNT(*input range, a, criterion range*)

@DMAX

The @DMAX function returns the largest value that fits the criteria in *criterion range*. *a* specifies which field column in the *input range* is to be maximized*.

Configuration

@DMAX(*input range, a, criterion range*)

@DMIN

The @DMIN function returns the smallest value that fits the criteria specified in the *criterion range*. The @DMIN function searches for this

---

* For details on using database functions, see chapter 9.

value in the field column that is *a* columns to the left of the first column in the *input range**.

Configuration
@DMIN(*input range, a, criterion range*)

@DSTD

@DSTD returns the standard deviation of the values that fit the criteria specified in the *criterion range*. The values used will be located *a* field columns to the left of the first column in the *input range**.

Configuration
@DSTD(*input range, a, criterion range*)

@DSUM

@DSUM returns the sum of the values that meet the criteria specified by the *criterion range*. The location of the values to be used is *a* field columns to the left of the first column of the *input range**.

Configuration
@DSUM(*input range, a, criterion range*)

@DVAR

The @DVAR function returns the variance of the values that match the criteria supplied in the *criterion range*. *a* specifies the location of the field column containing the values in relation to the first column of the *input range**.

Configuration
@DVAR(*input range, a, criterion range*)

---

* For details on using database functions, see chapter 9.

@ERR

@ERR returns the value ERR.

Configuration
@ERR

Example	Results
@IF(A1>10,5,@ERR)	ERR

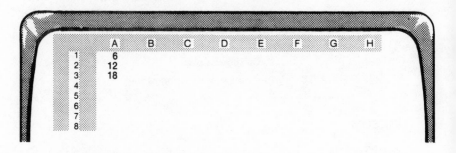

FIGURE 10-5. @ERR Example

@EXP

The @EXP function is used to calculate the exponential function.

Configuration
@EXP(*a*)

The value returned by @EXP is the mathematical function *e* raised to the power of the argument *a*. In 1-2-3, *e* is represented by 2.718281828459046.

Example	Result
@EXP(4)	54.59815

@FALSE

The @FALSE function has the value 0 (false). Notice that this function does not take an argument.

Configuration
@FALSE

Example

@IF(A1>10,@TRUE,@FALSE)

Result (using figure 10-5)

0

@FV

@FV calculates the future value of an ordinary annuity. An annuity can be defined as a series of equal cash flows at given intervals, at a given interest rate, for a specified number of periods. Future value is calculated according to the following formula:

$$FV = pmt * (((1+i)^n -1)/i)$$

i = periodic interest rate
n = number of payment periods
pmt = periodic payment amount

Configuration
@FV(pmt, i, n)

Example 1
If $1000 was deposited at the beginning of each year into an account for five years at 10% annual percent interest, the following would be entered to calculate the future value:

@FV(1000,.10,5)
Results: 6105.1

Example 2

	A	B	C	D
1	PAYMENT	$100.00		
2	INTEREST	0.0075		
3	NO. PERIODS	24		
4				
5				
6				
7				

@FV(B1,B2,B3)
Results: 2618.847

@HLOOKUP

@HLOOKUP compares the value of the *test* argument with the first row of the *table* and returns a value according to the value of *a*.

Configuration
@HLOOKUP(*test, table, a*)

table is a range consisting of at least 2 rows. If the table consists of only 1 row, ERR will be returned. Values that are to be compared with *test* must be located in the first row of the range. These values must be in increasing order from left to right.

1-2-3 compares *test* to the values in the first row of *table*. When *test* equals or exceeds a value, but is less than the next value, 1-2-3 finds the value that is *a* cells below and returns that as the function value. If *a* is greater than or equal to the total number of rows in the range or is less than 0, the value ERR will result. If *a* has a value greater than or equal to 0 but less than 1, results may be invalid.

An example of @HLOOKUP follows. This example determines a customer discount and freight amount for a customer order according to the quantity purchased.

	A	B	C	D	E	F
1	CUST	QTY	PRICE	DISCOUNT	FREIGHT	TOTAL
2	Bond	14	13.95			
3	Wilson	3	13.95			
4	Burns	56	13.95			
5	Larosa	0	13.95			
6	Lyons	15	13.95			
7						
8	TABLE					
9	0	1	4	15	50	
10	0	.25	.35	.40	.50	
11	0	1.50	2.50	0	0	
12						
13						
14						

FIGURE 10-6. HLOOKUP Example

To determine the discount for the customers on the worksheet in figure 10-6, the following formula would be entered in D3 and copied to D3..D6:

$$@HLOOKUP(B2,A\$9..E\$11,1)$$

To determine the freight, enter,

$$@HLOOKUP(B2,A\$9..E\$11,2)$$

in E2 and copy to E3..E6. Enter (+B2*C2*(1-D2))+E2 in F2 and copy to F3..F6 to determine the totals.

After these entries have been made, the worksheet should appear as depicted in figure 10-6a.

	A	B	C	D	E	F
1	CUST	QTY	PRICE	DISCOUNT	FREIGHT	TOTAL
2	Bond	14	13.95	0.35	2.50	129.45
3	Wilson	3	13.95	0.25	1.50	32.89
4	Burns	56	13.95	0.50	0.00	390.60
5	Larosa	0	13.95	0.00	0.00	0.00
6	Lyons	15	13.95	0.40	0.00	125.55
7						
8	TABLE					
9	0	1	4	15	50	
10	0	.25	.35	.40	.50	
11	0	1.50	2.50	0	0	
12						
13						

FIGURE 10-6a. HLOOKUP Example

For Bond's discount, @HLOOKUP (B2,A$9..E$11,1), 1-2-3 took the value of the *test* argument (B2), which was 14. This value was compared with the values in the first row of the *table* (0, 1, 4, 15, 50). Since fourteen was greater than four but less than fifteen, 1-2-3 returned the value .35. This was due to the fact that this value was 1 row down from four, and 1 was the value of the third argument.

@IF

The @IF function sets a condition in its first argument which results in the value of its second or third argument being returned.

Configuration
@IF *(expression, true clause, false clause)*

If *expression* evaluates as true (non-zero), than the *true clause* will result. If *expression* evaluates as false (zero), then the *false clause* will result. The *true* and *false clauses* can be either formulas, functions, or values. @IF is similar to a BASIC IF, THEN, ELSE statement.

Examples	Results (using figure 10-7)
@IF(A1>B1, C1, A1)	0
@IF(A5>B5, C5, A5)	6
@IF(A1<B1,(@IF(B1=C1, B1, C1)),A1)	6

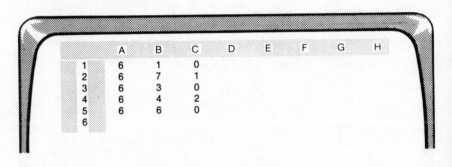

	A	B	C	D	E	F	G	H
1	6	1	0					
2	6	7	1					
3	6	3	0					
4	6	4	2					
5	6	6	0					
6								

FIGURE 10-7. @IF Example

@INT

The @INT function returns the integer portion of the argument.

Configuration
@INT(a)

Examples	Results
@INT(13.9)	13
@INT(-4.7)	-4

@IRR

The @IRR function determines an approximate internal rate of return (IRR) for a series of cash outflows and inflows at regular intervals. Internal rate of return can be defined as the discount rate at which the net present value (NPV) of the cash flows equals zero.

Configuration
@IRR(*guess,range*)

In order to determine the IRR, 1-2-3 uses an iterative process. Using an initial guess (the first argument) 1-2-3 calculates the discount rate at which the NPV of the second argument is equal to zero. If, within 20 iterations, 1-2-3 does not reach convergence within .0000001, ERR will be returned. The Lotus 1-2-3 manual suggests using an initial guess between 0 and 1.

More than one sign change in the series of outflows and inflows specified as the second argument can result in multiple IRR's. For example, the following series.

```
+10000    money received upon signing of a contract
-6000  ⎫
-1000  ⎬  business
-2000  ⎭  expenses
-4000
+20000    money received upon completion of contract
```

would result in different IRR's when different *guess* arguments are used.

If there is only one sign change as in the following series,

```
-98000    purchase a bond
+4000  ⎫
+4000  ⎬  interest income
+4000  ⎭
+104000   bond matures
```

then, any result other than ERR will be the correct IRR.

Examples	Results
@IRR(0.16,A1..A5)	.269707

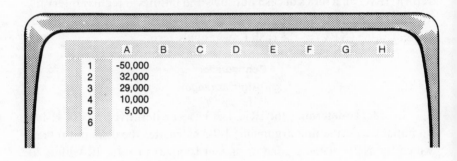

	A	B	C	D	E	F	G	H
1	-50,000							
2	32,000							
3	29,000							
4	10,000							
5	5,000							
6								

@ISERR

@ISERR returns a value of 1 (true) if the value of the argument is ERR. Otherwise, it returns a value of 0 (false).

Configuration
@ISERR

Example	Result
@ISERR(D4)	1 (true) if the value of D4 is ERR
	0 (false) if the value is not ERR.

@ISNA

The @ISNA function returns a value of 1 (true) if the value of the argument is NA. Otherwise, it will return a value of 0 (false).

Configuration
@ISNA(a)

Example	Result
@ISNA(D4)	1 (true) if the value in D4 is NA
	0 (false) if it is not NA

@LN

The @LN function returns the natural logarithm of the argument. Natural logarithms use a base of e (2.71828...). The natural log function is undefined for arguments less than or equal to zero. 1-2-3 returns the value, ERR, if the argument is zero or negative.

Configuration
@LN(*a*)

Examples	Results
@LN(7.39)	2.000127
@LN(−1)	ERR

@LOG

This function returns the base 10 logarithm of the argument. The logarithm is merely the power of 10 required to achieve the specified value. The @LOG function will return the value ERR if the value of the argument is zero or a negative number.

Configuration
@LOG(*a*)

For example, the logarithm of 100 is 2, since $10^2 = 100$. Similarly, the logarithm of 1000 is 3.

@MAX

The @MAX function returns the maximum value of all values in a list. The argument can be a series of values, one or more cell addresses, one or more ranges, or a combination of all three of these.

If the argument is a range, then blank cells will be ignored. If no entries are found in the range, the value ERR will be returned. In single cell references, a blank cell has the value of 0.

Configuration
@MAX(*list*)

Examples	Results
@MAX(A1..C5)	1008
@MAX(A1..A5,5000)	5000
@MAX(A2..C2)	ERR
@MAX(A2,B2,C2)	0

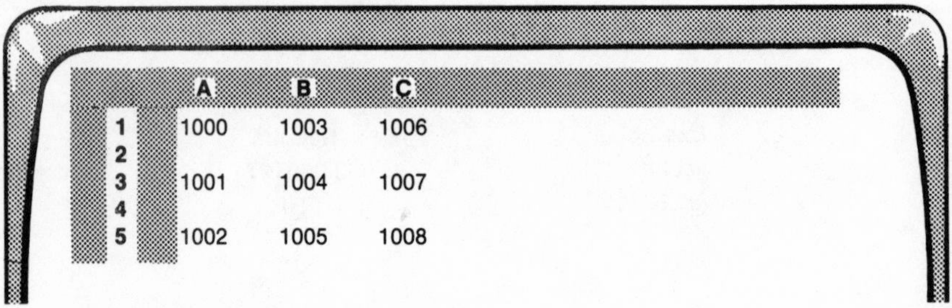

	A	B	C
1	1000	1003	1006
2			
3	1001	1004	1007
4			
5	1002	1005	1008

FIGURE 10-8. @MAX and @MIN Example

@MIN

The @MIN function returns the minimum value of all values in a list. The argument can be a series of values, one or more cell addresses, one or more ranges, or a combination of all three of these.

If the argument is a range, blank cells will be ignored. If no entries are found in the range, the value ERR will be returned. In single cell references, a blank cell has a value of 0.

Configuration

@MIN(*list*)

Examples	Results
@MIN(A1..C5)	1000
@MIN(A1,A2,A3,A4,A5))	0
@MIN(A2..C2)	ERR
@MIN(A2,B2,C2)	0

@MOD

The @MOD function returns the modulo or remainder of the first argument divided by the second argument. The actual calculation is: $a - (b * @INT(a/b))$. If the second argument is zero, 1-2-3 will return the value, ERR.

Configuration
@MOD(a,b)

Examples	Results
@MOD(23,8)	7
@MOD(C5,C8)	2
(where C5 = 17	
and C8 = 3)	

@MONTH

The @MONTH function returns the month number of a given date serial number.

Configuration
@MONTH(a)

a must be a number that represents the date serial number of a day between January 1, 1900 and December 31, 2099.

Examples	General Results Format	Date Results Format
@MONTH(20104)	1	01-JAN-00
@MONTH(3000)	3	03-JAN-00

If @MONTH is used with Date Format Options, the month number will appear where the day would normally be located. The month and year will be Jan and 00, respectively.

@NA

@NA returns the value NA.

Configuration

@NA

Example	**Result**
@IF(A1 > 10,5,@NA)	NA; where A1 = 6

@NPV

Configuration

@NPV(*i,range*)

where;   *i*   is the periodic interest rate.

@NPV will calculate the present value of a series of cash flows. It differs from @PV in that the cash flows do not have to be equal. @NPV assumes that the first cash flow occurs at the end of the first period. @NPV can be used within a formula to calculate the net present value of a series of cash flows where the initial cash flow occurs at the beginning of the first period.

initial cash flow + @NPV(*i,range*)

The initial payment can be a cash outflow such as purchasing a bond or an inflow, such as receiving a deposit on a building that is being sold. If the cash flows are equal in amount, it may be easier to use the @PV function and add the initial cash flow.

Example 1

To determine the present value of a 9% bond with a face value of $100,000 due in two years with semiannual payments of interest, the following formula could be used, if a yield of 12% was required:

@NPV(.06,A2..A5)

This calculation will result in a value of 94802.34.

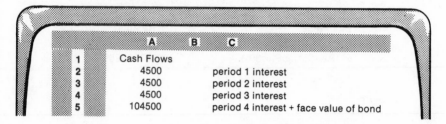

	A	B	C
1	Cash Flows		
2	4500		period 1 interest
3	4500		period 2 interest
4	4500		period 3 interest
5	104500		period 4 interest + face value of bond

Example 2

In this example, we will determine the net present value of an initial investment of $150,000 in a project that promises the following returns:

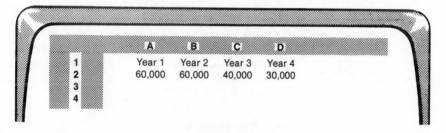

	A	B	C	D
1	Year 1	Year 2	Year 3	Year 4
2	60,000	60,000	40,000	30,000
3				
4				

If the required rate of return is 12%, use the following formula to calculate net present value:

$$-150000 + @NPV(.12,A2..D2)$$

This calculation will tell us that the project has a net present value of -1060. In other words, the series of cash inflows is worth less in today's dollars than the $150,000 initial investment.

@PI

The function @PI returns the value, π or 3.141592653589794. @PI does not take an argument. @PI can be used to convert degrees to radians for arguments in the @COS, @SIN, and @TAN functions. Radians can be calculated as follows:

$$degrees * @PI/180 = radians$$

Configuration
@PI

Examples	Results*
@PI	3.141592653589794
@TAN(35*(@PI/180))	0.700207538209710

@PMT

The @PMT function returns the payment per period for a given principal amount, interest rate, and number of periods. The calculation is made using the following formula:

$$PMT = principal * \frac{i}{1 - (1 + i)^n}$$

where;

i = interest rate per period
n = number of periods
PMT = payment per period

Configuration
@PMT(*principal,i,n*)

Example

Suppose that you want to purchase a condominium for $75,000. The bank will loan up to 85% of the appraised value (which is the same as the purchase price) or $63,750. The current fixed rate for 30 year mortgages is 14%, and payments are due the 1st of each month.

i = .14/12   (14% divided by 12 periods)
n = (30 * 12)   (30 years of 12 payments per year)
principal = 63,750

---

* Using a column-width of 18, Fixed format, 15 decimal places.

@PMT (D19, b24/12, a24·12)

@PMT(63750,.14/12,30*12) would result in a monthly payment of 755.3557.

@PV

@PV calculates the **present value** of an ordinary annuity according to the following formula:

$$PV = pmt * \frac{1-(1+i)^{-n}}{i}$$

where;

pmt = periodic payment amount
i = periodic interest rate
n = number of compounding periods

Configuration
@PV(*pmt,i,n*)

Suppose that Mr. Thomas won a magazine sweepstakes and was offered either $250,000 now or $50,000 a year for the next 10 years. If the expected interest rate is 12%, which prize is worth more in today's dollars*.

Computing the present value of $50,000 for 10 years at 12%, @PV(50000,.12,10) would result in $282,511.10. So $50,000 a year for the next 10 years would be worth more in today's dollars.

@RAND

The @RAND function is used to generate random numbers between 0.0 and 1.0. Note that @RAND does not require an argument.

Configuration
@RAND

---

* Tax implications are not considered.

Example	Result
@RAND	.147506

A different random number will be generated each time the worksheet is recalculated.

@ROUND

The @ROUND function rounds the first argument to the number of digits specified in the second argument. The second argument must be between –15 and +15 and will be converted to an integer for use in the function. For example, if the second argument is 1, the first argument will be rounded to the nearest tenth. If the second argument is –3, the first argument will be rounded to the closest multiple of 1000.

Configuration
@ROUND(a,b)

Examples	Results
@ROUND(42.6745,–1)	40
@ROUND(42.6745,0)	43
@ROUND(42.6745,0.3)	43
@ROUND(42.6745,1)	42.7
@ROUND(42.6745,5)	42.6745
@ROUND(1642,–3)	2000

@SIN

The @SIN function returns the sine of the angle specified as its argument. The argument is assumed to be in radians.

Configuration
@SIN(a)

Example	Result
@SIN(1.7)	.991664

@SQRT

@SQRT returns the square root of its argument.

Configuration

@SQRT(*a*)

Examples	**Results**
@SQRT(49)	7
@SQRT(D14)	square root of the value of cell D14

@STD

Configuration

@STD(*list*)

@STD returns the standard deviation of values in a list. In statistics, this is known as the standard deviation of a population. The standard deviation of a population assumes that the list contains all the values of all the items in a population. If the values in the list only represent part of the population, a **sample**, then the formula for a sample standard deviation should be used. A sample standard deviation is computed by taking the square root of the sample variance (see @VAR)

Sample Standard Deviation

@SQRT((@COUNT(*sample list*)/(@COUNT
(*sample list*)-1)) * @VAR(*sample list*))

If the argument of @STD is a range, blank cells will be ignored. If the @COUNT function would return a zero for the same argument, then @STD would return ERR. 1-2-3 calculates the @STD function using the following formula:

@SQRT(@VAR(*list*))

In the following example, the mean grade of a population consisting of an Economics class will be computed using @AVG. The class is one of four Econ classes taught by a certain professor. The standard deviation for the class is computed using the @STD function. Also, the sample standard deviation for all four classes is calculated using this class as the sample population.

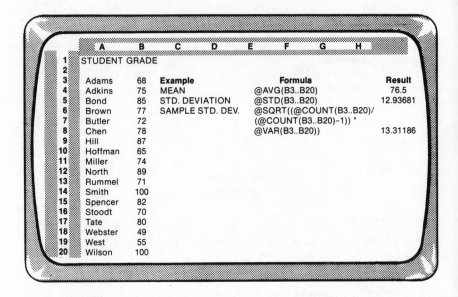

	A	B	C	D	E	F	G	H
1	STUDENT	GRADE						
2								
3	Adams	68	**Example**			**Formula**		**Result**
4	Adkins	75	MEAN			@AVG(B3..B20)		76.5
5	Bond	85	STD. DEVIATION			@STD(B3..B20)		12.93681
6	Brown	77	SAMPLE STD. DEV.			@SQRT(((@COUNT(B3..B20)/		
7	Butler	72				(@COUNT(B3..B20)–1)) *		
8	Chen	78				@VAR(B3..B20))		13.31186
9	Hill	87						
10	Hoffman	65						
11	Miller	74						
12	North	89						
13	Rummel	71						
14	Smith	100						
15	Spencer	82						
16	Stoodt	70						
17	Tate	80						
18	Webster	49						
19	West	55						
20	Wilson	100						

@SUM

The @SUM function returns the sum of values in a list. The argument can be either a range, references to single cells, or values.

Configuration

@SUM(*list*)

Examples	**Results**
@SUM(1000,1001,1002)	3003
@SUM(A2)	0
@SUM(A1..C5)	9036

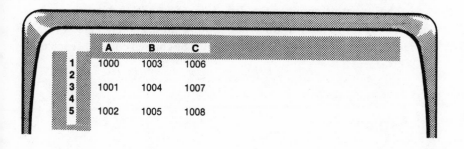

	A	B	C
1	1000	1003	1006
2			
3	1001	1004	1007
4			
5	1002	1005	1008

@TAN

The @TAN function returns the tangent of the argument where the argument is the angle in radians. Degrees can be converted to radians by multiplying the degrees by @PI/180.

Configuration
@TAN(a)

Examples
@TAN(D14)

@TAN(35*@PI/180)

Results
tangent of the
value of cell D14
0.713109

@TODAY

The @TODAY function returns the number of days that have elapsed between the current date and December 31, 1899. The number that results is a date serial number and is suitable for use in other 1-2-3 date functions.

Configuration
@TODAY

Example
@TODAY

Result
30682

This example assumes the date entered when 1-2-3 was input was Jan. 1, 1984. @TODAY does not require an argument. However, in order for it to work properly, the date must be entered correctly each time 1-2-3 is started.

@TRUE

This function has the value 1 (true). The @TRUE function does not take an argument.

Configuration

@TRUE

Example	**Result**
@IF(A1 > 6,@TRUE,@FALSE)	1; where A1 is a value greater than 6

@VAR

The @VAR function returns the population variance of values in a list. When range is used as @VAR's argument, blank cells will be ignored. If the @COUNT function would return a zero for the same argument, the value returned by @VAR will be ERR.

Configuration

@VAR(*list*)

The formula used to calculate a population variance is:

$$\frac{n \sum x^2 - (\sum x)^2}{n^2}$$

where; n = number of items in the argument

x = item in the argument list

To compute a sample variance, use the following formula:

(@COUNT(*list*)/(@COUNT(*list*)-1)) * @VAR(*list*)

Example 1

Suppose that the owner of a chain of retail stores wished to calculate the mean, variance, and standard deviation of the gross sales for each store. @VAR could be used as follows to make these calculations:

	A	B	C	D	E	F	G	H
22	STORE#	Sales	Example		Formula			Results
23	1	35444	MEAN		@AVG(B23..B34)			36698.66
24	2	36689	VARIANCE		@VAR(B23..B34)			7867439.
25	3	30632	STD. DEV.		@SQRT(@VAR(B23..B34))			2804.895
26	4	35101						
27	5	38012						
28	6	42985						
29	7	39433						
30	8	36642						
31	9	35242						
32	10	35611						
33	11	37903						
34	12	36690						
35								

Example 2

We will use the data from Example 1, but will assume that the stores listed are a sample from a total of 36 stores. To find the Variance and Standard Deviation for this sample population, we would use the following formulas:

Sample Variance (@COUNT(B23..B34)/(@COUNT(B23..B34)-1)) * @VAR(B23..B34)

Sample Standard Deviation @SQRT((@COUNT(B23..B34)/(@COUNT(B23..B34)-1)) * @VAR(B23..B34))

The results would be as follows:

Sample Variance	8582661
Sample Standard Deviation	2929.617

@VLOOKUP

@VLOOKUP compares the value of the *test* argument with the first column of the *table* and returns a value according to the value of *a*.

Configuration
@VLOOKUP(*test,table,a*)

table is a range consisting of at least 2 columns. If *table* has a width of only 1 column, or if the number of columns is $\leq a$, then ERR will be returned. If *a* is greater than 0 and less than 1, the results may be invalid.

Values that are to be compared with *test* must be located in the first column of the range. The values must be in increasing order from top to bottom.

1-2-3 compares *test* to the values in the first column of the *table*. When *test* equals or exceeds a value, but is less than the next value, 1-2-3 will find the value that is *a* cells to the right. This value will be returned as the function value.

In the following example of @VLOOKUP, we will determine the correct depreciation rate as of Dec. 31, 1983:

	A	B	C	D	E	F
		LIFE	DATE			DEPR
1						
2	ASSET	CODE*	PURCH	AGE	BASIS	RATE
3	DESK	2	JAN 82	2	500	
4	1981 BUICK	1	MAR 81	3	6500	
5	FILE CABINETS	2	MAR 79	4	640	
6			* 1 signifies a 3 year life			
7	TABLE		2 signifies a 5 year life			
8	AGE	3yr	5yr			
9	1	.25	.15			
10	2	.38	.22			
11	3	.37	.21			
12	4	0	.21			
13	5	0	.21			
14						

The following formula would be entered in F3 and copied to F4 and F5:

@VLOOKUP(D3,A10..C14,B3)

The results would be as follows:

	A	B	C	D	E	F
1		LIFE	DATE			DEPR
2	ASSET	CODE*	PURCH	AGE	BASIS	RATE
3	DESK	2	JAN 82	2	500	.22
4	1981 BUICK	1	MAR 81	3	6500	.37
5	FILE CABINETS	2	MAR 79	4	640	.21
6			* 1 signifies a 3 year life			
7	TABLE		2 signifies a 5 year life			
8	AGE	3yr	5yr			
9	1	.25	.15			
10	2	.38	.22			
11	3	.37	.21			
12	4	0	.21			
13	5	0	.21			
14						

@YEAR

@YEAR returns the year number of a given date serial number. The year number will be a number between 0 and 199, with zero representing the year 1900 and 199 representing 2099.

Configuration
@YEAR(a)

a must be a number that represents the date serial number of a day between January 1, 1900 and December 31, 2099.

Examples	General Format Results
@YEAR(20104)	55
@YEAR(3000)	8
@YEAR(70000)	191
@YEAR(30682)	84

This function will not return readable results while a Date Format Option is in effect.

11

Keyboard Macros

Introduction

Keyboard macros, or simply **macros**, allow the user to store a series of keystrokes in one or more worksheet cells and assign these keystrokes to one of the letter keys (A-Z). When the Alt key is pressed and held down concurrently with the assigned letter key, the 1-2-3 operations indicated by the stored keystrokes will be performed.

Macros can be a useful tool in a number of different 1-2-3 applications. For example, suppose that while a worksheet was being constructed, the user wished to save it on diskette at several different times. Assuming the spreadsheet was named SALES, the following keystrokes would be used to save it on diskette:

/FSSALES ⌐

Once SALES had been initially saved on the diskette, the following series of keystrokes would be required to save and replace the file:

/FSAVE ⌐ R

If this series of keystrokes was assigned to a macro named \S, then SALES could be subsequently saved and replaced by pressing the Alt and S keys.

In the remainder of this chapter, we will discuss Macro usage with 1-2-3. We will begin our discussion by describing a simple example of macro usage and will progress with more advanced examples of macro applications.

Macro Usage - An Elementary Example

We will expand on the example introduced in the last section to illustrate the steps involved in defining and invoking a macro. Suppose our worksheet appeared as follows:

	A	B	C	D
1		January	February	March
2	Widgets	8796.90	9056.87	9879.23
3	Gadgets	4673.39	4789.03	4573.77
4	Gizmos	3290.73	3562.91	3347.89
5				
6	Totals	16761.02	17408.81	17800.89
7				

Save the worksheet by using the following command:

/FS SALES ⌐

Suppose we revised our worksheet as follows,

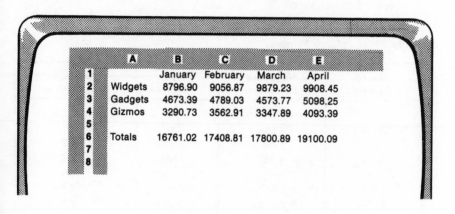

and wished to move the revised file in place of that currently stored in SALES. This could be accomplished with the following command:

/FSSAVE ⌐R

Since we have to save the revised worksheet regularly, we could conserve time by defining this command using a macro. Our first step in defining the macro would be to move the cell pointer to a cell which would not be used in the worksheet. Suppose we chose A10. Next, enter the command in that cell as follows:

'/FSSAVE~R

The apostrophe (') indicates that a label is being entered. Macros must be entered into the worksheet as labels. The tilde (~) is the macro symbol for enter. The various macro symbols are summarized in table 11-1.

Once the macro has been entered in the cell, it must be assigned a range name using the **R**ange **N**ame **C**reate command. Macro names must begin with a \ (backslash) and can contain only one other character. This character must be a letter of the alphabet or a 0 (zero). Since it may be difficult to remember which macro each one-character macro name represents, it is a good idea to use an adjacent cell to label the macro.

Suppose that we named the macro in our example \ A using / **RNC**.

By pressing down the Alt and A keys simultaneously, the worksheet will be saved on the diskette.

Table 11-1. Macro Symbols

Macro Symbol	Keyboard Equivalent	Macro Symbol	Keyboard Equivalent
~	⏎ (Enter key)	{Bs}	Backspace key
{Down}	↓ key	{Edit}	F2
{Up}	↑ key	{Name}	F3
{Right}	→ key	{Abs}	F4
{Left}	← key	{Goto}	F5
{PgUp}	PgUp key	{Window}	F6
{PgDn}	PgDn key	{Query}	F7
{Home}	Home key	{Table}	F8
{End}	End key	{Calc}	F9
{Del}	Del key	{Graph}	F10
{Esc}	Esc key	{?}	Pause for manual input

Advanced Macro Concepts

In the following sections, we will expand upon our discussion of macros by introducing the following topics:

Multiple cell macros

Auto-execute macros

Single step execution

Interrupting a macro

User input with macros

X commands

MULTIPLE CELL MACROS

In our definition of macros, we stated that the keystrokes used to define a macro could be stored in one or more cells. In our example, the macro was stored in a single cell. We will now illustrate how a macro can be stored in more than one cell. When entering complex macros, it is often preferable to spread the keystrokes over a series of cells. This will make both the macro and the accompanying documentation more readable.

The following illustration depicts our example with the macro defined over several cells:

	A	B	C	D	E
1		January	February	March	April
2	Widgets	8796.90	9056.87	9879.23	9908.45
3	Gadgets	4673.39	4789.03	4573.77	5098.25
4	Gizmos	3290.73	3562.91	3347.89	4093.39
5					
6	Totals	16761.02	17408.81	17800.89	19100.09
7					
8					
9	/fs	File Save			
10	save	Filename			
11	~	Enter key			
12	R	Replace			
13					
14					

When / **RNC** was executed to name the macro, only A9 was indicated as the macro. It was not necessary to indicate the entire range, as 1-2-3 will continue to read cells beneath the one specified in / **RNC** as part of the macro. When a non-label cell (blank, formula, or number) is entered, 1-2-3 will consider the macro to have ended.

AUTO-EXECUTE MACROS

An **auto-execute** macro is automatically executed when the worksheet is loaded using / **F**ile **R**etrieve. An auto-execute macro is created like any other macro, but is assigned the name \ 0. Auto-execute macros can not be issued via the keyboard using the Alt key.

Suppose the worksheet appeared as follows;

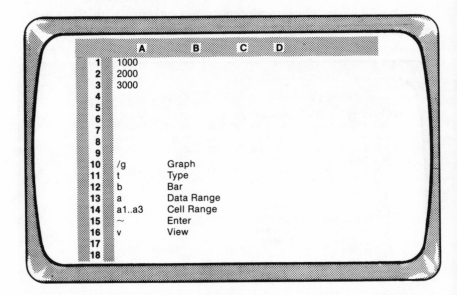

and A10 had been defined as \0. Next, suppose that we executed / **FS** and saved the worksheet as TEST152. We could then issue / **WEY** to erase the worksheet. If TEST 152 was then read into the worksheet by issuing the **File Retrieve** command, \0 would be automatically executed, and a simple bar graph would be displayed on the screen.

SINGLE STEP EXECUTION

In certain instances, the programmer may wish to slow down macro execution. This can be expecially useful when a macro is not executing as intended and requires debugging. In the single-step mode, 1-2-3 will pause after each macro keystroke is executed. Execution will not continue until a key has been pressed.

The single step mode is invoked by pressing the Alt and Help keys simultaneously. When 1-2-3 is in the single step execution mode, SST will be displayed in the upper right-hand corner of the screen rather than CMD. By pressing the Alt and Help keys a second time, the single step mode will be turned off.

INTERRUPTING MACRO EXECUTION

A macro can be interrupted during execution by simultaneously pressing the Control and Scroll Lock keys. If the macro is waiting for a keyboard entry before continuing execution, Control-Scroll Lock can again be pressed to interrupt execution. When macro execution is interrupted, 1-2-3 will return to the Ready mode.

USER INPUT WITH MACROS

1-2-3 allows macros to pause during execution in order to accept user input from the keyboard. When any of the following commands are inserted in a macro, it will pause for a keyboard entry:

?

/XM

/XL

/XN

When ? is used in a macro, 1-2-3 will stop executing the macro sequence and will instead wait for a keyboard entry. When the Enter key is pressed, 1-2-3 will accept the keyboard entry, and will continue with macro execution. An example of the use of ? is given below:

/CA1..A5 ~ {?} ~

In the preceding example, macro execution would stop allowing the user to enter the range into which A1..A5 would be copied.

The following X commands:

/XM

/XL

/XN

also cause macro execution to stop in order to allow a keyboard entry. These commands will be discussed in the following section.

X Commands

The X commands allow 1-2-3 to be used much like a computer programming language such as BASIC or FORTRAN. The X commands control the command execution sequence in a macro. The X commands are summarized with their equivalent BASIC statement in table 11-2. Each command will be discussed in detail in the following sections.

Table 11-2. X Commands

X Command	Command Description & BASIC Equivalent
X Programming Commands	
/XI *condition* ~	Equivalent of IF-THEN statement in BASIC. Sets a condition which will determine execution flow.
/XG *location* ~	Equivalent of GOTO statement in BASIC. Alters execution flow to specified *location*.
/XC *location* ~	Equivalent of GOSUB statement in BASIC. Calls the subroutine at the indicated *location*.
/XR	Equivalent of RETURN statement in BASIC. Returns from subroutine.
/XQ	Ends macro execution. Equivalent of END in BASIC.
X Input Commands	
/XM	Allows the user to choose from a menu. Execution will branch depending upon the menu choice.
/XL *message* ~ *location* ~	Displays a prompt in the control panel. Accepts a label entry from the keyboard and places same in the *location* specified. Similar to BASIC's INPUT statement.
/XN	Identical to /XL except that it accepts a numeric entry.

/XI

The /XI command branches macro execution depending upon the execution of a condition indicated with the command. /XI is used with the following format:

/XI *condition* ~ ...

The *condition* will evaluate as either true (non-zero) or false (zero). If the *condition* evaluates as true, macro execution will continue in the same cell immediately after the ~. If the condition evaluates as false, macro execution will branch to the cell immediately below that containing the /XI statement. An example of /XI is given below:

```
/XI COUNTER < = LIMIT ~/XG AGAIN ~
/XQ
```

In the preceding example, Lotus would continue the macro at AGAIN if the cell COUNTER had a value less than or equal to the cell LIMIT. If the value of cell COUNTER exceeded the value of cell LIMIT, the command /XQ would be executed.

/XG

The /XG command is used to branch macro execution to a specified cell location. /XG is similar to BASIC's GOTO command. /XG is used with the following format:

/XG *location* ~

location indicates a cell address, range, range name, or macro name to which execution will be branched. In the following example,

/XG TEST2 ~

macro execution will branch to the range named TEST2.

/XC
/XR

/ **XC** is used to branch macro execution to a specified subroutine. When / **XR** is encountered in that subroutine, execution will resume with the macro command immediately following / **XC**. / **XC** and / **XR** must be specified in pairs. Otherwise, an error will occur. / **XC** or / **XR** are similar to BASIC's GOSUB and RETURN statements respectively. They are used in the following configuration:

> /**XC** *location* ~
> /**XR**

An example of the use of / **XC** and / **XR** follows:

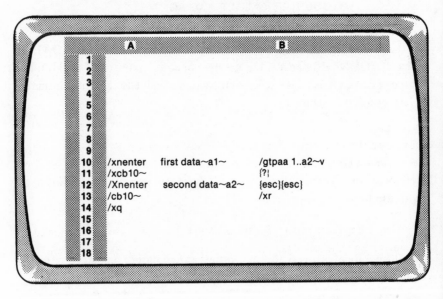

In this example, we will assume that macro \A had been defined as A10. When the Alt and A keys are pressed, the user will be prompted to enter data in A1. When that data has been entered, the instruction in A11 will cause execution to branch to the subroutine at B10 where a pie graph will be displayed. In B11, {?} requests a user input. When this input is received, / **XR** will return execution to A12, where a second data entry will be prompted for. Again, execution is branched to the subroutine at B10 where a pie graph will be displayed. The user will be prompted for an entry. This entry will result in the execution of / **XR**, which will return execution to A14 where the macro will end.

/XL
/XN

The / **XL** command allows the user to input a label or literal consisting of up to 240 characters. The entry will be automatically prefixed with the ' label prefix. The / **XN** command allows user input of values and ranges (including range names). / **XL** and / **XN** are used with the following configurations:

/**XL** *message* ~ *location* ~
/**XN** *message* ~ *location* ~

message is a string up to 39 characters in length, and *location* is the cell where the user input will be stored. If *location* is a range, the user input will be stored in the upper left-hand cell in the range.

If user input for the / **XL** command cannot be evaluated by 1-2-3, an error message will be displayed. The user, after pressing the Enter or ESC keys, can then re-input. An example of the usage of / **XN** is given in the example on page 272.

/XQ

The / **XQ** command causes macro execution to end. When macro execution ends, the CMD indicator in the upper right-hand corner of the screen will be replaced with READY.

/XM

/ **XM** allows the user to choose from a menu during macro execution. This menu is only accessible during macro execution and can have a width of up to 8 columns and a depth of up to 2 rows. / **XM** is used with the following configuration:

/**XM** *location* ~

location refers to the upper left-hand corner of the range containing the menu. *location* may be specified as a cell address, range, or range name.

The first row of the menu consists of the menu selections. The second row consists of descriptions of these selections. When the menu is created, certain rules must be observed for / **XM** to execute properly. These include:

- Up to eight menu choices can be entered.
- Blank cells are not allowed between menu choices.
- The cell to the right of the final menu selection must be blank.
- The menu choice should fit in the space allowed for that column.
- Do not use menu selections that begin with identical first letters. Doing so would limit the user's ability to denote a selection by entering just the first letter.

When / **XM** is executed, the macro will pause. A menu will be displayed in the control panel that is identical to the various menus displayed by 1-2-3 commands. The menu selections will be displayed in line 2 of the control panel, and the descriptions will be displayed in line 3. The user can indicate a menu selection by using the menu pointer or by entering the first letter of the menu selection.

When a menu selection has been made, macro execution will continue with those keystrokes just below the menu description in the same column as the menu selection.

	AA	BB	CC	DD
1	ENTER	PRINT	SAVE	QUIT
2	input data	print copy	store spreadsheet	Exit to Ready mode
3	/RI field ~	/PPR chart ~ GQ	/FSTable7~R~	/XQ
4	/XG	/XG start ~	/XG start~	
5				

FIGURE 11-1. / **XM** Example

Figure 11-1 contains an example of a menu created with / **XM**.

The second line of the menu is a description field. As each choice in the menu is pointed to, the associated descriptive field will appear. If the pointer was on PRINT in the example in figure 11-1, the second line would display "Print copy".

When the menu choice is selected by pointing to the choice and pressing the Enter key, the commands listed below the descriptive field will be executed. In our example, if Print was selected, 1-2-3 would execute the lines / **PPR** chart ~ GQ.

12

1-2-3 Example Models

Introduction

In this chapter, we will present a number of pre-designed 1-2-3 models.* Each model will be presented with step-by-step instructions for both entry and usage. Although these models can be used to solve specific problems, the purpose of this chapter is to provide practical examples of fairly involved 1-2-3 models that can be analyzed by the reader. Hopefully, the insight gained from these models will assist the reader when he or she attempts to build his or her own models.

---

* The models were created with an IBM PC with 256K of RAM and a B&W graphic monitor.

Loan Amortization Model

The purpose of this model is to prepare a loan amortization schedule based on the following input:

- a known loan or periodic payment amount
- an interest rate
- the number of payments

If the loan amount is known, the payment amount will be calculated using the @PMT function. If the payment amount is known, the original loan amount will be calculated using the @PV function.

GLOBAL SETTINGS

The global settings should be as follows:

Recalculation	Format	Label Prefix	Column Width
MANUAL NATURAL	(F2)	'	9

SETTING UP THE WORKSHEET

1. Enter the following labels:

Cell	Entry
D2	LOAN AMT
D3	INT%PER YR
D4	TOTAL#PMTS
D5	'#PMTS PER YR
D6	INPUT PMT
D7	CALC PMT
D8	PV OF LOAN
A11	PMT
A12	NO.
B10	TOTAL
B11	PMT
B12	AMT
C11	PRINCIPAL
C12	PMT
D11	INT
D12	PMT
E11	PRINCIPAL

E12	BALANCE
F10	PRINCIPAL
F11	PAID
F12	TO DATE
G10	INT
G11	PAID
G12	TO DATE

2. Center the labels using /**R**ange **L**abel-Prefix **C**enter. Specify the range A10..G12.

3. Format the following ranges with /**R**ange **F**ormat:

Range	Format	Decimal Places
C3..C3	Percent	2
C4..C5	Fixed	2
A15..A375	Fixed	0

4. Use /**R**ange **N**ame **La**bels to name the cells to the left of D2..D8. This will make the formulas more meaningful than referencing cell addresses.

User Step 1:	Select /**R**ange **N**ame Labels (/**RNL**)
User Step 2:	Select **L**eft
User Step 3:	Type D2..D8↵

5. Enter the formulas to calculate the payment amount and present value of the loan.

Cell	Formula
C7	@PMT(LOAN AMT, INT%PER YR/#PMTS PER YR, TOTAL#PMTS)
C8	@PV(@MAX(INPUT PMT, CALC PMT), INT%PER YR/#PMTS PER YR, TOTAL# PMTS)

6. To enter the lines as shown on the worksheet in figure 12-1, follow the steps outlined below. These lines are not essential to the operation of the model, but they do make it more readable.

User Step 1:	Place pointer on A9 and type \--↵.
User Step 2:	Select /**C**opy.
User Step 3:	Specify A9 as the FROM range and press ↵.
User Step 4:	Specify B9..G9 as the TO range and press ↵.

User Step 5:   Repeat User Steps 1-5 for A13 and B13..G13

7. The following formulas should be entered to construct the amortization schedule:

Cell	Entry	Description
E14	@MAX(LOAN AMT, PV of LOAN)	Indicates the loan amount to be used in the schedule.
A15	@IF((A14+1)>$TOTAL #PMTS, @NA, A14+1)	This formula sets up a condition to check whether the loan has been fully amortized. It asks if the previous payment number plus 1 is greater than the total number of payments. If it is, the value NA will be entered. Otherwise, the new payment number will be entered.
B15	@IF(@ISNA(A15),@NA, @MAX($INPUT PMT, $CALC PMT))	If the value in the payment number column is NA, the value NA will be returned. Otherwise, the payment amount should be entered.
C15	+B15-D15	This formula calculates the principal payment amount by subtracting the interest payment (D15) from the total payment (B15).
D15	@IF(@ISNA(A15),@NA, ($INT%PER YR/$#PMTS PER YR) *E14)	If the value in the payment number column is A15, then NA will be returned. Otherwise, the interest portion of the payment will be calculated.
E15	@IF(@ISNA(A15),@NA, E14-C15)	If the value in the payment number column is NA, then NA will be returned. Otherwise, the amount of the principal payment will be subtracted from the previous principal balance.
F15	@SUM(C15..C15)	Calculates the totals of the principal and interest amounts paid including this payment.
G15	@SUM(D15..D15)	

8. The next step is to copy the formulas in A15..G15 to the rest of the worksheet.

User Step 1:	Select /Copy
User Step 2:	Specify A15..G15 as the FROM range and press ↵.
User Step 3:	The TO range can vary depending on the term of the loan. For loans up to 5 years, use A16..G65. For loans up to 10 years use A16..G135. In our example, we input the range for loans up to 30 years, A16..G375.

9. To protect the cell formulas from possibly being overwritten or erased, turn the global protection on by selecting / **WGPE**. Then, unprotect the user input cells, C2..C6, using / **RU**.

10. Use / **File Save** to save the model as a form for future use.

11. The following cells will require user input:

Cell	Description	Entry Required
C2	LOAN AMT	Original amount of loan, if known — otherwise, 0.
C3	INT % PER YR	Annual interest rate entered as a decimal amount.
C4	TOTAL # PMTS	A value or a formula representing the number of periodic payments to be made during the term of the loan.
C5	# PMTS PER YR	A number or value representing the number of payments made per year.
C6	INPUT PMT	0, if payment amount is unknown and the amount of the loan was input in C2. If the amount of the payment is known but the loan amount is unknown, input the payment amount.

12. After the required user entries have been made, press the F9 (Calc) key to calculate the formulas.

Model Usage Example

The worksheet depicted in figure 12-1 resulted from following these User Steps with the model previously described.

User Step 1:   Make the following cell entries

Cell	Entry
C2	40000
C3	.1325
C4	120
C5	12
C6	0

User Step 2:   Press the F9 (Calc) key

1-2-3 Response: Depicted in figure 12-1

Printing the Schedule

User Step 1:	Select /Print Printer.
1-2-3 Response:	Displays Printer menu
User Step 2:	Select Range
1-2-3 Response:	Enter Print range:A1
User Step 3:	Type or point to A14..G134⌐
1-2-3 Response:	Returns to Printer menu
User Step 4:	Select Options
1-2-3 Response:	Displays Options menu
User Step 5:	Select Borders
1-2-3 Response:	Columns Rows
User Step 6:	Select R
1-2-3 Response:	Enter Border Rows:A1
User Step 7:	Type or point to A9..G13⌐
1-2-3 Response:	Returns to Options menu
User Step 8:	Select Quit
1-2-3 Response:	Returns to Printer menu
User Step 9:	Make sure printer is on line. Select Align, then Go.
1-2-3 Response:	Sends information directly to the printer then returns to the Printer menu. The printout will be similar to that depicted in figure 12-2.
User Step 10:	Select Quit to return to the Ready mode.

A1:   READY

A	B	C	D	E	F	G
1						
2		40000.00	LOAN AMT			
3		13.25%	INT% PER YR			
4		120	TOTAL #PMTS			
5		12	#PMTS PER YR			
6		0.00	INPUT PMT			
7		603.16	CALC PMT			
8		40000.00	PV OF LOAN			
9						
10		TOTAL				PRINCIPAL	INT
11	PMT	PMT	PRINCIPAL	INT	PRINCIPAL	PAID	PAID
12	NO.	AMT	PMT	PMT	BALANCE	TO DATE	TO DATE
13							
14					40000.00		
15	1	603.16	161.49	441.67	39838.51	161.49	441.67
16	2	603.16	163.27	439.88	39675.24	324.76	881.55
17	3	603.16	165.07	438.08	39510.16	489.84	1319.63
18	4	603.16	166.90	436.26	39343.27	656.73	1755.89
19	5	603.16	168.74	434.42	39174.53	825.47	2190.30
20	6	603.16	170.60	432.55	39003.92	996.08	2622.86

CAPS

A124: (F0) @IF(A123+1 > $TOTAL #PMTS,@NA,A123+1)   READY

A	B	C	D	E	F	G
116	102	603.16	489.57	113.58	9797.17	30202.83	31319.04
117	103	603.16	494.98	108.18	9302.19	30697.81	31427.22
118	104	603.16	500.44	102.71	8801.74	31198.26	31529.93
119	105	603.16	505.97	97.19	8295.77	31704.23	31627.12
120	106	603.16	511.56	91.60	7784.22	32215.78	31718.72
121	107	603.16	517.20	85.95	7267.01	32732.99	31804.67
122	108	603.16	522.92	80.24	6744.10	33255.90	31884.91
123	109	603.16	528.69	74.47	6215.41	33784.59	31959.37
124	110	603.16	534.53	68.63	5680.88	34319.12	32028.00
125	111	603.16	540.43	62.73	5140.45	34859.55	32090.73
126	112	603.16	546.40	56.76	4594.05	35405.95	32147.49
127	113	603.16	552.43	50.73	4041.62	35958.38	32198.21
128	114	603.16	558.53	44.63	3483.10	36516.90	32242.84
129	115	603.16	564.70	38.46	2918.40	37081.60	32281.30
130	116	603.16	570.93	32.22	2347.47	37652.53	32313.52
131	117	603.16	577.24	25.92	1770.23	38229.77	32339.44
132	118	603.16	583.61	19.55	1186.62	38813.38	32358.99
133	119	603.16	590.05	13.10	596.57	39403.43	32372.09
134	120	603.16	596.57	6.59	.00	40000.00	32378.68
135	NA	NA	NA	NA	NA	NA	NA

CAPS SCROLL

FIGURE 12-1. Loan Amortization Worksheet

- Saving the entire worksheet

User Step 1:	Select /File **S**ave
1-2-3 Response:	Enter save file name:
User Step 2:	Type LOAN ↵
1-2-3 Response:	Saves worksheet as a worksheet file under the filename, LOAN. Returns to the Ready mode.

- Saving only the worksheet values (as opposed to formulas)

User Step 1:	Select /**FX**
1-2-3 Response:	Formulas Values
User Step 2:	Select **V**
1-2-3 Response:	Enter xtract filename:
User Step 3:	Type LOANVAL↵
1-2-3 Response:	Enter xtract range:A1..A1
User Step 4:	Specify A1..G134 and press↵
1-2-3 Response:	Saves the worksheet containing values instead of formulas under the filename LOANVAL. Returns to the Ready mode.

PMT NO.	TOTAL PMT AMT	PRINCIPAL PMT	INT PMT	PRINCIPAL BALANCE	PRINCIPAL PAID TO DATE	INT PAID TO DATE
				40000.00		
1	603.16	161.49	441.67	39838.51	161.49	441.67
2	603.16	163.27	439.88	39675.24	324.76	881.55
3	603.16	165.07	438.08	39510.16	489.84	1319.63
4	603.16	166.90	436.26	39343.27	656.73	1755.89
5	603.16	168.74	434.42	39174.53	825.47	2190.30
6	603.16	170.60	432.55	39003.92	996.08	2622.86
7	603.16	172.49	430.67	38831.44	1168.56	3053.52
8	603.16	174.39	428.76	38657.04	1342.96	3482.29
9	603.16	176.32	426.84	38480.73	1519.27	3909.13
10	603.16	178.26	424.89	38302.46	1697.54	4334.02
11	603.16	180.23	422.92	38122.23	1877.77	4756.94
12	603.16	182.22	420.93	37940.01	2059.99	5277.87
13	603.16	184.23	418.92	37755.77	2244.23	5596.79
14	603.16	186.27	416.89	37569.50	2430.50	6013.68
15	603.16	188.33	414.83	37381.18	2618.82	6428.51
16	603.16	190.41	412.75	37190.77	2809.23	6841.26
17	603.16	192.51	410.65	36998.26	3001.74	7251.91
18	603.16	194.63	408.52	36803.63	31960.	7660.43
19	603.16	19	406.37	36606.85	330	66.81
20	603.16		404.20	36407.89		01
21	603.16		402.00	36206.74	26	
22	603.16		399.78	36003.3	04.23	3180
23	603.0	511.00			32215.78	3171.0
24	600	517.20			32732.99	31804.00
25		522.92			33255.90	31884.90
26		528.69			33784.59	31959.37
27	.16	534.53	68.0	00080.88	34319.12	32028.00
	03.16	540.43	62.73	00140.45	34859.55	32090.73
	603.16	546.40	56.76	4594.05	35405.95	32147.49
	603.16	552.43	50.73	4041.62	35958.38	32198.21
4	603.16	558.53	44.63	3483.10	36516.90	32242.84
115	603.16	564.70	38.46	2918.40	37081.60	32281.30
116	603.16	570.93	32.22	2347.47	37652.53	32313.52
117	603.16	577.24	25.92	1770.23	38229.77	32339.44
118	603.16	583.61	19.55	1186.62	38813.38	32358.99
119	603.16	509.05	13.10	596.57	39403.43	32372.09
120	603.16	596.57	6.59	.00	40000.00	32378.68

FIGURE 12-2. Print out of Loan Amortization

Budget Model

In this model, three worksheets will be used in the example. These are depicted in figures 12-3, 12-4, and 12-5.

GLOBAL SETTINGS

The global settings used for all three worksheets are:

Recalculation	Format	Label Prefix	Column Width
AUTO NATURAL	(F0)	'	9

SETTING UP THE WORKSHEET

In the worksheet depicted in figure 12-3, formulas will be entered in B19..N19, N6..N10, and N14..N17.

All of the other entries are either label or numeric entries to be made by the user. Column A was given a column-width of 15 by using / **WCS**et. The month labels were right-justified by using / **RLR**ight and specifying the range B3..N3.

In the worksheet, the following formulas were entered to calculate the totals:

Cell	Entry
B19	@SUM(B6..B17)
N6	@SUM(B6..M6)

These formulas were copied using the following procedure:

User Step 1:	Select /**C**
1-2-3 Response:	Enter range to copy FROM:A1..A1
User Step 2:	Type or point to B19..B19↵
1-2-3 Response:	Enter range to copy TO:A1..A1↵
User Step 3:	Type or point to C19..N19↵
1-2-3 Response:	Copies formula in B19 to C19..N19 and returns to Ready mode.
User Step 4:	Select /**C**
1-2-3 Response:	Enter range to copy FROM:A1..A1
User Step 5:	Type or point to N6..N6↵
1-2-3 Response:	Enter range to copy TO:A1..A1
User Step 6:	Type or point to N7..N10↵
1-2-3 Response:	Copies formula in N6 to N7..N10 and returns to the Ready mode.

User Step 7: Repeat user steps 4-6, but in step 6 specify N14..N17 as the range.

The user should save the accounting department personnel budget worksheet under the filename ACCTPERB using /File Save before setting up the next worksheet.

	A	B	C	D	E	F	G	H	I	J
1	BUDGET — PERSONNEL			ACCOUNTING DEPT			Filename — ACCTPERB			
2										
3		JAN	FEB	MAR	APR	MAY	JUN			
4	HOURLY									
5										
6	JOHN MOHR	950	950	950	950	950	950			
7	SUSAN DUNN	800	800	800	800	800	800			
8	JANE COHEN	1050	1050	1050	1050	1050	1050			
9	BOB MILLER	1250	1250	1250	1250	1250	1250			
10	JIM PETRIE	1440	1440	1440	1440	1440	1440			
11										
12	SALARIED									
13										
14	DOUG PLANT	1580	1580	1580	1580	1750	1750			
15	MIKE SPEHER	1750	1750	1750	1750	1750	1750			
16	BARBARA BEHL	2050	2050	2050	2050	2050	2050			
17	KITTY SANDERS	3100	3100	3100	3100	3100	3100			
18										
19	TOTALS	13970	13970	13970	13970	14140	14140			
20										

	K	L	M	N	O	P	Q	R	S	T
1										
2										
3	JUL	AUG	SEP	OCT	NOV	DEC	TOTAL			
4										
5										
6	950	950	1050	1050	1050	1050	1180			
7	880	880	880	880	880	880	10080			
8	1050	1050	1050	1050	1050	1050	12600			
9	1250	1250	1250	1250	1350	1350	15200			
10	1440	1440	1440	1560	1560	1560	17640			
11										
12										
13										
14	1750	1750	1750	1750	1750	1750	20320			
15	1750	1900	1900	1900	1900	1900	21750			
16	2050	2050	2050	2050	2050	2050	24600			
17	3100	3100	3100	3300	3300	3300	37800			
18										
19	14220	14370	14470	14790	14890	14890	171790			
20										

FIGURE 12-3. Accounting Department Personnel Budget

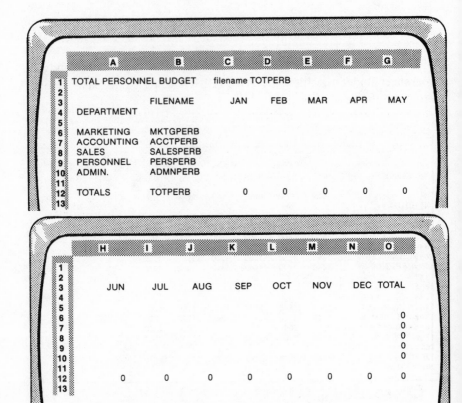

FIGURE 12-4. Total Personnel Budget Worksheet

The following cell entries were made and / Copy was used to copy them to the appropriate cells:

Cell	Entry	Range copied to
C12	@SUM(B6..B10)	D12..O12
O6	@SUM(B6..M6)	O7..O10

The column-width of column A was set to 15 using / **WCSet**. The month label entries were right-justified using / **RLR**ight for the range C3..D3.

The column labeled FILENAME is provided so the user can enter the name of the file containing details of that department's personnel budget.

This worksheet should be saved under the filename TOTPERB before setting up the next worksheet.

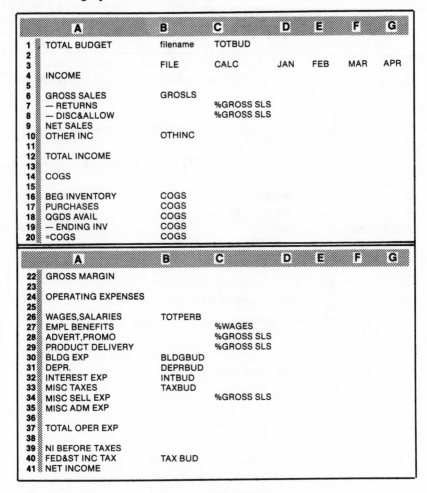

	A	B	C	D	E	F	G
1	TOTAL BUDGET	filename	TOTBUD				
2							
3		FILE	CALC	JAN	FEB	MAR	APR
4	INCOME						
5							
6	GROSS SALES	GROSLS					
7	— RETURNS		%GROSS SLS				
8	— DISC&ALLOW		%GROSS SLS				
9	NET SALES						
10	OTHER INC	OTHINC					
11							
12	TOTAL INCOME						
13							
14	COGS						
15							
16	BEG INVENTORY	COGS					
17	PURCHASES	COGS					
18	QGDS AVAIL	COGS					
19	— ENDING INV	COGS					
20	=COGS	COGS					

	A	B	C	D	E	F	G
22	GROSS MARGIN						
23							
24	OPERATING EXPENSES						
25							
26	WAGES,SALARIES	TOTPERB					
27	EMPL BENEFITS		%WAGES				
28	ADVERT,PROMO		%GROSS SLS				
29	PRODUCT DELIVERY		%GROSS SLS				
30	BLDG EXP	BLDGBUD					
31	DEPR.	DEPRBUD					
32	INTEREST EXP	INTBUD					
33	MISC TAXES	TAXBUD					
34	MISC SELL EXP		%GROSS SLS				
35	MISC ADM EXP						
36							
37	TOTAL OPER EXP						
38							
39	NI BEFORE TAXES						
40	FED&ST INC TAX	TAX BUD					
41	NET INCOME						

FIGURE 12-5. Total Budget Worksheet*

---

* The worksheet would extend to column P, so that each month would be represented as well as a total column.

In the Total Budget worksheet, column B is provided so the filename of files containing details of that information can be entered. Column C is provided so if the amounts are based on a calculation, a short description can be entered. Save this worksheet under the filename TOTBUD

CALCULATING THE TOTAL PERSONNEL BUDGET

To calculate the Total Personnel Budget, we will use /File Xtract Values to extract totals from each department's personnel budget. As an example, we will use the accounting department personnel budget (figure 12-3).

- Use /File Xtract to create a file containing the total accounting department personnel budget values by month.

User Step 1:	/File Retrieve ACCTPERB file and place pointer on B19.
User Step 2:	Select /FX
1-2-3 Response:	Formulas Values
User Step 3:	Select V
1-2-3 Response:	Enter Xtract filename:
User Step 4:	Type ACCTPERT↵
1-2-3 Response:	Enter xtract range:B19..B19
User Step 5:	Type or point to B19..N19 and press ↵

- Incorporate accounting department personnel budget totals by month in the Total Personnel Budget.

User Step 1:	/File Retrieve TOTPERB file and place pointer on C7.
User Step 2:	Select /File Combine.
1-2-3 Response:	Copy Add Subtract
User Step 3:	Select C
1-2-3 Response:	Entire File Named Range
User Step 4:	Select E
1-2-3 Response:	Enter name of file to combine:
User Step 5:	Make sure the diskette containing the file to combine is in the data drive*.
User Step 6:	Type ACCTPERT and press ↵

---

* Usually drive B.

1-2-3 Response:

	A	B	C	D	E	F	G
1	TOTAL PERSONNEL BUDGET		filename TOTPERB				
2							
3			JAN	FEB	MAR	APR	MAY
4	DEPARTMENT	FILENAME					
5							
6	MARKETING	MKTGPERB					
7	ACCOUNTING	MKTGPERB	13970	13970	13970	13970	14140
8	SALES	SALESPERB					
9	PERSONNEL	PERSPERB					
10	ADMIN.	ADMNPERB					
11							
12	TOTALS	TOTPERT	13970	13970	13970	13970	14140
13							

	H	I	J	K	L	M	N	O
1								
2								
3	JUN	JUL	AUG	SEP	OCT	NOV	DEC	TOTAL
4								
5								
6								0
7	14140	14220	14370	14470	14790	14890	14890	171790
8								0
9								0
10								0
11								
12	14140	14220	14370	14470	14790	14890	14890	171790
13								

The remaining department personnel budgets would be incorporated in the Total Personnel Budget using / File Combine. The finished worksheet might appear as follows:

	A	B	C	D	E	F	G
1	TOTAL PERSONNEL BUDGET		filename TOTPERB				
2							
3			JAN	FEB	MAR	APR	MAY
4	DEPARTMENT	FILENAME					
5							
6	MARKETING	MKTGPERB	10000	10000	10000	10000	10000
7	ACCOUNTING	MKTGPERB	13970	13970	13970	13970	14140
8	SALES	SALESPERB	13000	13000	13000	13000	13000
9	PERSONNEL	PERSPERB	8500	8500	8500	8500	8500
10	ADMIN.	ADMNPERB	20000	20000	20000	20000	20000
11							
12	TOTALS	TOTPERT	65470	65470	65470	65470	65640
13							

Worksheet continued on next page

	H	I	J	K	L	M	N	O
1								
2								
3	JUN	JUL	AUG	SEP	OCT	NOV	DEC	TOTAL
4								
5								
6	10000	10000	10000	10800	10800	10800	10800	123200
7	14140	14220	14370	14470	14790	14890	14890	171790
8	13000	13000	14000	14000	14000	14000	14000	161000
9	8500	8500	8500	8500	8500	8700	8700	102400
10	20000	23000	23000	23000	23000	23000	23000	258000
11								
12	65640	68720	69870	70770	71090	71390	71390	816390
13								

INCORPORATING THE PERSONNEL BUDGET IN THE TOTAL BUDGET

The totals for the Total Personnel Budget worksheet, C12..N12, could then be placed in a file named TOTPERT using / **FXV**. This file could be incorporated in the Total Budget (filename TOTBUD) by using / **F**ile **C**ombine **C**opy at D26. If the file being combined was TOTPERT, the following would result:

A22:   'GROSS MARGIN   filename TOTBUD

	A	B	C	D	E	F	G
22	GROSS MARGIN						
23	OPERATING EXP.						
24	WAGES,SALARIES	TOTPERB		65470	65470	65470	65470
25	EMPL BENEFITS		WAGES				
26	ADVERT,PROMO		%GROSS SLS				
27	PRODUCT DELIVERY		%GROSS SLS				
28	BLDG	BLDGBUD					
29	DEPR.	DEPRBUD					
30	INTEREST EXP	INTBUD					
31	MISC TAXES	TAXBUD					
32	MISC SELL. EXP		%GROSS SLS				
33	MISC ADM EXP						
34							
35	TOTAL OPER EXP						
36							
37	NI BEFORE TAXES						
38	FED&ST INC TAX TAXBUD						
39	NET INCOME						
40							
41							

The appropriate files would be incorporated into TOTBUD for each category dependent on a file for its values (i.e. Gross Sales, COGS, BLDG, etc.)

Formulas would be entered for all the accounts requiring a calculation of their values (i.e. RETURNS, DISC&ALLOW, EMPL BENEFITS, etc.). Formulas would also be entered to calculate TOTAL INCOME, NET SALES GROSS MARGIN, TOTAL EXP, NI BEFORE TAX, and NET INCOME. The formulas need only be entered in cells in column D. They can then be copied to the other cells.

Accounts Receivable Model

In this model, a list of invoices will be searched for those invoices that are unpaid. The unpaid invoices (or receivables) will be **aged** as of a particular date. With this model, the user can also search for a particular customer's unpaid invoices and age the receivables from that customer.

The aging process groups the unpaid invoice amounts into the following categories. It is assumed that the terms are net 30 days from date of invoice.

Category	Description
Current	Includes unpaid invoices that are less than 31 days old days at the date of the report.
31-60	Includes unpaid invoices between 31 and 60 days old at the date of the report.
61-90	Includes unpaid invoices between 61 and 90 days old at the report date.
91+	Includes all unpaid invoices over 90 days old at the date of the report.

GLOBAL SETTINGS

The global settings should be as follows:

Recalculate	Format	Label Prefix	Column Width
AUTO NATURAL	(F2)	'	9

SETTING UP THE WORKSHEET

1. Enter the following labels:

Cell	Entry		Cell	Entry	
A1	CUSTOMER		G100	REPORT DATE	
B1	INVOICE		H100	DATE	
C1	INVOICE		I100	DATE	criterion field
D1	Y/N		J100	DATE	for Data names functions
A2	NAME		K100	DATE	
B2	AMOUNT		E101	N	
C2	DATE		E103	CURRENT	
D2	PAID		E104	'31-60	
E100	PAID	criterion field names for **Data** Query	E105	'61-90	
F100	NAME		E106	'90+	

2. Center the labels using /**R**ange **L**abel-Prefix **C**enter. Specify the range A1..D2. and E100..K100

3. Copy the field names to the output range.

> User Step 1:   Select /**C**opy
> User Step 2:   Specify A1..C2 as the FROM range and press ↵
> User Step 3:   Specify A100 as the TO range and press ↵

4. Format the following ranges with /**R**ange **F**ormat:

Range	Format
G101	Date1
C3..C99	Date1
C102..C198	Date1

5. Use /**R**ange **N**ame **L**abels **D**own and specify G100, to give the range name, REPORT DATE, to G101.

6. Enter data into the worksheet by typing in the following entries:

Cell	Entry
A3	DOME INC
A4	PAPERWORKS

Cell	Entry	Cell	Entry
A5	A.B. CO.	C4	@DATE(83,4,23)
A6	B SMITH CO.	C5	@DATE(83,5,9)
A7	SPENCER CO.	C6	@DATE(83,6,1)
A8	FORREST MFG	C7	@DATE(83,6,11)
A9	SAVEX	C8	@DATE(83,7,28)
A10	GENERIC PRODUCT	C9	@DATE(83,9,9)
A11	ESSEL LTD	C10	@DATE(83,9,30)
A12	DOME INC	C11	@DATE(83,10,31)
A13	SPENCER CO.	C12	@DATE(83,11,6)
A14	A.B. CO.	C13	@DATE(83,12,1)
A15	DOME INC	C14	@DATE(83,12,19)
B3	56.45	C15	@DATE(83,12,24)
B4	460	D3	N
B5	50	D4	Y
B6	43.85	D5	Y
B7	538.45	D6	Y
B8	323.8	D7	Y
B9	26.65	D8	Y
B10	87.5	D9	Y
B11	37	D10	Y
B12	168.3	D11	N
B13	98.75	D12	Y
B14	20.8	D13	N
B15	233.05	D14	Y
C3	@DATE(83,4,19)	D15	N

7. Move the cell pointer to the specified column to set the following column widths using / Worksheet Column Set Width. After completing this step, the worksheet should resemble that depicted in figure 12-6, when the cell pointer is located at A1.

Column	Width
A	18
C	10
D	2
E	7
F	16
G	10

8. Enter the following formulas and values in the following cells:

Cell	Entry
F103	@DSUM(A101..C198,1,H100..H101)
F104	@DSUM(A101..C198,1,I100..I101)-F105-F106
F105	@DSUM(A101..C198,1,J100..J101)-F106
F106	@DSUM(A101..C198,1,K100..K101)
H101	+C102+30 > = $REPORT DATE
I101	+C102+30 < $REPORT DATE
J101	+C102+60 < $REPORT DATE
K101	+C102+90 < $REPORT DATE

9. Using / Data Query, define the Input range as A2..D99, the Output range as A101..C198, and the Criterion range as E100..F101. Return to the Ready mode by selecting Quit.

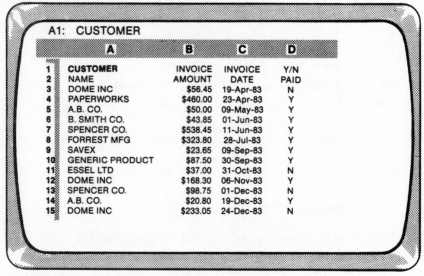

FIGURE 12-6. Worksheet Appearance after Completion of Step 7.

10. Press Home. Then, place the pointer on A11 and select / Worksheet Windows Horizontal.

11. Select / WWUnsync.

12. Adjust the window so the worksheet resembles figure 12-7.

A100:   CUSTOMER

	A	B	C	D	E	F	G
1	CUSTOMER	INVOICE	INVOICE	Y/N			
2	NAME	AMOUNT	DATE	PAID			
3	DOME INC	$56.45	19-Apr-83	N			
4	PAPERWORKS	$460.00	23-Apr-83	Y			
5	A.B. CO.	$50.00	09-May-83	Y			
6	B. SMITH CO.	$43.85	01-Jun-83	Y			
7	SPENCER CO.	$538.45	11-Jun-83	Y			
8	FORREST MFG	$323.80	28-Jul-83	Y			
9	SAVEX	$23.65	09-Sep-83	Y			
10	GENERIC PRODUCT	$87.50	30-Sep-83	Y			

	A	B	C	D	E	F	G
100	CUSTOMER	INVOICE	INVOICE		PAID	NAME	REPORT DATE
101	NAME	AMOUNT	DATE		N		
102							
103					CURRENT	$0.00	
104					31-60	$0.00	
105					61-90	$0.00	
106					90+	$0.00	
107							

FIGURE 12-7. Worksheet After Step 12

13. Enter the REPORT DATE in cell G101.

Cell	Entry
G101	@DATE(83,12,31)

14. Enter the / Data Query menu by typing / DQ. Select Extract. Then, exit to the Ready mode by selecting Quit.

15. The screen should resemble the one depicted on the next page. The unpaid records are in the range A102..C105. The amount from each period that is not paid is located in cells F103..F106.

	A	B	C	D E	F	G
1	CUSTOMER	INVOICE	INVOICE	Y/N		
2	NAME	AMOUNT	DATE	PAID		
3	DOME INC	$56.45	19-Apr-83	N		
4	PAPERWORKS	$460.00	23-Apr-83	Y		
5	A.B. CO.	$50.00	09-May-83	Y		
6	B. SMITH CO.	$43.85	01-Jun-83	Y		
7	SPENCER CO.	$538.45	11-Jun-83	Y		
8	FORREST MFG	$323.80	28-Jul-83	Y		
9	SAVEX	$23.65	09-Sep-83	Y		
10	GENERIC PRODUCT	$87.50	30-Sep-83	Y		

	A	B	C	D E	F	G
100	CUSTOMER	INVOICE	INVOICE	PAID	NAME	REPORT DATE
101	NAME	AMOUNT	DATE	N		31-Dec-83
102	DOME INC	$56.45	19-Apr-83			
103	ESSEL LTD.	$37.00	31-Oct-83	CURRENT	331.80	
104	SPENCER CO.	$98.75	01-Dec-83	31-60	0.00	
105	DOME INC	$233.05	24-Dec-83	61-90	37.00	
106				90+	56.45	

16. To find the amount for a specific customer, enter the following label in cell F101:

DOME INC

17. Pressing the F7 key will execute the last **D**ata **Q**uery command issued. The result is shown below.

	A	B	C	D E	F	G
1	CUSTOMER	INVOICE	INVOICE	Y/N		
2	NAME	AMOUNT	DATE	PAID		
3	DOME INC	56.45	19-Apr-83	N		
4	PAPERWORKS	460.00	23-Apr-83	Y		
5	A.B. CO.	50.00	09-May-83	Y		
6	B. SMITH CO.	43.85	01-Jun-83	Y		
7	SPENCER CO.	538.45	11-Jun-83	Y		
8	FORREST MFG	323.80	28-Jul-83	Y		
9	SAVEX	23.65	09-Sep-83	Y		
10	GENERIC PRODUCT	87.50	30-Sep-83	Y		

	A	B	C	D E	F	G
100	CUSTOMER	INVOICE	INVOICE	PAID	NAME	REPORT DATE
101	NAME	AMOUNT	DATE	N	DOME INC	31-Dec-83
102	DOME INC	56.45	19-Apr-83			
103	DOME INC	233.05	24-Dec-83	CURRENT	233.05	
104				31-60	0.00	
105				61-90	0.00	
106				90+	56.45	

Forecasting Model

This forecast model is based on the belief that in the **short run**, future trends tend to be an extension of past trends. No forecasting method can predict the future exactly, but forecasting methods can establish trends based on the past.

This forecasting model uses a method called **trend-adjusted exponential smoothing**. Exponential smoothing is used in lieu of the weighted moving average because its calculation is more efficient and can be just as effective. Alpha, the weighting factor, can be adjusted to improve the accuracy of the forecast. The best alpha to use is determined by experimentation but it should always be less than one. Trend-adjustment calculates the rate at which a trend is changing and adjusts the exponentially smoothed forecast figure for this.

GLOBAL SETTINGS

The global settings would be as follows:

Recalculation	Format	Label Prefix	Column Width
AUTO NATURAL	(F2)	'	9

SETTING UP THE WORKSHEET

1. Enter the following labels:

Cell	Entry	Cell	Entry
A10	MONTH	B10	SALES
A12	JANUARY	C8	SALES
A13	FEBRUARY	C9	LAST
A14	MARCH	C10	MONTH
A15	APRIL	D10	ALPHA
A16	MAY	E7	'(ALPHA)*
A17	JUNE	E8	'(SALES
A18	JULY	E9	LAST
A19	AUGUST	E10	MONTH)
A20	SEPTEMBER	F10	'(1-ALPHA)
A21	OCTOBER	G7	PREVIOUS
A22	NOVEMBER	G8	FORECAST
A23	DECEMBER	G9	OF LAST
B9	ACTUAL	G10	MONTH

Cell	Entry	Cell	Entry
H6	'(1-ALPHA)*	M9	'*(OLD
H7	'(PREVIOUS	M10	TREND)
H8	FORECAST	N9	TREND
H9	OF LAST	N10	ADJ.
H10	MONTH)	O8	TREND-
I8	FORECAST	O9	ADJUSTED
I9	FOR	O10	FORECAST
I10	MONTH	P12	J
J6	CHANGE IN	P13	F
J7	FORECAST	P14	M
J8	FROM PREV	P15	A
J9	MONTH'S	P16	M
J10	FORECAST	P17	J
K7	ALPHA*	P18	J
K8	CHANGE	P19	A
K9	IN	P20	S
K10	FORECAST	P21	O
L9	OLD	P22	N
L10	TREND	P23	D
M8	'(1-ALPHA)		

2. Right justify the labels using / **R**ange **L**abel-Prefix **R**ight. Specify the range B6..O10.

3. To enter the line under the labels as shown on the worksheet in figure 12-8, follow the steps outlined below. This line is not essential to the operation of the model, but it does make it more readable.

User Step 1:	Place pointer on A11 and type \-↵
User Step 2:	Select /**C**opy
User Step 3:	Specify A11 as the FROM range and press ↵
User Step 4:	Specify B11..O11 as the TO range and press ↵

4. Enter these formulas into the following cells:

Cell	Entry
C13	+B12
C14	+B13
D13	.7
D14	.7
E13	+C13*D13
E14	+C14*D14

Cell	Entry	Cell	Entry
F13	1-D13	K14	+D14*J14
F14	1-D14	L13	+N12
G14	+I13	L14	+N13
H13	@IF(E13=0,@NA,F13*G13)	M13	+F13*L13
H14	@IF(E14=0,@NA,F14*G14)	M14	+F14*L14
I13	+E13+H13	N13	(D13*J13)+(F13*L13)
I14	+E14+H14	N14	(D14*J14)+(F14*L14)
J14	+I14-I13	O13	+I13+N13
K13	+D13*J13	O14	+I14+N14

5. Copy the formulas to the other cells requiring formulas.

> User Step 1: Select /**C**
>
> User Step 2: Specify C14..O14 as the FROM range and press ↵.
>
> User Step 3: Specify C15..O23 as the TO range and press ↵.

6. Cells B12 through B23 and G13 are user input cells. If global protection is enabled, the user input cells should have their protection lifted using / **RU**. The following data was entered in the user input cells in our model:

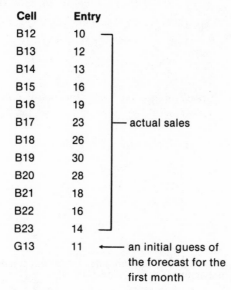

Cell	Entry	
B12	10	
B13	12	
B14	13	
B15	16	
B16	19	
B17	23	— actual sales
B18	26	
B19	30	
B20	28	
B21	18	
B22	16	
B23	14	
G13	11	← an initial guess of the forecast for the first month

The worksheet should resemble that depicted in figure 12-8. To view a graph* of the forecast versus actual of the data entered in step 6, execute the following steps:

● Specifying the values to be used in the graph

User Step 1:	/Graph
1-2-3 Response:	Displays /Graph menu
User Step 2:	Select X
1-2-3 Response:	Enter X-axis range:A1
User Step 3:	Specify P12..P23↵
1-2-3 Response:	Returns to /Graph menu
User Step 4:	Select A
1-2-3 Response:	Enter first data range:A1
User Step 5:	Specify B12..B23↵
1-2-3 Response:	Returns to /Graph menu
User Step 6:	Select B
1-2-3 Response:	Enter second data range:A1
User Step 7:	Specify the range O12..O23 and press ↵
1-2-3 Response:	Returns to the /Graph menu

---

* Graphs cannot be displayed on the Monochrome monitor but can be saved for future printing with PrintGraph.

H4:

	A	B	C	D	E	F	G	H
	MONTH	ACTUAL SALES	SALES LAST MONTH	ALPHA	(ALPHA)* (SALES LAST MONTH)	(1-ALPHA)	PREVIOUS FORECAST OF LAST MONTH	(1-ALPHA) (PREVIOUS FORECAST OF LAST MONTH)
12	JANUARY	10.00						
13	FEBRUARY	12.00	10.00	0.70	7.00	0.30	11.00	3.30
14	MARCH	13.00	12.00	0.70	8.40	0.30	10.30	3.09
15	APRIL	16.00	13.00	0.70	9.10	0.30	11.49	3.45
16	MAY	19.00	16.00	0.70	11.20	0.30	12.55	3.76
17	JUNE	23.00	19.00	0.70	13.30	0.30	14.96	4.49
18	JULY	26.00	23.00	0.70	16.10	0.30	17.79	5.34
19	AUGUST	30.00	26.00	0.70	18.20	0.30	21.44	6.43
20	SEPTEMBER	28.00	30.00	0.70	21.00	0.30	24.63	7.39
21	OCTOBER	18.00	28.00	0.70	19.60	0.30	28.39	8.52
22	NOVEMBER	16.00	18.00	0.70	12.60	0.30	28.12	8.44
23	DECEMBER	14.00	16.00	0.70	11.20	0.30	21.04	6.31

P4:

	I	J	K	L	M	N	O	P
	FORECAST FOR MONTH	CHANGE IN FORECAST FROM PREV MONTH'S FORECAST	ALPHA* CHANGE IN FORECAST	OLD TREND	(1-ALPHA) *(OLD TREND)	TREND ADJ.	TREND-ADJUSTED FORECAST	
12								J
13	10.30		0.00	0.00	0.00	0.00	10.30	F
14	11.49	1.19	0.82	0.00	0.00	0.83	12.32	M
15	12.55	1.06	0.74	0.83	.025	0.99	13.54	A
16	14.96	2.42	1.69	0.99	0.30	1.99	16.95	M
17	17.79	2.83	1.98	1.99	0.60	2.57	20.36	J
18	21.44	3.65	2.55	2.57	0.77	3.33	24.76	J
19	24.63	3.19	2.24	2.22	1.00	2.23	27.86	A
20	28.39	3.76	2.63	3.23	0.97	3.60	31.99	S
21	28.12	-0.27	-0.19	3.60	1.08	0.89	29.01	O
22	21.04	-7.08	-4.96	0.89	0.27	-4.69	16.34	N
23	17.51	-3.52	-2.47	-4.69	-1.41	-3.87	13.64	D

FIGURE 12-8. Sales Forecast Model after Data Input

- Selecting the type of graph to be displayed

User Step 1:	Select Type from the /Graph menu.
1-2-3 Response:	Displays Type menu
User Step 2:	Select Line.
1-2-3 Response:	Returns to/Graph menu

- To view the graph, select View. The graph depicted will resemble that shown in figure 12-9.

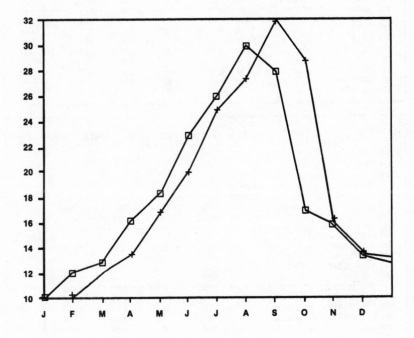

FIGURE 12-9. Sales Forecast Graph

- Labels and a legend can be placed on the graph using the following steps:

User Step 1:	Select Options from the /Graph menu
1-2-3 Response:	Displays Options menu
User Step 2:	Select Legend

1-2-3 Response:	Displays **L**egend menu
User Step 3:	Select **A**
1-2-3 Response:	Enter legend for A-range:
User Step 4:	Type in the following — ACTUAL ↵
1-2-3 Response:	Returns to **O**ptions menu

FORECAST VS ACTUAL

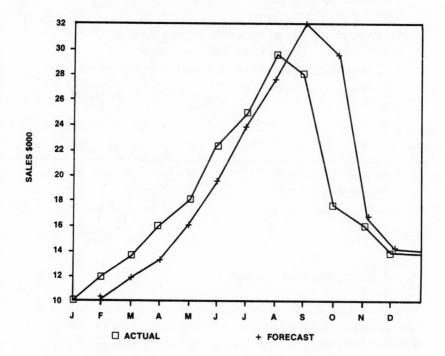

FIGURE 12-10. Forecast Model Graph with Titles and Legend

User Step 5:	Select **L**egend.
1-2-3 Response:	Displays **L**egend menu
User Step 6:	Select **B**
1-2-3 Response:	Enter legend for B-range:
User Step 7:	Type in the following — FORECAST ↵

1-2-3 Response:	Returns to **O**ptions menu
User Step 8:	Select **T**itles
1-2-3 Response:	Displays **T**itles menu
User Step 9:	Select **F**irst
1-2-3 Response:	Enter graph title, top line:
User Step 10:	Type in the following — FORECAST VS ACTUAL↵
1-2-3 Response:	Returns to **O**ptions menu.
User Step 11:	Select **T**itles
1-2-3 Response:	Displays **T**itles menu.
User Step 12:	Select **Y**-axis
1-2-3 Response:	Enter Y-axis title:
User Step 13:	Type in the following — SALES $000↵
1-2-3 Response:	Returns to **O**ptions menu.
User Step 14:	Select **Q**uit
1-2-3 Response:	Returns to /**G**raph menu.
User Step 15:	*Select **V**iew.
1-2-3 Response:	Figure 12-10

7. To save the model with all the formulas, use / **F**ile Save. If only the values need to be saved, use / **F**ile **X**tract Values.

Cash Disbursements Model

The cash disbursements model enables the user to enter check information, an account number and the check amount. The amount will automatically be distributed to the correct account. Each account is totaled and the sum of the account totals is compared to the sum of the check amounts. If a difference exists, Err will be returned so as to notify the user that an account number was entered incorrectly.

The model was set up to accommodate 50 checks and 7 different accounts. It can be expanded to accommodate more checks and/or accounts. The size of the model is limited by the amount of RAM available.

GLOBAL SETTINGS

The following global settings are used:

Recalculation	Format	Label Prefix	Column Width
MANUAL NATURAL	(F2)	'	8

SETTING UP THE WORKSHEET

1. Enter the following label entries:

Cell	Entry	Description
A5	Payee	——— To whom the check is written
A6	=	
C57	-	
A58	Totals	
B4	Check	
B5	No.	To label column containing the check number
C4	Check	To label the column containing the
C5	Amount	check amount
D4	Account	Account number where the cash disburse-
D5	No.	ment is to be charged
E2	Office	
E3	Exp	
E5	40001	
F3	Advert	
F5	40002	
G3	Travel	
G5	40003	
H2	Sales	
H3	Comm	Various account titles and
H5	40004	corresponding numbers
I2	Inv	
I3	Purch	
I5	40005	
J3	Misc	
J5	40099	
K2	Tax	
K3	Deposits	
K5	11700	

2. / Copy the double dash line at A6 across the worksheet to separate the column labels, making the worksheet more readable.

User Step 1: /Copy

1-2-3 Response: Enter range FROM:A6..A6

User Step 2:	Specify A6 and press ↵
1-2-3 Response:	Enter range to copy TO:A6
User Step 3:	Specify B6..K6 and press ↵

/ Copy the line at C57 across the worksheet to separate the totals.

User Step 1:	Select /C
User Step 2:	Specify C57 as the FROM range and press ↵
User Step 3:	Specify D57..K57 as the TO range and press ↵

3. Center the labels in the ranges A2..K5 using / Range Label-Prefix Center.

4. Format the following ranges with / Range Format:

Range	Format	Decimal Places
B7..B56	Fixed	0
D7..D56	Fixed	1
A1	Date1	
E5..K5	Fixed	1

5. Use / Worksheet Column-Width Set to widen column A to 15.
6. To create the column labels titles rows, follow these steps:

User Step 1:	Place pointer on A7.
User Step 2:	Select /Worksheet Titles Horizontal.

7. The following formulas should be entered to do the acutal distribution of the check amounts to the accounts and to total the columns:

Cell	Entry	Description
E7	@IF($D7=E$5,$C7,0)	If the account number in column D is equal to the account number at the top of this column, enter the check amount in this cell. Otherwise, enter a zero.
E58	@SUM(E7..E56)	Totals the amounts in the Office Exp column
C58	@IF(@SUM(C7..C56)=@SUM(E7..K56),@SUM(C7..C56),@ERR)	This formula compares the sum of the checks to the sum of the accounts. If they are different, then ERR will be returned. Otherwise, the sum of the checks will be returned. Differences may occur if account numbers were not entered or were entered improperly.

8. / Copy the formulas to appropriate ranges.

Copy FROM	Copy TO
E7	E7..K56
E58	F58..K58

After completion of this step, the worksheet should resemble that depicted in figure 12-11. To position the worksheet as shown in figure 12-11, press the F5 (GoTo) key and specify A49*.

A49:

	A	B	C	D	E	F	G
1							
2					OFFICE		
3					EXP	ADVERT	TRAVEL
4		CHECK	CHECK	ACCOUNT			
5	PAYEE	NO.	AMOUNT	NO.	40001.0	40002.0	40003.0
6	:==:
49					0.00	0.00	0.00
50					0.00	0.00	0.00
51					0.00	0.00	0.00
52					0.00	0.00	0.00
53					0.00	0.00	0.00
54					0.00	0.00	0.00
55					0.00	0.00	0.00
56					0.00	0.00	0.00
57					---------------------------
58	Totals		0.00		0.00	0.00	0.00
59							
60							
61							
62							

FIGURE 12-11. Cash Disbursements Model after Step 8

* The actual worksheet extends through column K and can be viewed in windows by using the pointer movement keys.

9. Turn on the cell protection by selecting / **W**orksheet **G**lobal **P**rotection **E**nable. Use / **RU**n protect to turn off the protection for the following user input cells:

       A1

       A7..D56

10. At this point, save the worksheet using / **FS** so it can be re-used as a form for input.

USING THE MODEL

User Step 1:	To enter the date in cell **A1**, press the F5 (goto) key to move the cell pointer to cell A1. Enter the date with the @DATE function.* Press PgDn then PgUp to restore the previous worksheet position.
User Step 2:	Place the cell pointer on A7 and type the payee name and press →.
User Step 3:	Type the check number and press →.
User Step 4:	Type the check amount and press →.
User Step 5:	Type the account number and press ↵.
User Step 6:	Press ← three times, and then ↓.
User Step 7:	Repeat User Steps 2 through 6 until all the checks (up to 50 per worksheet) have been entered.
User Step 8:	Press F9 (calc) to calculate the totals.

An example of the model with input is shown in figure 12-12.

- Saving the Results

  Save the worksheets using /**FXV** under a different name from the form containing the formulas. Suggestion: use CD followed by the date. For example, CD15MAR4 for March 15, 1984.

- Printing the results

User Step 1:	Select /**PP**
User Step 2:	Select **R**ange and specify A1..K58
User Step 3:	Select **O**ptions margins and specify **R**ight and **L**eft margins that allow 105 characters to be printed. Select **Q**uit to return to the **P**rinter menu.

User Step 4: Adjust paper and select **A**lign. Make sure the printer is on line.

User Step 5: Select **G**o. See figure 12-13 for results.

User Step 6: Select **Q**uit to return to the Ready mode.

A7:

	A	B	C	D	E	F	G
1							
2					OFFICE		
3					EXP	ADVERT	TRAVEL
4		CHECK	CHECK	ACCOUNT			
5	PAYEE	NO.	AMOUNT	NO.	40001.0	40002.0	40003.0
6							
7	LG & E	100	5.00	40001.0	5.00	0.00	0.00
8	BELL TELEPHONE	101	10.00	40001.0	10.00	0.00	0.00
9	POSTMASTER	102	3.50	40099.0	0.00	0.00	0.00
10	AMERICAN EXPRES	103	50.55	40003.0	0.00	0.00	50.55
11	IRS	104	500.00	11700.0	0.00	0.00	0.00
12	DD&D AD AGENCY	105	410.00	40002.0	0.00	410.00	0.00
13	D HANCOCK	106	120.00	40004.0	0.00	0.00	0.00
14					0.00	0.00	0.00
15					0.00	0.00	0.00
16					0.00	0.00	0.00
17					0.00	0.00	0.00
18					0.00	0.00	0.00
19					0.00	0.00	0.00
20					0.00	0.00	0.00

A45: U

	A	B	C	D	E	F	G
1	15-Mar-84						
2					OFFICE		
3					EXP	ADVERT	TRAVEL.
4		CHECK	CHECK	ACCOUNT			
5	PAYEE	NO.	AMOUNT	NO.	40001.0	40002.0	40003.0
6	==!						
45					0.00	0.00	0.00
46					0.00	0.00	0.00
47					0.00	0.00	0.00
48					0.00	0.00	0.00
49					0.00	0.00	0.00
50					0.00	0.00	0.00
51					0.00	0.00	0.00
52					0.00	0.00	0.00
53					0.00	0.00	0.00
54					0.00	0.00	0.00
55					0.00	0.00	0.00
56					0.00	0.00	0.00
57				--			
58		Totals	1099.05		15.00	410.00	50.55

FIGURE 12-12. Cash Disbursements Model with User Input

15-Mar-84

PAYEE	CHECK NO.	CHECK AMOUNT	ACCOUNT NO.	OFFICE EXP 40001.0	ADVERT 40002.0	TRAVEL 40003.0	SALES COMM 40004.0	INV PURCH 40005.0	MISC 40099.0	TAX DEPOSITS 11700.0
LG & E	100	5.00	40001.0	5.00	0.00	0.00	0.00	0.00	0.00	0.00
BELL TELEPHONE	101	10.00	40001.0	10.00	0.00	0.00	0.00	0.00	0.00	0.00
POSTMASTER	102	3.50	40099.0	0.00	0.00	0.00	0.00	0.00	3.50	0.00
AMERICAN EXPRES	103	50.55	40003.0	0.00	0.00	50.55	0.00	0.00	0.00	0.00
IRS	104	500.00	11700.0	0.00	0.00	0.00	0.00	0.00	0.00	500.00
DD&D AD AGENCY	105	410.00	40002.0	0.00	410.00	0.00	0.00	0.00	0.00	0.00
D HANCOCK	106	120.00	40004.0	0.00	0.00	0.00	120.00	0.00	0.00	0.00
				0.00	0.00	0.00	0.00	0.00	0.00	0.00
				0.00	0.00	0.00	0.00	0.00	0.00	0.00
				0.00	0.00	0.00	0.00	0.00	0.00	0.00
				0.00	0.00	0.00	0.00	0.00	0.00	0.00
				0.00	0.00	0.00	0.00	0.00	0.00	0.00
				0.00	0.00	0.00	0.00	0.00	0.00	0.00
				0.00	0.00	0.00	0.00	0.00	0.00	0.00
				0.00	0.00	0.00	0.00	0.00	0.00	0.00
				0.00	0.00	0.00	0.00	0.00	0.00	0.00
				0.00	0.00	0.00	0.00	0.00	0.00	0.00
				0.00	0.00	0.00	0.00	0.00	0.00	0.00
				0.00	0.00	0.00	0.00	0.00	0.00	0.00
				0.00	0.00	0.00	0.00	0.00	0.00	0.00
				0.00	0.00	0.00	0.00	0.00	0.00	0.00
				0.00	0.00	0.00	0.00	0.00	0.00	0.00
				0.00	0.00	0.00	0.00	0.00	0.00	0.00
Totals		1099.05		15.00	410.00	50.55	120.00	0.00	3.50	500.00

FIGURE 12-13. Printed Results of Cash Disbursement Model

Appendix A.
ASCII Codes

In the following table, the ASCII codes recognized by 1-2-3 are listed with their corresponding character and **set-up** string values. A set-up string is one or more characters which are sent to the printer to control its output. For the first thirty-two ASCII characters, control codes must be entered into the set-up string using the following configuration:

xxx

xxx represents the character's ASCII codes denoted with three digits. The remaining ASCII characters can be entered either as the character itself or in the *xxx* configuration.

ASCII Code (Decimal)	Character	Setup String	ASCII Code (Decimal)	Character	Setup String
0	^@	\\000	25	^Y	\\025
1	^A	\\001	26	^Z	\\026
2	^B	\\002	27	[ESCAPE]	\\027
3	^C	\\003	28	FS	\\028
4	^D	\\004	29	GS	\\029
5	^E	\\005	30	RS	\\030
6	^F	\\006	31	US	\\031
7	^G	\\007	32	(SPACE)	\\032
8	^H	\\008	33	!	\\033
9	^I	\\009	34	"	\\034
10	^J	\\010	35	#	\\035
11	^K	\\011	36	$	\\036
12	^L	\\012	37	%	\\037
13	^M	\\013	38	&	\\038
14	^N	\\014	39	`	\\039
15	^O	\\015	40	(	\\040
16	^P	\\016	41	)	\\041
17	^Q	\\017	42	*	\\042
18	^R	\\018	43	+	\\043
19	^S	\\019	44	`	\\044
20	^T	\\020	45	-	\\045
21	^U	\\021	46	.	\\046
22	^V	\\022	47	/	\\047
23	^W	\\023	48	0	\\048
24	^X	\\024	49	1	\\049

APPENDIX A. ASCII Codes (cont).

ASCII Code (Decimal)	Character	Setup String	ASCII Code (Decimal)	Character	Setup String
50	2	\050	89	Y	\089
51	3	\051	90	Z	\090
52	4	\052	91	[	\091
53	5	\053	92	\	\092
54	6	\054	93	]	\093
55	7	\055	94	^	\094
56	8	\056	95	—	\095
57	9	\057	96	`	\096
58	:	\058	97	a	\097
59	;	\059	98	b	\098
60	<	\060	99	c	\099
61	=	\061	100	d	\100
62	>	\062	101	e	\101
63	?	\063	102	f	\102
64	@	\064	103	g	\103
65	A	\065	104	h	\104
66	B	\066	105	i	\105
67	C	\067	106	j	\106
68	D	\068	107	k	\107
69	E	\069	108	l	\108
70	F	\070	109	m	\109
71	G	\071	110	n	\110
72	H	\072	111	o	\111
73	I	\073	112	p	\112
74	J	\074	113	q	\113
75	K	\075	114	r	\114
76	L	\076	115	s	\115
77	M	\077	116	t	\116
78	N	\078	117	u	\117
79	O	\079	118	v	\118
80	P	\080	119	w	\119
81	Q	\081	120	x	\120
82	R	\082	121	y	\121
83	S	\083	122	z	\122
84	T	\084	123	{	\123
85	U	\085	124	¦	\124
86	V	\086	125	}	\125
87	W	\087	126	~	\126
88	X	\088	127	DEL	\127

Appendix B.
The Translate Utility

Introduction

The Translate Utility allows the 1-2-3 user to transfer data files between 1-2-3 and other programs as follows:

File Source	File Destination
1-2-3	dBASE-II
1-2-3	DIF
dBASE-II	1-2-3
Visicalc	1-2-3
DIF	1-2-3

Procedure

Before files can be translated, their filenames must include the current filename extension. The filename can be changed using either 1-2-3's File Manager program or DOS's RENAME command. The correct filename extensions are as follows:

File Source	Extension Needed
dBASE-II	.DBF
DIF	.DIF
Visicalc	.VC

Once the filename extensions have been changed, select Translate from the Lotus Access System menu. A prompt will appear requesting that the PrintGraph Program diskette be loaded in drive A. The Translate program resides on this diskette. Once Translate has been loaded, the following menu selections will be displayed:

VC to WKS	Translate a Visicalc .VC file to a 1-2-3 worksheet file.

DIF to WKS	Translate a .DIF data file to a 1-2-3 worksheet file.
WKS to DIF	Translate a 1-2-3 worksheet file to a .DIF data file.
DBF to WKS	Translate dBASE-II data file to a worksheet file.
WKS to DBF	Translate 1-2-3 worksheet file to a dBASE-II data file.
Quit	Exit Translate

Once the menu selection has been made, Translate will prompt for the source drive — the drive containing the files to be translated. Once the source drive has been selected, a list of filenames with a filename extension matching that specified in the menu selection will be displayed beneath the control panel. For instance, if the menu selection was,

WKS to DBF

all 1-2-3 worksheet files would be displayed. Select the file to be translated by highlighting it. When the desired file is highlighted, it can be selected by pressing the Esc key.

Translate will next prompt for the destination drive to receive the translated file. A message will appear similar to the following:

Translate s:TEXTA.WKS d:TEXTB.DBF

s and d denote the source and destination drives respectively. The user will be prompted as follows,

Yes   No   Quit

to determine whether he or she wishes to proceed with the translation as indicated. Indicate "Yes" to proceed with the translation. The computer's keyboard will be locked out during the translation process. If "No" is indicated, translate will return to the file specification step. "Quit" returns the program to the Translate menu.

Index

ABOUT THE
WEBER SYSTEMS, INC. STAFF

In 1982, Weber Systems, Inc. began a start-up publishing division specializing in books related to the personal computer field. They initially published three books, and within a year, expanded their list to eighteen machine-specific titles, with fourteen more scheduled for early 1984.

All Weber Systems USER'S HANDBOOKS are created by an in-house editorial staff with extensive backgrounds in computer science and technical writing. The three basic tenets of their publishing philosophy are: quality, timeliness and maintenance (frequent updating).

Weber Systems is located in Cleveland, Ohio.